Louvre

Portrait of a Museum

Louvre - Frontispiece

Louvre
Portrait of a Museum

Conceived and photographed
by Nicholas d'Archimbaud

Text by Bruno de Cessole,
Annie Forgeau, Frédéric Valloire,
Anne Chêne, and Yves Saint-Hilaire

Stewart, Tabori & Chang

NEW YORK

Originally published in France as *Louvre* by Éditions Robert Laffont, Paris in 1997.

Published in 1998 by and distributed in the U.S. by
Stewart, Tabori & Chang,
a division of U.S. Media Holdings, Inc.
115 West 18th Street, New York, NY 10011

Distributed in Canada by
General Publishing Company Ltd.
30 Lesmill Road
Don Mills, Ontario, Canada M3B 2T6

Sold in Australia by
Peribo Pty Ltd.
58 Beaumont Road
Mount Kuring-gai, NSW 2080, Australia

Distributed in all other territories by
Grantham Book Services Ltd.
Isaac Newton Way, Alma Park Industrial Estate
Grantham, Lincolnshire, NG31 9SD, England

Library of Congress Cataloging-in-Publication Data

Archimbaud, Nicholas d'.
[Louvre. English]
Louvre : Portrait of a Museum / conceived and photographed by Nicholas d'Archimbaud ;
text by Bruno de Cessole. . .
p. cm.
Includes bibliographical references and index.
ISBN 1-55670-625-1
1. Louvre (Paris, France) 2. Musée du Louvre 3. Paris (France) — Buildings, structures, etc.
4. Louvre (Paris, France) — Pictorial works. 5. Musée du Louvre — Pictorial works.
6. Paris (France) — Buildings, structures, etc. — Pictorial works. I. De Cessole, Bruno II. Title.
N2030.A9213 1998
708.4'361 — dc21
96 — 17163
CIP

Printed in France

10 9 8 7 6 5 4 3 2 1

To My Bear, Victor, and to Mummy,

"And the family, deep-rooted

On the garden slope she has sown,

Blossoms anew from year to year"

LAMARTINE

L O U V R E

"The museum offers us not everyday reality but a personal vision transmuted into art. A masterpiece is both idea and execution: but the idea is nothing without the artist's hand." This observation of Renoir's holds doubly true for the Louvre. On the one hand, the museum houses and exhibits masterpieces from the entire family of the arts without distinction as to national origin (although French art is the most fully represented there). Detached from their creators, artistic masterpieces live on, sovereign and timeless; beyond admiration, they summon up perplexity in the face of the mystery of creation.

On the other hand, the Louvre is the reflection of the personal vision of kings and queens who stubbornly pursued the original "grand design" of completing the great museum. It also reflects the ideals of generations of collectors, who have passed down to us their own vision of perfection and beauty. Ever since antiquity, collecting has been a princely privilege. A sovereign worthy of the name was not just a victorious conqueror and vigilant administrator, but an enlightened protector of arts and letters — for the success of a country's artists reflected glory on the monarch and his regime. The first to transform the original Louvre fortress into a museum was François I, who was also the founder of France's royal collections. From his campaigns in Italy, he brought back works by Titian and Raphael. Leonardo da Vinci, Benvenuto Cellini, Sebastiano del Piombo, Niccolo d'Abbate, and Francesco Primaticcio were among the Italian artists he invited to the French court. He staked everything on artistic splendor and began to accumulate paintings, sculptures, and other decorative objects in his chateaux. Visitors to the Louvre who marvel at Mona Lisa's smile owe the experience to this first of France's patron-kings.

This embryo of what became the royal collections would be enriched in varying degrees by each succeeding French monarch. Henri IV decorated the palace with the works of his predecessors. His widow, Marie de Medici, commissioned from Peter-Paul Rubens the series of canvases that once adorned the Luxembourg Palace and are now the pride of the Louvre. Although Louis XIII lacked artistic vision, his chief minister, Cardinal Richelieu, was a collector who (like Mazarin later on) bequeathed his treasure to the French crown. But it was above all to Louis XIV, and to the systematic purchasing policies he entrusted to Colbert that the royal collections owed their true growth. By the year of the Sun King's death, they had grown from two hundred to two thousand pieces — marking the 17th century as France's golden age of collecting. The next two reigns, those of Louis XV and XVI, could not compete in terms either of the quantity or the quality of purchases. But by the end of the 18th century, the comte d'Angivillers had amassed important collections through judicious purchases and commissions — and Louis XVI, responsive to the public mood, envisaged converting the Louvre's Grande Galerie into a Muséum Royal des Arts. The Revolution — which had stood by while the nation's artistic heritage was vandalized — then took up the king's unrealized project: in 1873, the Muséum Central des Arts was born, designed to house "humankind's universal patrimony," confiscated from the royal collections, Church holdings, émigrés, and external enemies.

This policy of fruitful plundering was promoted on an even vaster scale by Napoleon Bonaparte, initially as First Consul and finally as Emperor of the French. He brought to the Louvre (rechristened the Musée Napoléon) art treasures looted from virtually every part of Italy. When the Empire fell, the Louvre was forced to return the bulk of this war booty — in the teeth of fierce opposition from its curator, Vivant Denon. Despite the gaps thus created in its holdings, the museum continued to enlarge and above all to diversify its collections.

Interest in antiquity, abetted by the contemporary neoclassical decorative style and provided with a ready-made ideology by both the Republic and the Empire, was directly responsible for the division of

the Museum into separate departments. By 1800, the Musée des Antiques exhibited Greek and Roman remains seized in Italy by Bonaparte's troops. In the wake of his Egyptian expedition, the rediscovery of the civilization of Ancient Egypt led to Champollion's first steps into Egyptology, and then (in 1826, under the Restoration) to the foundation of the Musée Egyptien. Champollion, the decipherer of hieroglyphics, was its first curator. In 1847, Louis-Philippe inaugurated the Musée Assyrien, created to house the yield from Paul-Emile Botta's digs at Khorsabad. Through acquisitions, confiscations, and bequests, all seven departments thus slowly emerged. They were distributed among the museum's three major "geographic" areas — Denon, Sully, and Richelieu — that form the physical skeleton of the Louvre: the three original departments (Greek and Roman Antiquities, Egyptian Antiquities, and Near Eastern Antiquities) were joined by the Department of Sculptures and the Department of Decorative Arts. Thus, having begun life as a museum of paintings, the heir to the royal collections, the Louvre was utterly transformed during the 19th century by its acquisition of a steady stream of specialized collections. Curators like Champollion abandoned the practice of displays organized on esthetic lines, and began to exhibit the Louvre's possessions according to period and style: paintings were broken down into schools; separate rooms were fitted out to display each different period of Greek art. A few oases were set aside for diehard lovers of older methods of exhibition, such as the Salon Carré's eclectic display of masterpieces. (In 1914, these too were dispersed, on "pedagogical" grounds.) Even in its late 18th-century "prehistory" (when Hubert Robert was medidating on the possibilities of the ideal museum), the Louvre was already very much a museum conceived by artists for artists. In the beginning, it was a place where one sought instruction, where copyists learned their trade by reproducing the works of the masters. For them, the judges' bench was the masterpieces gazing down on them. Next, a separation was established between the art of the past and contemporary work. Inaugurated during the Restoration, the Luxembourg museum, home of living artists, rose in opposition to the Louvre, shrine of dead genius. It was at this point that management of the museum passed from the hands of artists to those of art historians and archaeologists. This did not mean that individual tastes and idiosyncracy were henceforth banished, for they were abundantly represented in the donations made by collectors. (As Sauvageot, La Caze, His de la Salle, Gatteau, Davillier, Rothschild, Caillebotte, Camondo, Thomy-Thiéry, Moreau-Nélaton, Besteigui, David-Weill, Niarchos, and Grog-Carven), without whose generosity the Louvre would not be the museum it is. Unlike Mazarin (who reviewed his collections shortly before death with the sigh, "I must leave all this behind! What trouble I went to to acquire these things! I shall never see them where I am going!"), the great private collectors were set on emulating the spirit of royal patronage. Perhaps this is because our civilization, with its increasingly ephemeral products, seeks security in the values of stability and timelessness represented by the museum, the cathedral in our new religion of art. Hundreds of thousands of visitors annually, if unwittingly, confirm Henri Matisse's remark: "I believe in the need for museums. The works of the great masters are our foundation and our model: it is always from a forerunner that we solicit the basic components of our language."

Eight Centuries of History

The story of the Louvre is even older than the stones from which it was built. Where crowds of tourists now gather, at the entrance to the new pyramid designed by the architect I.M.Pei, Neolithic tribes hunted in prehistoric times. Layer after layer of history has been superimposed on the site of the world's largest museum. On this spot dedicated to remembering, every king and every generation has left a characteristic mark, never quite obliterating what had gone before. But before we hurry into this centuries-old history – which would take a lifetime to explore fully – let us pause to look briefly at three of the story's towering protagonists.

Before he left for the Crusades in 1190, Philip Augustus, the king of France, ordered a rampart built around Paris to protect it from attack. At the western approaches to his city, on the banks of the Seine, he built a sturdy keep, itself protected by a fortress overlooking the river.

As the city's guardian, the tower of the Louvre (as it became known) also housed the royal treasury and notable prisoners. The Louvre remained a fortress until the end of the 14th century, when Charles V decided to add it to his list of royal residences. He had a fortified wall built around Philip Augustus's old walls, thus enclosing the Louvre within the city's perimeter. A learned king and a lover of architecture, Charles asked his personal architect, Raymond du Temple, to transform the forbidding old fortress into a sumptuous dwelling. In 1367 Charles's great library of 973 books was moved into the falconry tower, which was known thereafter as the Library Tower. The history of the Louvre as a repository of culture had begun.

After the dark decades of the Hundred Years' War, the French Renaissance burst upon the country. In 1528 Francis I, greatest of the Valois kings, pulled down the keep and the Gothic castle of the Louvre. He gave the architect Pierre Lescot the task of building an "urban château" to rival the great châteaux of the Loire Valley. Work had only just begun when the king died, but his successors remained faithful to Francis I's dream of seeing the Italian Renaissance bloom under French skies.

THE MASSACRE OF ST. BARTHOLOMEW'S DAY

The Massacre of St. Bartholomew's Day is the most tragic event in the Louvre's long history. Henry of Navarre's retinue of Huguenots was killed in the courtyard of the Louvre. Religious wars between Catholics and Protestants had supposedly come to an end with the truce concluded in 1570 at Saint Germain. Nevertheless, Charles IX's mother, Catherine de Médicis, was disturbed by the influence that a prominent Protestant, Admiral Gaspard de Coligny, was gaining over her son. With the encouragement of the duke of Guise, leader of the Catholic extremists, she tried to have him murdered on August 22, 1572. But Coligny was merely wounded, and the Protestants sought revenge. Spurred on by Guise, Catherine decided to have the Protestants eliminated altogether. At 3.00 a.m., on August 24, under orders from Charles IX, nearly 3,000 Protestants were killed, including Admiral Coligny.

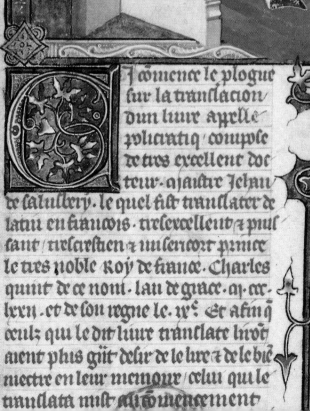

J cōmence le plogue
sur la translacion
dun liure apelle
policratiq compose
de tres excellent doc
teur ā faistre Jehan
de salusbery le quel fist translater de
latin en francois tresexcellent z puil
sant treschrestien z misericort prince
le tres noble roy de france Charles
quint de ce nom lan de grace m̄ cc
lxxj et de son regne le xj et afin q
ceulx qui le dit liure translate liront
aient plus grant desir de le lire z de le bie
mettre en leur memoire celui qui le
translata mist au comencement

eat vn plogue a
lp q la ꝺ mendaa
iue on du liure
ꝛ t z du trs no
ꝛ sapi ble roy qui le
ꝛ eua fist trsslater
au et qui afflut prudenaa pu
z caplo Ceste parole dit q
lomon est benoit qui treuue sapiece
et qui afflue largement de prude
ce Le tres glorieus docteur mō
seigneur saint ambroise en con
siderant diuerses opinions de bea
titude et beliate que plusieurs genz
ont par le monde et par especial
de tele cōme on la puet auoir en

HENRY IV'S "GRAND DESIGN"

above right
Louvre and Tuileries
under Louis XIII:
Panoramic Elevation
*This engraving shows
the Louvre's long
facade (the Grande
Galerie), running
parallel to the banks of
the Seine.*

above
Assassination of
Henry IV
*On May 14, 1610, as
Henry IV was leaving
the Louvre to visit his
ailing minister, the
duke of Sully, he
received two mortal
knife wounds from the
Catholic extremist
Ravaillac.*

On his deathbed, the last of the Valois kings, Henry III, appointed Henry of Navarre as his successor. By the time Henry IV ascended to the throne in 1589, France had been ravaged by civil war, and the Louvre was severely dilapidated. The new king undertook to transform the Louvre into a symbol of the throne, housing both the seat of government and the king's private residence.

Earlier, Catherine de Médicis had asked the architect Philibert Delorme to construct an Italian-style palace surrounded by gardens (known as the Tuileries) to the west of the Louvre: unfortunately, the Tuileries palace remained unfinished. Pursuing one of Charles IX's projects, Henry IV developed a "grand design." His aim was to link the Louvre with the Tuileries palace by two parallel 480-yard-long galleries, one

along the bank of the Seine, the other to its north, and to replace the slums between the two arms with open squares. Henry IV lacked the time and the money to carry out his plan, but his concept was visionary; this is what the Louvre would look like in the 19th century.

At the time of Henry's death in 1610, the only completed areas were the Grande Galerie and the Pavillon de Flore, which linked the Louvre to the Tuileries. His successor, Louis XIII, asked the painter Nicolas Poussin to decorate the Grande Galerie, and he gave the architect Jacques Lemercier the task of quadrupling the size of the Cour Carrée (which meant doubling the size of the Lescot Wing) and building the Pavillon de l'Horloge. As late as the 19th century, each succeeding ruler attempted to complete Henry IV's "grand design."

center left
The Grand Design
*To symbolize the power
of the Bourbon
monarchy, Henry IV
conceived his grand
design of quadrupling
the area of the Cour
Carrée, linking the
Louvre to the Tuileries
palace with two long
galleries running north
and south, and
demolishing the slum
dwellings in between.
Incomplete at his death
but continued by
succeeding rulers, its
was finally completed
in the 19th century
under Napoleon III.*

PARIS, CAPITAL CITY

below right
Elevation of the
Tuileries Palace
*Begun by Catherine de
Médicis, the Tuileries
palace was finally
completed under Louis
XIV. The facade, like
that of the Louvre, was
punctuated at
intervals by square
pavilions, a style that
became a model for
French classicism.*

Between 1594, when Henry IV triumphantly entered Paris, and 1660, when Louis XIV made his first ceremonial appearance there, Paris developed into the capital city of the kingdom. With its seventeen districts, 20,000 houses, and 400,000 inhabitants, it also became the biggest city in Europe. The first Bourbon kings made Paris their main residence. Under royal patronage, Paris experienced unprecedented

architectural development, along with a great artistic and intellectual flowering. The Louvre changed radically: the Luxembourg Palace and the Palais-Royal were built, along with Place Royale, the town houses of the Marais district, and the hospitals of Saint-Louis, la Pitié, la Charité, and Bicêtre, while the Ile-Saint-Louis was divided into lots. At the same time, Cardinal Richelieu founded the Académie Française.

right
Henry IV
*"Paris is worth a
mass," Henry of
Navarre is believed to
have said before
agreeing to convert to
Catholicism to gain the
throne of France.
Paris, like the rest of
France, had suffered
during the religious
wars. It took twenty
years of "good King
Henry's" conciliatory
rule for France to
recover its former glory
and wealth.*

Louis XIV and the Glory of Classicism

above right
Equestrian Statue of Louis XIV Reaching Place Louis-le-Grand, Edme Bouchardon
The absolute rule of Louis XIV meant that an image of the Sun King – inspired by the famous Roman statue of the emperor Marcus Aurelius – stood in every major square in France. Bernini's project for a statue was rejected, and this version by Edme Bouchardon became the model for the whole kingdom.

Louis XIV was nicknamed "Louis the God-Given" because he was born some twenty years after Louis XIII and Anne of Austria were married in 1638. He owed his miraculous birth to a stormy night when Louis XIII had been obliged to spend a rare moment together with his queen in the Louvre.

When Louis was still a boy-king, during the aristocratic uprising known as the Fronde against the king's Italian-born chief minister, Cardinal Jules Mazarin, he and his mother were forced to leave the Louvre under cover of darkness. The experience left its mark on the future absolute monarch: he moved his court from the Louvre to Saint-Germain-en-Laye in 1666 and then to Versailles after 1682. In the forty-four years between 1671 and his death in 1715, Louis XIV made only twenty-four appearances in Paris and spent not a single night in the capital.

Although other huge construction projects were commissioned by this sovereign with a passion for architecture, the Louvre was not neglected. As early as 1657 the young king, with his chief architect Louis Le Vau, resumed work on Henry IV's "grand design." The east wing, a last vestige of the medieval Louvre, was demolished; the north wing was finished; the south wing doubled in size; and the Petite Galerie was rebuilt and extended after a fire destroyed it in 1661. A gallery and pavilion completed the facade of the Tuileries palace. Inside, the royal apartments were decorated with carved ceilings, wood paneling, and gilded stucco, laden with the royal symbols of fleurs-de-lys, crowns, honors, and trophies.

The death of Cardinal Mazarin in 1661 left Louis alone at last at the helm of state, and henceforth he ruled as an

center left
View of Château and Gardens of Versailles, Pierre Patel
This painting by Patel shows the state of construction in 1668 and gives some idea of the power and grandeur of the château and its park, which were designed by Le Vau, Hardoin-Mansart, and Le Nôtre.

below
Imaginary View of the Colonnade, Pierre-Antoine Demachy
Not until the reign of Louis XV was the facade of the Colonnade in the Louvre finished, completed on the courtyard side by a top floor.

absolute monarch, without even the help of a prime minister. Jean-Baptiste Colbert, although a statesman of outstanding ability, merely executed the royal will. Appointed superintendent of buildings in 1664, Colbert worked hard to reconcile the Sun King's dreams of grandeur with economic realities. His strategy is detectable in the conflicts that flared over the Louvre's east wing between the architects Louis Le Vau, François d'Orbay, Charles Le Brun, François Mansart, and the Perrault brothers, on the one hand, and Gian Lorenzo Bernini, the Italian genius of the Baroque, on the other.

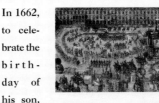

In 1662, to celebrate the birthday of his son, Louis XIV held a "carrousel," or parade, that dazzled all of Europe. Inspired by medieval tournaments, the celebration combined military displays with mythological tableaux. It was held in a vast square amphitheater built between the Louvre and the Tuileries, with seats for 15,000 spectators. Five horseback quadrilles with Roman cavalry were led by the king in person. After a flamboyant parade, the horsemen competed in tests of skill. The carrousel symbolized for everyone present the king's dominion over his own nobles – and the whole world. Henceforth the chances of another revolt – like that of the aristocratic Fronde – were much smaller. It was on this occasion that Louis XIV adopted the sun as his emblem, as well as a Latin motto, *Nec Pluribus Impar*, signifying his ability to rule over several kingdoms at once.

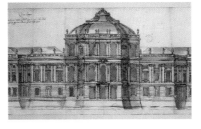

Unfortunately for the Louvre, Bernini's ambitious projects were rejected – for reasons of both climate and expediency – in favor of the dull Colonnade by the Perrault brothers, a project that took ten years to complete, and remained roofless for a century. French classicism had defeated Italian Baroque.

Meanwhile, Louis XIV had moved to Versailles. There he gave free rein to his monumental visions, leaving the Louvre to become the abode of academies of intellectuals, of artists' studios, and of "temple merchants," whose small businesses prospered under the sign of the royal lilies.

When Louis XIV died in 1715, his successor was only five years old. Power lay in the hands of a regency council presided over by Philip of Orléans, the young king's uncle. From 1715 to 1718 the government ruled from the Louvre, but when Louis XV reached his majority in 1723, he returned the court to Versailles.

Abandoned by the crown, the Louvre turned into a "Spanish tavern." Its rooms were made available to artists, craftsmen, and the fortunate recipients of ministerial largesse. Outside, stalls and bars favored by the colorful low life of Paris were run by none other than members of the Royal Swiss Guard, who turned into wine merchants and even brothel-keepers. Scandalized at the anarchy and decadence that ruled the palace, Louis XV and his superintendent of buildings, the marquis of Marigny, Madame de Pompadour's brother, agreed to undertake improvements. The king's favorite architect, Jacques-Ange Gabriel, restored the Colonnade and cleared a square in front of the Louvre. But these essential measures were interrupted by the royal financial problems.

It was now that the idea of a Louvre dedicated to the arts was born. Ever since Francis I, kings had increasingly adorned their palaces with precious objects, tapestries, and paintings. Louis XIV had increased the Royal Collections from two hundred to more than two thousand paintings. The Painting Academy, housed in the Louvre since 1692, had developed the custom of exhibiting its members' works in the Grande Galerie. In 1737 one section of

the gallery, the Salon Carré, became the site of regular exhibitions. The journalist Lafont de Saint-Yenne made the proposal, taken up by Diderot in his *Encyclopedia*, that the Louvre should become a museum and that the public should have access to the Royal Collections. Under Louis XVI Marigny's successor, the count of Angivillers, proposed making the Grande Galerie into a Musée de France. The French Revolution delayed this project, although the idea had been welcomed by an enlightened public and approved by the first mod-

ern museum conservationists. Finally the Legislative Assembly adopted the project in its decree of May 26, 1791, assigning to the Louvre and Tuileries palaces "the habitation of the king and the reunion of all monuments of the sciences and the arts and the principal establishments of public instruction."

Not until the monarchy fell, at the end of 1792, was the Musée de la Nation, combining the Royal Collections with those formerly belonging to the Church and the émigrés, turned into tangible reality.

DAYS OF REVOLUTION AT THE LOUVRE

The life of the monarchy came to an end in 1792 against the backdrop of the Louvre and the Tuileries. On October 6, 1789, the king and his family were brought to the Tuileries under guard by Paris's revolutionary political organizations. On June 20, 1792, sans-culottes broke into the palace and put a revolutionary bonnet on the king's head but failed to persuade him to relinquish the right of veto granted him by the Constitution. In July the duke of Brunswick threatened

Paris with retaliation if anything happened to the royal family, provoking a group of insurrectionists to attack the Tuileries. Louis XVI yielded and declared himself in the Assembly's care. But the protesters rejected this capitulation, and a bloodthirsty massacre of the king's followers ensued. Soon after, Louis XVI was suspended by the Assembly and imprisoned in the Temple. After a sham trial, he climbed the scaffold to his death on January 21, 1793.

NAPOLEON AND THE MUSÉE DES VICTOIRES

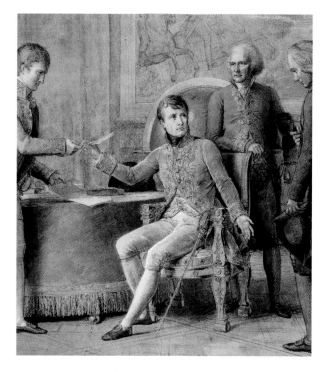

On October 17, 1792, the revolutionary minister of the interior, Jean-Marie Roland, met with painter Jacques-Louis David, known as "Raphael of the sans-culottes," who would later become the first administrator of the Louvre. Roland defined for the painter his conception of what the museum should be: "It must nourish a taste for the fine arts, create new art lovers, and serve as a school for artists; it must be open to all. The monument must be a national one." In September of the following year, the public was admitted to the Salon Carré and the Grande Galerie, where paintings were now grouped in schools.

In July 1798 a triumphal procession brought works that French troops had pillaged in Italy to the Louvre, including the *Dying Gladiator*, the *Venus de Milo*, and the horses from St. Mark's Basilica in Venice. To welcome these prestigious guests, a new department was created on the ground floor of the Louvre. The Antiquities Room was inaugurated by Napoleon Bonaparte in November 1800, a year after the coup d'état in which he threw out the Directory and had himself appointed first consul. Settling into the palace of kings, Bonaparte muttered, "It's nothing to be in the Tuileries; the game is to remain there."

As early as 1803 the museum was renamed the Musée Napoléon. The following year, Napoleon broke all ties with the royal past of France when,

below
Napoleon Bonaparte
A greater administrator than a warrior, Napoleon Bonaparte was perhaps most of all a great self-publicist. A pure product of the 18th century in his culture and strategy, he used art and the press to promote himself in a way that prefigures the image-obsessed dictators of the 20th century.

bottom right
Laocoön Room, Benjamin Zix
On November 9, 1800, Bonaparte declared the Antiquities Room in the Louvre open to the public. Most of the pieces came from church collections taken over by the Republic. One of the most striking exhibits was the Laocoön group, which stunned the general's entourage.

left
Signing the Concordat, drawing, Baron François Gérard
Signed in Paris by the consulate and the Holy See on July 15, 1801, the Concordat established a new status for the post-Revolutionary French Church, defining its relationship with the state. Napoleon understood that settling this question was essential for peace within France.

left center
Presentation of the Consular Act, Jean Duplessis-Bertaux
This engraving shows François de Barthélemy, president of the Senate, presenting First Consul Bonaparte with the constitutional act establishing the Consulate for life in July 1802. It was the first step toward the hereditary Empire, proclaimed less than two years later.

NAPOLEONIC SPOILS AND THE REVIVAL OF TASTE

The first Louvre museum commissioners (four painters and a geometrician) intended to give prominence to French works, which until then had been considered inferior to Italian art. But the influx of foreign works soon dwarfed the size of the French collection. Although they administered the greatest storehouse of stolen property in Europe, the commissioners' consciences were clear. They believed that France had saved these works from the decay inevitable in their countries of origin. As the revolutionaries had once wanted, the Louvre was also fulfilling a didatic mission. Vivant Denon's policies at the Louvre undoubtedly changed public taste. This administrator was also largely responsible for reviving interest in the early Italian artists, the so-called Primitives, as well as Etruscan art.

on his orders, the duke of Enghien, a Bourbon, was seized in German territory by French troops and executed. The Senate approved the first consul's ascent to the rank of hereditary emperor, and the investiture was held on December 2, 1801. Obsessed by grandeur – "beauty lies in greatness alone" –

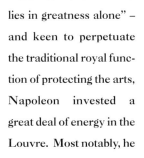

and keen to perpetuate the traditional royal function of protecting the arts, Napoleon invested a great deal of energy in the Louvre. Most notably, he revived the "grand design" of the Bourbon kings, continuing the work, with his architects Pierre Fontaine and Charles Percier, of linking the palaces. Stallkeepers and artists were evicted, a Roman triumphal arch was added to the Carrousel, and spoils from Napoleon's campaigns enriched the collections. He was aided considerably in this task by his capable lieutenant Dominique-Vivant Denon, once a figure of the ancien régime. In Napoleon's energetic hands, the Louvre grew in size and glory to become a center of European art, in a manner unprecedented since the reign of another great conqueror, Louis XIV.

From Faraway Worlds
to a Short-Lived Republic

right

Charles X

This younger brother of Louis XVI succeeded Louis XVIII. Ill advised by a short-sighted entourage, he provoked the 1830 revolution. Its "Trois [Journées] Glorieuses" put an end to Bourbon rule in France.

above

The Obelisk at the Bastille

Erected on the Place de la Bastille, the obelisk commemorates the "Trois Glorieuses" – the three-day revolution of 1830 – and its victims.

center bottom

Ruins of the Tuileries Palace

Paris Communards set fire to the Tuileries palace – a much-hated symbol of power – in 1871.

Napoleon's conquests and Denon's cultural policies had made the Louvre the world's richest museum. But when Louis XVIII came to the throne in 1815, he faced the obligation of returning the works of art to their countries of origin. Ordered to return the marvels, Denon replied that he would give in only to bayonets. And give in he finally did – to the British victor of Waterloo, the duke of Wellington. More than five thousand works of art made their way back home; only a hundred of the most imposing works remained in the Louvre.

The Tuileries palace recovered its status as the center of power, and unlike Napoleon, the king opened large areas of it to the public. The architect Fontaine extended the north wing of the palace to the Pavillon de Rohan and

redesigned the interior of the Louvre. New aquisitions, including the famous *Venus de Milo*, completed the museum's antiquities collection.

But it was Louis's successor, Charles X, who presided over the true modernization of the old Louvre. On the first floor of the south wing, Charles X inaugurated the museum that bears his name. Medieval and Renaissance art returned to favor in the wake of the Romantic movement. Soon thereafter, thanks to the Egyptologist Jean-François Champollion, Egyptian art made a spectacular entrance.

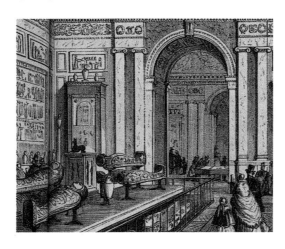

Under Louis Philippe, the Louvre acquired an Assyrian museum – just before France's third revolution broke out in 1848. It brought to an end the entire French tradition of monarchy and ushered in the era of popular rule.

left

Louis Philippe

One hand on his heart, signifying his honest intentions (the other, not shown, is holding the French Republican flag instead of the white royal banner), Louis Philippe presents himself as guarantor of the harmony between monarchy and liberty. Less than twenty years later, the so-called bourgeois king was deposed in yet another revolution.

center top

Louis XVIII

Louis XVIII's engraved features appear on the Charter, a liberal constitution that the king officially endorsed in 1814. Despite many concessions, it displeased both the old revolutionaries and those loyal to the fallen Emperor Napoleon.

center left

The Egyptian Museum

Entrusted to the care of Champollion under Charles X, the Egyptian Museum was housed on the second floor of the Cour Carrée, in rooms specially designed by the architect Fontaine.

The People's Revenge

The Revolution of 1848, which toppled Louis Philippe, was marked by a vengeful spirit as the people turned on the symbols of monarchy. Gustave Flaubert's novel *Sentimental Education* vividly illustrates this spirit. "The throne was picked up and passed unsteadily from hand to hand across the room. . . . An explosion of frenzied joy

followed, as if, in place of the throne, a future of boundless joy had appeared; and the mob . . . smashed or tore up mirrors, curtains, chandeliers, sconces, tables, chairs . . . in the mounting fury the continuous din was swollen by the sound of broken glass and crystal, which tinkled as it fell like the keys of a harmonica."

Riding on lyrical illusions, incarnated by the poet Alphonse Lamartine, the Second Republic was proclaimed on February 25, 1848. In November, a new constitution gave legislative power to an assembly elected for three years by universal suffrage and executive power to a president elected for four years. The president was not allowed either to dissolve the assembly or to stand for election to it. The regime was doomed to failure. On December 10, Louis-Napoleon, nephew of Napoleon I, was elected president by a landslide. Three years later, on December 2, 1851, a coup d'état, followed by a referendum, enabled the "little Napoleon" (as Victor Hugo called him) to follow in the steps of the great Bonaparte. Under Napoleon III's capable rule, an increasingly liberal Second Empire brought economic prosperity to France, but fell to defeat by the Prussians in 1870. On September 4 of that year, Léon Gambetta and Jules Favre proclaimed the beginning of the Third Republic at the Hôtel de Ville in Paris.

In the meantime, the Louvre had benefited considerably from imperial largesse. No less a builder than his uncle, Napoleon III was responsible for finally completing Henry IV's "grand design." In March 1852 he

instructed his architect Ludovico Tullio Visconti to complete this ambitious project, with the object of making the Louvre not only a center of the arts but also the hub of a centralized state system. From the telegraph office to the nation's stables, from printing presses to barracks, everything would have to pass through the main administrative offices at the Louvre.

As Napoleon III also wished, Visconti's intention was to preserve the diversity of styles that corresponded to the different periods of the Louvre's construction. But Visconti died prematurely, in 1853. His successor, Hector Lefuel, was a loyal follower of the city planner Baron Haussmann, at that time engaged in pulling down old Paris. Lefuel wanted to do away with the past and impose the electic and ostentatious "Napoleon III" style. He destroyed Henry IV's Pavillon de Flore and

the Grande Galerie, then rebuilt them on a more massive scale. In 1866, bright with gilt and bristling with sculptures, the new Louvre was more or less finished. Lefuel would gladly have pursued this extravaganza further, but in 1870 the Second Empire fell before the Prussians, and the city rose in revolt. The Paris Commune wanted to go much further toward popular rule than the "bourgeois" Second Republic had done. On May 23, 1871, faced with a national army that had regained control of France, Communards set fire to the Tuileries palace and the Pavillon Richelieu, along with the city hall and other symbolic monuments. Thanks to its curator, its guards, and an army detachment, the Louvre was saved. Now that Tuileries – symbol of national power – no longer stood beside it, the Louvre could fulfill its mission unimpeded, as a temple to the arts.

above right
Visconti Presents Plans for the New Louvre to Napoleon III
In March of 1852, Napoleon III gave Visconti the task of completing the Louvre. Highly respectful of the past, Visconti here shows the emperor and his wife his plans for the new building, the character of which "would be taken religiously from the old Louvre."

center right
Prussian Bombardment of Paris, 1871
In early January 1871, the Prussians set up long-range artillery on the hills of Clamart, Châtillon, and Fontenay in order to force an early capitulation by Paris. Neighborhoods along the Seine suffered particularly heavily, and on July 26 Paris surrendered.

below
Barricade, 1871, Edouard Manet
Manet, who sympathized with the Communards,

illustrates here the terrible repression launched by Louis-Adolphe Thiers when his troops reconquered Paris. Communards not executed on the spot were sentenced to penal servitude or deported to New Caledonia.

below left center
Tuileries in Flames During Bloody Week
Burned by the Communards as a hated symbol of power, the Tuileries palace looks heavenward from its blackened walls and empty windows. In 1883 the Third Republic made a purely political decision to tear down the monument, which could have been rebuilt.

THE REPUBLIC ABHORS A RUIN

In the aftermath of the Commune, the charred skeleton of the Tuileries palace was a Parisian scandal. Of the former glory of this residence of kings and emperors only the facades remained intact. Baron Haussmann, an inveterate demolisher of the old Paris, nonetheless insisted that restoration and reconstruction were possible. After ten years of proposals and disagreements, politics won out

over aesthetics. "There is no beauty or grandeur in the ruins," Jules Ferry decided. "They are simply ugly and sad." The writer Émile Zola suggested that they be "pulled down to extend the Champs-Élysées as far as the Carrousel." In 1882 the Third Republic opted for demolition and hired the entrepreneur Achille Picart to perform the task. A few relics of the palace were bought by artists and social leaders.

From the Third Republic to the present, the history of the Louvre has been one of vaulting ambition and an insatiable quest for ever more space.

From the Second Empire onward, government ministries had wrested firm footholds for themselves in the palace of the arts. The most powerful of them, the Finance Ministry, was housed in the Rivoli Wing and had the full run of the sumptuous apartments of the Pavillon Turgot. In 1900 the Musée des Arts Décoratifs occu-

pied the Pavillon Marsan and the adjacent wing. Only in 1960 was the National Lottery administration cleared from Pavillon de Flore, and in 1989 the Ministry of Finance finally agreed to relinquish the Rivoli Wing. The muscum was by now suffering from a desperate lack of space, even though the Maritime Museum, Ethnographic Museum, and museums of Asiatic arts,

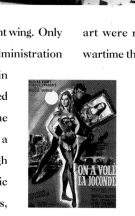

modern art and painting, and painting of the second half of the 19th century had all moved elsewhere.

The last decades of the 19th century and the first decades of the 20th were the Louvre's most uneventful period in centuries. The most noteworthy event was the theft of Leonardo's world-famous *Mona Lisa* (known to the French as *La Joconde*); stolen in 1911, it was recovered in Italy and returned in 1914.

During the First and Second World Wars, works of art were removed from the gaze of visitors. In wartime the Louvre's masterpieces – from the *Venus de Milo* to the *Apollo Belvedere*, from Watteau's *Gilles* to Ingres's *Grande Odalisque* – were sent away for some country air. Nevertheless, Nazi occupiers were able to siphon off several thousand works. Worst of all, they burned the modern paintings, which

they considered decadent, on a bonfire in front of the Jeu de Paume.

Not until the 1980s did the Louvre make newspaper headlines again. As rulers have always done, François Mitterrand, president of France until 1995, was eager to leave his mark on a public monument. The Louvre was his opportunity to rival Pericles, Augustus Caesar, Lorenzo de Medici, and Louis XIV. In the space of ten years, the Louvre

has not only seen the number of its rooms (and its capacity to receive visitors) increase, it has also managed to exhibit many treasures that were formerly hidden away in its reserves and improve the display of major works. It has had a spectacular face-lift, metamorphosing into a true city within the city. Here it is on the eve of a new millennium: very different from the fairy-tale castle of the duke of Berry but every bit as stunning.

GARDEN IN THE CITY

The Tuileries were originally Italian-style gardens, enhanced by shrub-lined flowerbeds, ornamental pools, and statuary. The landscape artist Bernard Palissy even built an artificial grotto there, and Henry IV planted mulberry trees and installed a silkworm nursery. Then André Lenôtre turned it into a garden *à la française*. On the two esplanades overlooking the Place de la Concorde, Napoleon III built the Pavillon de l'Orangerie and the Pavillon du Jeu de Paume. Except for a single section reserved for Louis Philippe and Napoleon III, the garden has been open to the public since Henry IV. In 1991 the landscape artist Jacques Wirtz renewed the section known as the Carrousel, while Pascal Cribler, Louis Kenech, and François Roubaud introduced more varied flora and established more amenities for strollers.

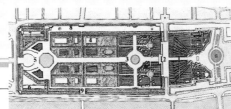

Architecture

The Louvre is nearing the end of its latest metamorphosis – the Grand Louvre project. The large-scale plans brought to fruition over the past ten years by architect I.M. Pei and his associates have added 20th-century elements to the many architectural styles that have succeeded one another at the museum since the time of Philip Augustus. Pei's two guiding principles – a resolutely contemporary contribution, coupled with a deliberate enhancement of elements from the past – highlight the Louvre's personality at each stage of its history. Before the Grand Louvre project, the public had never been able to visit the medieval castle of the Louvre, the Napoleon III apartments, the Cour Lefuel, and the Second Empire stables. These pages trace the development of the Louvre's architecture, first outdoors, then inside, focusing on decorative details as well as broad outlines. Photographs capture the masterpieces created over the centuries and the unceasing evolution of taste and style.

3. Caryatid Room

12. Anne of Austria's Apartments

13. Galerie d'Apollon

16. Winged Victory Staircase

19. Grande Galerie

21. Stables, Riding School

25. Lion Gate

31. Carrousel Triumphal Arch

33. Statue of Louis XIV

39. Pei Staircase

40. Café Richelieu

41. Ministry of State Apartments

42. Cour Marly

46. One of 83 Statues of Famous Men

47. Lefuel Staircase

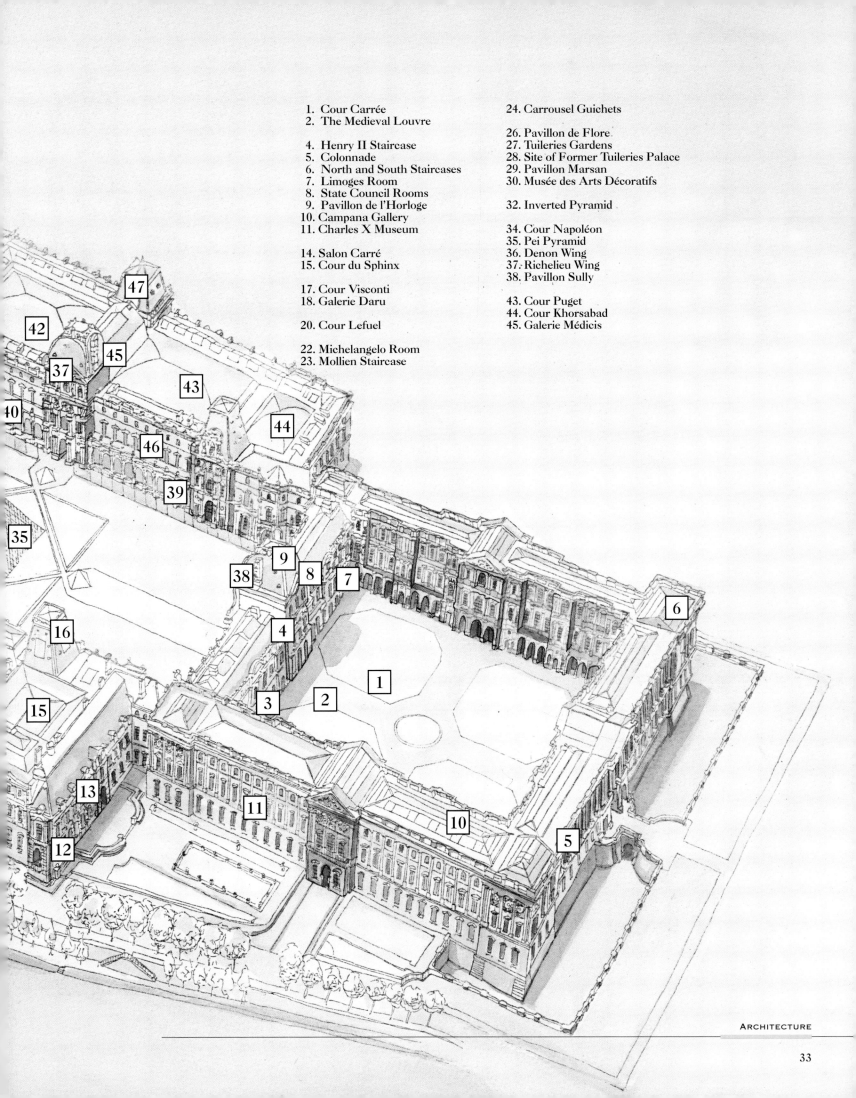

1. Cour Carrée
2. The Medieval Louvre

4. Henry II Staircase
5. Colonnade
6. North and South Staircases
7. Limoges Room
8. State Council Rooms
9. Pavillon de l'Horloge
10. Campana Gallery
11. Charles X Museum

14. Salon Carré
15. Cour du Sphinx

17. Cour Visconti
18. Galerie Daru

20. Cour Lefuel

22. Michelangelo Room
23. Mollien Staircase

24. Carrousel Guichets

26. Pavillon de Flore
27. Tuileries Gardens
28. Site of Former Tuileries Palace
29. Pavillon Marsan
30. Musée des Arts Décoratifs

32. Inverted Pyramid

34. Cour Napoléon
35. Pei Pyramid
36. Denon Wing
37. Richelieu Wing
38. Pavillon Sully

43. Cour Puget
44. Cour Khorsabad
45. Galerie Médicis

The Louvre is a book of stone in which eight centuries of French architecture have been chronicled. From Philip Augustus's late-12th-century keep to François Mitterrand's Grand Louvre of 1981, kings, emperors, and statesmen have doubled as builders; between fifteen and twenty great architects have helped direct the extraordinary enterprise.

The Louvre's history is a long and multifaceted one. Its architecture has had to adapt to its many changes of vocation, to serve the needs of fortress, palace, royal residence, and national museum. Under Philip Augustus it was the kingdom's most beautiful castle, its innovative construction eagerly imitated at Château Gaillard, Mont-Saint-Michel, and Dourdan. Kings incarcerated important prisoners here, along with arms and treasure. Until Charles X transformed it into a royal residence, the ancient fortress remained a picture-book castle; as it was painted by the Limburg brothers in their *Very Rich Hours of the Duke of Berry*.

In 1546 Francis I spearheaded the Louvre's decisive transformation. In a brilliant stroke he selected the architect Pierre Lescot and the sculptor Jean Goujon to direct the work. Lescot and Goujon went on to define the principles of what became French classicism. Their design for the west and south wings of the Cour Carrée would serve as yardsticks for the Louvre's later development. Henry IV – the king who first articulated the goal of linking the Louvre to the Tuileries palace by means of two long galleries on the north and south sides – respected this architectural language when he began his "grand design" by building one of the galleries, on the south (or river) side.

Respecting the style established by Lescot, Louis XIII, Louis XIV, and Napoleon I enlarged the courtyard fourfold. Under Napoleon III architect Hector Lefuel completed the "grand design" by building a second connecting gallery on the north side, parallel to Henry IV's south wing.

Most recently, the architect I. M. Pei was equally convinced of the impossibility of breaking with the past. Determined both to innovate and to remain faithful to the Louvre's quintessentially French character, he designed his glass pyramid to draw all the hues of the Paris skies into the ancient royal palace, now the world's largest museum.

---

right
Stucco figure, Michel Anguier
Decorating the apartments of Anne of Austria, this stucco celebrates the beauty and grace of the female body. It is a theme that recurs throughout the Louvre, from its caryatid sculptures to its allegories and figures of the Fates.

above
Caryatids, Rue de Rivoli, Second Empire
The word "caryatid" evokes ancient Greece – more specifically, the Peloponnesian city of Karyai, which gave its name to these women-as-columns. They support the cornices on all the Louvre's facades; this one looks out on the Rue de Rivoli.

center below
The Caryatids; Peace and War, Pavillon Sully, Second Empire
These caryatids were sculpted by Charles Simart, who also carved the pediment of the Pavillon Denon. Pierre-Jules Cavelier sculpted the figures of Peace and War flanking the clockface. Cavelier carved a number of other works at the Louvre under Napoleon III: the caryatids on the Richelieu pediment, the Petite Galerie, the statue of Pierre Abelard, and the west face of the Pavillon de Flore.

right
The Richelieu Wing, seen from the Denon Wing
Seen through the transparent Pei Pyramid, the old Louvre (the Denon Wing, through which visitors formerly entered the museum) gazes out on the Richelieu Wing, an area of 22,000 square meters (144,000 square feet), formerly occupied by the Ministry of Finance.

PAVILLON SULLY

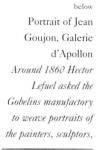

The Cour Carrée

The Cour Carrée symbolizes the birth of the Louvre we see today. Conceived in the mid-16th century by Pierre Lescot and Jean Goujon, it established a model that was followed by all successive architects who have worked on the complex.

Francis I deserves lasting praise for his boldness and taste in choosing two nearly unknown young artists to work on the Louvre. As far back as 1528 Francis had expressed his determination "to repair and put some order into our old Louvre castle." But at that stage he simply tore down the great tower, filled in the moats, and cleared the approaches to the river to give the Louvre an unobstructed view of the Seine.

For more than twenty years, Francis preferred the game-rich forests of the Loire valley and the lush parks of the Île-de-France, where he could hunt deer and indulge in the pleasures of courtly life. He built a château at Chambord and embellished Amboise, Fontainebleau, Saint-Germain-en-Laye, and the Spanish city of Madrid before turning again to his Parisian palace in 1540.

At the end of that year he invited two renowned Italian architects, Giacomo da Vignola and Sebastiano Serlio, to Paris. But their proposals for remodeling the Louvre were unacceptable: France was the only country in Europe to reject the reigning Baroque style. The

Compass, Square, and Chisel

On August 2, 1546, Francis I commissioned his architect Pierre Lescot to replace the west wing of the castle with a series of *hôtels*, or town houses, in the new Renaissance style. Lescot's facade is composed of a forward wing graced by columns and framed by inset wings. An arcade of fully rounded arches runs along the ground floor, which is surmounted by the second floor and then a mansard floor with a

pitched roof. The sculpture was entrusted to Jean Goujon in 1549: allegorical figures frame the bull's-eye windows above the doors, and decorate lintels and window pediments. In his reference work *The Most Excellent Buildings of France*, Androuet du Cerceau immortalized this facade, in which the sculptor's chisel and the architect's compass achieve a strking mutual enhancement.

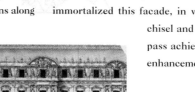

left
The Glass Pyramid,
I. M. Pei, 1988

right
Science Holding her
Caduceus,
Cour Carrée,
West Facade,
Jean Goujon

right
Drawing of East
Facade, Gian
Lorenzo Bernini
*Bernini's study for the
east facade of the
Louvre was among
several projects
submitted by this
renowned Baroque
architect. They were
judged unsuitable to
French tastes and
eventually rejected.*

previous double page
Nature Holding Her
Cornucopia,
Cour Carrée,
West Facade,
Jean Goujon
*Goujon sculpted the
figures of nature and
science on the west side
of the Cour Carrée in
symmetrical positions.
For the humanists of
the Renaissance, nature
and science promised
to reveal the secrets of
divine order, masked
by the world's
apparent disorder.*

top left
Pediment, Minerva
Rewarding the Fine
Arts and Sciences,
Cour Carrée, South
Facade, Eustache
Le Sueur, 1814
*Minerva is surrounded
by the muses of
astronomy with her
globe, painting with
her palette, and music
with her trumpet.*

below
Glory Distributing
Crowns, Colonnade,
Pierre Cartellier
*In 1807 Cartellier
sculpted this ornate*

*tympanum of Glory in
Neoclassical style, at
the center of the
Colonnade. The
symmetrical
compositions were
inspired by an antique
cameo.*

left below
Drawing
of East Facade,
Charles Le Brun
*Proposed for the east
wing of the Louvre,
this drawing exploits
the existing theme of
alternating apertures
and arcades. Le Brun
conceived the Colonnade
with Le Vau and
Perrault in 1667;
the appendage of
Perrault's name was
hasty.*

Italians left, for much the same reason that Gian Lorenzo Bernini would depart a century later.

The departure of the Italians freed Lescot to transform the Louvre into the first monument of French Renaissance architecture. An enormous cathedral planned for Beauvais had collapsed disastrously, announcing the final flickering of the Gothic style. Thus Lescot opted for radical innovation: he imposed a strong geometrical framework on the west and south wings of the Cour Carrée, the perfect support for Goujon's sculptures and bas-reliefs. Goujon, a scholar and friend of the poet Pierre de Ronsard, brought the facades of the Louvre to florid life with forests, fountains, harvests, nymphs, fluttering draperies, and the svelte thighs of divine huntresses – in short, with all the abundant sensuality so

dear to the king. After the wars and misery of the 15th century, France was reborn; in keeping with the new peaceful spirit, Goujon's work exalted the beauty of women and children.

All the Louvre's subsequent architects have respected the language of Lescot and Goujon. In 1805 Napoleon vehemently opposed a proposal by Charles Percier and Pierre Fontaine to destroy Goujon's masterpieces: "Architects seek to adopt a single order and change everything else, but finances, common sense, and good taste are of a different mind. Each of the parts that exist must retain the character of its own century." As a result, the wings designed by Lescot and Goujon have survived; Jean-Baptiste Carpeaux's Pavillon de Flore possesses the same grace and strength as Goujon's caryatids.

THE COLONNADE

The Colonnade's history began in 1664, when Jean-Baptiste Colbert was appointed Louis XIV's superintendent of buildings. Rejecting Louis Le Vau's project for the east facade, he sent an emissary to Rome to seek further ideas. Disappointed by the proposals brought back, Colbert presented Le Vau's proposal to Gian Lorenzo Bernini. Although offended at being consulted after other Italians, Bernini nevertheless worked for four months, endlessly correcting and altering his drawings.

But his vision did not suit the minister's pragmatic concerns. "Don't talk to me of anything small," Colbert had warned Bernini. Meanwhile, French architects had launched a campaign against the Italian project – which ended with Bernini's return to Rome. Colbert invited Le Vau, Le Brun, Claude, and Perrault to design a new project. In May 1666 two drawings were presented to the king: one with a colonnade, the other without. Louis XIV chose the Colonnade.

above right

Quays of the Seine,
Frieze, detail
*Executed in the reign
of Henry IV, this frieze
on the Seine quayside
is possibly by the
Lheureux brothers. It
was completed during
the Second Republic by
Félix Duban, who also
adopted the theme of
children.*

below

Guichets
*"The guards on watch
at the Louvre's gates
do not in the least
defend our kings,"
wrote the poet
François de Malherbe.
He meant that the
Louvre's Swiss Guards*

*and sentinels could bar
the common people
from entering the
palace gates – but not
death. After the
French crown moved
to Versailles, these*
guichets, *or
passageways, became
galleries occupied by
dealers in engravings.*

THE SEINE FACADE

By an ironic twist of fate, Napoleon III completed the "grand design" that kings could never bring to fruition. For ten years, with the growing support of financiers, the prince-president and emperor-to-be set more than five hundred men to work – by day and by night, thanks to the first arc lamps. But scarcely was the Louvre linked to the Tuileries palace when the Tuileries went up in flames!

Henry IV, the first monarch to attempt to connect the two buildings, envisaged a long gallery on the Seine side to accomplish it. As soon as he arrived in triumph in Paris in 1594, he commissioned his architects, Louis Métezeau and Jacques Androuet du Cerceau, to design the enormous space running along the Seine to the Pavillon de Flore, a length of more than 1,350 feet. Work

began in 1595, and was completed 1608.

From these gallery windows the court could admire waterborne fetes on the Seine – a fashionable amusement all through the 16th, 17th, and 18th centuries.

Historians have left descriptions of an extraordinary "river pageant" that was staged in 1550 to celebrate Henry II's victory over the English at Boulogne. In an enormous "Rococo chaos," Orpheus played his harp while Hercules severed the Hydra's heads; Neptune surged from a rock to hand his trident to the king, declaring in verse that he abdicated his power over the deeps. Multitudes of boats decked out to look like dolphins and whales streamed up and down the river. Two seahorses drew a triumphal chariot, while ships simulated a naval battle to the thunder of cannonfire.

left center

Riverside Facade
seen from accross
the Seine
*To gaze at this facade
is to return to the time
of Henry IV. The road
leading west out of
Paris came this way,
while from under the
windows the hubbub of
the busy riverside port
of Saint-Nicholas
could be heard.*

below center

The Pont des Arts
*This graceful
footbridge links the
Louvre, a temple of
art, to the Académie
Française, a temple of
learning. Now
restored, the bridge is
once again a place
where – as the Georges
Brassens song suggests
– lovers can stroll
hand in hand.*

right

Facade,
Grande Galerie
*When Henry IV first
envisioned the Grande
Galerie, he told the
Swiss humanist
Thomas Platter that he
wanted "to be able to
wander, and to watch
happenings on the
Seine in front of the
palace." The spectacle
is not very different
today, except, of course,
that the boats are
power-driven.*

right
The Louvre, from
the Île de la Cité
*It takes considerable
imagination to
visualize Pierre
Lescot's Louvre as it
once appeared from the
Île de la Cité. The
island was still
cluttered with medieval
buildings, while the
quays were much closer
to the water than
today.*

left
Lion,
Antoine-Louis Barye
*On the quays in front
of the Lion Gate, this is
one of the two lions
designed by Barye, a
leading animal
sculptor under
Napoleon III. The
sculptures reflect
Barye's Romantic taste
for animal combats, as
well as his knowledge
of anatomy, gained at
the Museum of
Natural History.*

previous double page
Medusa's Head,
Wendling, Armand,
and Yan
*This war trophy with
Medusa's head was
sculpted in 1851 under
Félix Duban's
direction. For his
reconstruction of this
entire section of the
quay, Duban copied
designs from the time
of Henry IV.*

left center
Riverside Figures
*Overlooking the Seine,
these statues were
installed by Lefuel
around 1858 to
decorate niches that
had remained
untenanted since
Duban's restoration.*

bottom center
Section of
Charles IX Balcony,
Félix Duban
*Under the Second
Republic, the architect
Félix Duban, a student
of the great Eugène
Viollet-le-Duc,
redecorated a large part
of the Louvre in
Renaissance style. This
is part of the Charles
IX facade, from which,
according to legend, the
king fired at
Protestants on
St. Bartholomew's Day.*

above
Bacchus Pediment,
Florence Walter and
Victor Corbet
*This pediment, sculpted
in 1850-1851, shows
a head of Bacchus with
harvest spirits.*

From the east side of the Galerie Henry IV, we can still admire an intact frieze of children frolicking in the water, and a decorative field glorifying the king, in which dolphins, scepters, and crowns, as well as the scales of justice and the sheaves of abundance, also stand out from the background.

The only remaining traces of the Grande Galerie's west side are a handful of photographs taken by Edouard Baldus in 1861. Just afterward Lefuel began to tear down the Pavillon de Flore and about a third of the Grande Galerie as far as the Pavillon Lesdiguières. The plan outraged the press, but Lefuel went ahead, building a new Pavillon de Flore, a more elaborate wing, and the triple triumphal arch forming the Grands Guichets passageway to the Seine. The decor

of these new facades was inspired by the Lescot Wing, although they were marked as well by an exuberance that Lefuel's enemies called "sophisticated candy." But Lefuel deserves recognition for hiring two of the best sculptors of his time, Jean-Baptiste Carpeaux and Antoine-Louis Barye. On the south face of the Pavillon de Flore, Carpeaux carved a large bas-relief, *Flora Crouched Laughing at the Children Around Her*, undoubtedly the most famous sculpture on the outside of the Louvre. Barye's *River* and *Stream*, represented by two young reclining bodies crowned with reeds, can still be seen. They originally flanked the equestrian statue of Napoleon III, which was torn down in 1870 and replaced with Antonin Mercié's *Spirit of the Arts.*

right center

Pavillon de Rohan
and Pavillon Marsan
*The Pavillon de
Rohan was begun
under Napoleon I by
Charles Percier and
Pierre Fontaine and
completed during the
Restoration. The
Pavillon Marsan was
reconstructed in 1871
by Hector Lefuel.*

right center, below

Allegorical Figures,
Top of Pavillon
Marsan
*This decorative theme
– two winged political
allegories and the
initials "R.F."
(République
Française) – was
originally intended for
the government's
general accounting
office, which was to be
housed in the pavilion.
This never came to pass,
and in 1905 the Musée
des Arts Décoratifs
was inaugurated here.
In 1997 a fashion
museum opened in the
pavilion.*

left

Restoration with Her
Carriage, Carrousel
Triumphal Arch
*Napoleon had the
horses from St. Mark's
in Venice placed on top
of the Carrousel
Triumphal Arch.
When the Empire
collapsed, they were
returned to Italy, and
the imperial eagles and
bees were replaced with
the fleur-de-lys.*

below

Carrousel
Triumphal Arch
*This monumental yet
graceful triumphal
arch once served as the
entrance to the Tuileries
palace. Its exorbitant
price of one million
francs was paid by the
Grand Army. The
large marble reliefs
glorifying Napoleon's*

*campaigns were carved
by the best sculptors of
the period: Michel
Clodion, Pierre
Cartellier, Louis-Pierre
Deseine, and Eustache
Le Sueur*

above

The Peace of
Presbourg, Carrousel
Triumphal Arch,
Eustache Le Sueur
*This bas-relief, carved
in 1810 by Le Sueur,
represents the treaty
signed on December 26,
1805, following
Napoleon's victory at
Austerlitz.*

THE CARROUSEL

Carrousels were sumptuous royal displays – equestrian parades – staged for foreign sovereigns, royal weddings, and coronations. The carrousel of June 5, 1662, staged by Louis XIV for his mother, Anne of Austria, gave its name to the present square, the Place du Carrousel. More ambitious than previous carrousels, this one went down in history because the young king leading the horsemen was dressed as an emperor of antiquity.

It was on the Place du Carrousel that Napoleon honored his armies by erecting a triumphal arch. Its style, inspired by the Arch of Septimus Severus in Rome, reflects Napoleon's strong affinity for antiquity. The arch was originally surmounted by four horses that had been removed from St. Mark's Basilica in Venice following the French victories in Italy. But they were returned to Venice in 1815. Louis XVIII replaced them with François Bosio's *Restoration with Her Carriage*, a group that lacks the beauty and history of the horses. Ironically, the "Venetian" horses were themselves spoils of war, having been seized from the Hippodrome in Constantinople during the Crusade of 1204.

Although the legendary horses are gone, four magnificent bas-reliefs of rivers, sculpted in the Louvre's finest tradition, can be admired under the vault of the arch. The eye can then travel across the Place de la Concorde to the Arc de Triomphe and then onward to the Grande Arche at La Défense – an immense perspective left open by the removal of the Tuileries palace.

THE PAVILLON DE ROHAN

On March 12, 1853, Louis-Napoleon entrusted completion of the Louvre to Ludovico Visconti. Three months later the architect began by constructing the Pavillon de Rohan, thus inaugurating the largest building site of the whole Second Empire. The son of a former curator of the Louvre's paintings and antiquities, Visconti was a classicist with profound respect for the past. The facade of the Pavillon de Rohan, with its false arcades and columns, resembles the side facing the Seine. The large figure known as *La France Artiste*, carved by Georges Diebolt, is inspired by the Molière fountain, designed at an earlier date by Visconti himself.

THE COUR NAPOLÉON

The Cour Napoléon did not take on its present appearance until 1852, when Napoleon III launched his large-scale construction projects. He accepted Ludovico Visconti's proposal to build three courtyards to the north and two to the south. Five years later they formed the Cour Napoléon as we see it today.

While the Second Republic had sought to transform the Louvre into an "intellectual Mecca," Napoleon III's plans for the Louvre were somewhat less ambitious. He wanted the renovated and expanded museum to become the seat of government, an imperial city-within-a-city, complete with government ministries, military barracks, armed forces, telegraph services, and police.

Visconti, who envisaged facades inspired by Lescot's earlier work, was felled by a heart attack in 1853 and left the construction site unfinished. Lefuel, his successor, was less circumspect. Without calling into question Visconti's overall concept, he raised each facade by one floor and decorated them with a profusion of sculptures exalting Napoleon III's reign.

Taking the Pavillon de l'Horloge as his model, Lefuel constructed the pavilions of the Cour Napoléon. He dedicated the northern ones to the great ministers of the ancien régime, and those on the southern side to leading officials of the Napoleonic Empire. Caryatids supported pediments representing themes of peace, law, the arts, and abundance, already repeatedly adopted by the Louvre's earlier architects. On the terrace Lefuel placed eighty-three giant statues of illustrious men from literature, the arts, the Church, and the State. To give the courtyard greater unity, he decided in

THE RUE DE RIVOLI

The Rue de Rivoli runs along the full length of the Richelieu Wing on the side of the Place du Palais Royal. This wing was returned to the museum when the Finance Ministry found new quarters. The street was built at the beginning of Napoleon I's empire by the architects Charles Percier and Pierre Fontaine, with the intention of building a wing to connect the two palaces on the northern side. The Galerie Napoléon stretched from the Pavillon Marsan to the Saint-Napoléon Chapel, near the Pavillon Beauvais.

Not until the Second Empire and Baron Haussmann's urban overhaul did the administration tear down the squalid tenements located to the east of the Pavillon de Rohan – "the warts on the face of Paris," as Honoré de Balzac described them in *La Cousine Bette*. Once the square was cleared, it became possible to link the Louvre and the Tuileries on the north side. Visconti then built the Pavillon de Rohan and part of the adjoining wing, which was completed after his death by Lefuel.

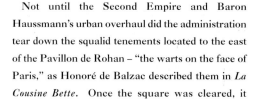

1856 to renovate the decor on the Old Louvre wing, connecting the Beauvais with the Rotonde d'Apollon, at the far end of the courtyard.

When the Cour Napoléon was inaugurated in 1857, majestically opening onto the Carrousel and the Tuileries palace, Napoleon III could honestly claim that completion of the Louvre was not "a passing whim, but the realization of a grand design instinctively approved by the nation for more than a hundred years."

The emperor did not know how truthfully he spoke. The Cour Napoléon reflects not merely three or four centuries of history: between 1980 and 1985, excavations revealed a wealth of ancient treasures buried in its sub-

strata. The digs, led by the archaeologist Pierre-Jean Trombetta, furthered knowledge of how the site of the Louvre had been occupied since prehistoric times. Ten thousand years ago, in the area where the Carrousel now stands, distant ancestors of Parisians worked with stone to make arrowheads and harpoons. About five thousand years later, agriculture was practiced here, while cattle were raised during the Gallo-Roman period. Around the 7th century, the first houses were built on the stones now trodden by visitors from around the world. The Cour Napoléon is not only the Louvre's most ancient shrine of human remembrance but its most modern and timeless symbol.

left
Caryatids,
Pavillon Richelieu
The decor on this
pavilion was sculpted
by François-Joseph
Bosio, Joseph-Michel-
Ange Pollet, and
Pierre-Jules Cavelier.

right

The Pavillon
Richelieu
The pavilion here is
seen reflected through
one of the three small
pyramids. This one
stands above the hall
leading to the Pavillon
Richelieu, home to the
Departments of
Sculpture, Decorative
Arts, and Near
Eastern Antiquities.

center right

France-Soir,
January 23, 1984
Several influential
figures took up arms
against the Pei project.
So did the daily
France-Soir. *The*
controversy raged for
several months. But
President Mitterrand's
and the museum's
unwavering support
finally won its
adversaries round. By
May 1984, the battle of
the pyramid was over.

previous double page

The Pyramid
At night, the Pyramid
is transformed into a
"filigree that glistens
like the silken strands
of a spider's web," as
François Chaslin
wrote in the book Les
Paris de François
Mitterrand (The
Many Parises of
François
Mitterrand).

below

Drawing of a
Connecting Joint
From the Pyramid's
Structure, designed
and drawn by I. M. Pei
Architects in the United
States often execute their
own final drawings and
handle all the
technological details.
Their French
counterparts usually
entrust their drawings
to the engineering firm,
which then becomes the
main contractor.

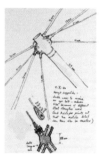

center below

Putting the Final
Touches to the
Louvre,
Magazine Illustration,
dated January 12, 1867
In 1866 archaeologists
discovered the
foundations of a
medieval fortress in
the Cour Carrée.

right

The Pyramid
Respecting the "flesh
tones" of the Louvre
and preserving the
immense perspective
stretching all the way
to La Défense, Pei
requested the most
transparent glass for
its construction.

THE GLASS PYRAMID

As tends to happen with great works of art, the Pyramid quickly became such an obvious part of the Louvre's landscape that the unprecedented artistic and technological challenges of its construction have virtually been forgotten.

In November 1983 I. M. Pei submitted to President François Mitterrand a proposal for a glass pyramid at the center of the Cour Napoléon. The news stunned France and triggered virulent reactions. Some poured scorn on the idea of inviting a Chinese architect, domiciled in America, to redesign the historic heart of the French capital.

Unlike Bernini, however Pei had immediately understood what the Louvre required. In the end his audacity carried the day because he was able to convince people that he had made the best possible choice. Today, with the exception of a handful of diehard opponents, the glass pyramid on its aluminum framework has won unanimous acceptance. This weightless covering has at last given the Louvre a vast, welcoming, and luminous entrance. Its geometry seems perfect to stimulate the mind and prepare it for the treasures inside.

I. M. PEI

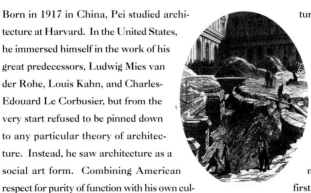

Born in 1917 in China, Pei studied architecture at Harvard. In the United States, he immersed himself in the work of his great predecessors, Ludwig Mies van der Rohe, Louis Kahn, and Charles-Edouard Le Corbusier, but from the very start refused to be pinned down to any particular theory of architecture. Instead, he saw architecture as a social art form. Combining American respect for purity of function with his own culture's reverence for the past, Pei's East Wing at the National Gallery in Washington is renowned for its elegance, its harmonious ordering of proportions, and its effortless integration into its surroundings. Throughout its history, the Louvre has kept pace with the unfolding centuries. The glass Pyramid, an abode of light, reflects the museum's contemporary image – and its first step into the new millennium.

The Medieval Louvre

The Grand Louvre project not only prepared the museum for the 21st century, it also restored the former palace's ties to its past, which started with Philip Augustus in the 12th century. Once the modern Louvre decided that the Pyramid would be built, a team of archaeologists, led by Michel Fleury, spent the two years before construction began carrying out excavations in the Cour Carrée. As a result, visitors entering from the Sully corridor now encounter the foundations of the medieval Louvre.

(The remains on the south and west were destroyed by Lescot's construction work.) They can almost touch the enormous, exquisitely fitted honey-colored stone blocks, punctuated here and there by hearts engraved by medieval laborers. Walking around the keep, the towers, and the curtain walls gives visitors a sense of the proportions of the ancient stronghold. They can also admire the base of the large spiral staircase leading to Charles VI's library. The historian Sauval considered this staircase one of the architectural masterpieces of the Middle Ages.

Visitors with a particular interest in medieval France will admire the fragments of a royal helmet and the crown of golden fleurs-de-lys discovered at the bottom of the keep. Both are now displayed in the windows of the Saint-Louis Room. The motto "En Bien" can still be read between the fleurs-de-lys on the crown, set on an azure background. An inventory of the king's stables, dating back to 1411, mentions this helmet, strongly suggesting that it belonged to Charles VI.

below
New Underground Rooms, Louvre
This 19th-century engraving recalls the unexpected discovery in 1882 of the Saint-Louis Room.

above
Pietà, Anonymous German Master
This Pietà *from Saint-Germain-des-Prés, painted by a German master living in Paris around 1500, is in the Louvre's Department of Paintings. Saint-Germain-des-Prés is shown in the foreground; in the middle distance is the Louvre fortress; to its right, the riverside facade of the Hôtel de Bourbon, which no longer exists. In the background is the convent of Saint-Pierre de Montmartre.*

above left
Medieval Moats
The moats to the north and east of the medieval Louvre were cleared during the digs of 1983-1985. In the Middle Ages, water lapped at the base of these beautiful carved stones.

below left
Saint-Louis Room
The columns and arches of the Saint-Louis Room, located in the west wing of the Cour Carrée, were rebuilt in the 13th century under Philip Augustus. The beauty of the room suggests that the fortress might already have served as a residence in medieval times.

right
Medieval Foundations
In 1866, at Baron Haussmann's request, Adolphe Berty conducted digs in the Cour Carrée. They led to the discovery of the foundations of the medieval Louvre. Pressured by Napoleon III to move quickly, Berty had only four months to complete his surveying. By contrast, Michel Fleury and his team dug from 1983 to 1985 and carried their research to term.

THE HENRY II STAIRCASE

right

Ceiling Decor, Henry II Vestibule, Georges Braque
In 1953 Georges Salles, director of the Musés de France, commissioned these birds from Braque for the center panel of the ceiling in Henry II's vestibule, designed by Scibecq de Carpi. It was the last contemporary work to enter the Louvre.

below

Vaulting, Henry II Staircase
On the foundations of the west wing (which was torn down in

1546), Pierre Lescot built a Renaissance corps de logis for Henry II. A vaulted staircase with a sculpted and coffered ceiling links Jean Goujon's Caryatid Room to the Salle des Gardes, or guardroom, on the first floor.

Together with the Caryatid Room, the Henry II Staircase, which looks as if it were carved from a single block of white stone, is the showpiece of the 16th-century Louvre. Its vaulting, sculpted by Jean Goujon, is a pure joy to contemplate.

Feast your eyes on the lissom grace of Diana the huntress, her light skirt seemingly fluttering in the breeze. Admire the unassuming elegance of the tall children on the staircase landings, and savor the splendor of the reclining fawns, described by a single curve running from shoulder to hindquarters and back up to the knees. Even the hounds, amazingly alive, are a pleasure to the eye.

At each step the visitor encounters images of young pages in bright silk livery, beautiful young women from the queen's "flying squadron" in gold

and silken dresses, musicians in red and yellow standing beside archers of the royal bodyguard, and all the other denizens of this glittering, elegant court, wholly given over to poetry and music.

These were the days of the great poets of the Pléiade movement. Like the sculptors of the day, they felt a strong sense of kinship with nature, cultivating beauty and admiring pagan antiquity. They were fond of love poetry, which could verge – like Pierre de Ronsard's *Folâtreries*, which officials sought to ban in 1553 – on the licentious. Henry II reigned over a festive court, renowned for its unfettered exuberance. Its spirit still graces the vaulting of this great staircase and the other rooms dating from the Renaissance Louvre.

below

Grapes and Faun Heads, Henry II Staircase

right

Diana the Huntress, Henry II Staircase
Diana appears on the staircase ceiling. In her 1678 novel, La Princesse de Clèves, *Madame de Lafayette describes the cult of female beauty in the days of Henry II this way: "Never have magnificence and gallantry shone so brightly as in the king's last days."*

below left

Faun, Ceiling of Henry II's Bedchamber
This ceiling is a hymn to hunting, sensuality, and the beauty of children and animals. In Greek mythology fauns were fertility divinities – and assiduous pursuers of nymphs. It is no surprise to find them in the bedchamber of a king whose court was famed for its amorousness.

Francis I was determined in transforming the Louvre, to enhance it with a sumptuous reception hall. The result was the present-day Caryatid Room. At one end stood the royal box; at the other Jean Goujon's four caryatids upheld the musicians' gallery.

Like their counterparts in the Cour Carrée, these figures have lost none of their youthful bloom. Their fluid forms seem susceptible only to the currents and breezes of water and air. Sculpted by an artist who was isolated from the tumults of his times, these caryatids are possessed of a profound serenity. Yet they were silent witnesses to the turbulent and romantic era of the Valois dynasty. The days of Lescot and Goujon were a time of sumptuous fetes, like the one Henry III organized for his comely

favorite, the duke of Joyeuse. There were fights pitting lions against dogs – until the day when the king, tormented by a nightmare, had all the animals killed

with muskets. There were also the adventures of the duke of Alençon: kept under surveillance at the Louvre, he managed to escape with the assistance of his sister, Queen Margot, who lowered him on a rope to the moat below her window. But it was also during these years that the Louvre witnessed one of French history's grimmest massacres. In 1572, two days after the marriage of Marguerite of Valois to Henry of Navarre, Catherine de Médicis convinced her son Charles IX that Protestant leaders were plotting against him and should be eliminated. The weak-minded king eventually gave the fatal order and unleashed his archers and crossbowmen. Even at the Louvre the walls were spattered with blood. The only survivors – the future Henry IV and the prince of Condé – hid in the king's bedchamber. Years later Henry IV confided to his physician, Ambroise Paré, that he was still haunted by nightmares from the St. Bartholomew's Day Massacre.

left
Centaur Ridden
by Love
*Set between two of
Jean Goujon's
caryatids, this centaur
is a Roman copy – as
are all the antique
sculptures in this room.
According to legend,
centaurs were a wild
and brutal race who
lived in Thessaly and
Arcadia.*

center below
Session,
Caryatid Room,
Charles de Wailly
*The Louvre's Cabinet
of Drawings owns
drawings for several
museum projects (the
Grande Galerie and
the museum entrance)
conceived by de Wailly,
who executed this
drawing in 1796.
This architect and
decorator also designed
the Odéon theater in
Paris.*

below
Balcony with Bronze
Bas-relief
*Goujon's four
caryatids support a
gallery where
musicians sat during
balls given at the
Valois court. It was
decorated with a series
of these bronze bas-
reliefs.*

above left
Caryatid Room
*The Caryatid Room,
built by Pierre Lescot
in 1550, displays the
museum's collection of
Greek sculpture from
the Hellenistic period.*

left center
Fireplace,
Caryatid Room
*At the far end of the
Caryatid Room is this
fireplace, designed by
Charles Percier and
Pierre Fontaine. It
was installed by the
Italian marble and
mosaic worker
Francesco Belloni.
The architects placed
two large marble
figures, probably from
Goujon's workshop, on
either side.*

above
Sleeping
Hermaphrodite,
Caryatid Room
The Sleeping
Hermaphrodite
*breathes an ambiguous
sensuality. Nudity is
used as an occasion for
studying the beauty of
the human body.*

The Apartments of
Anne of Austria

Anne of Austria was the widow of Louis XIII and regent of France in the middle of the 17th century, when she remodeled the apartments of the country's queen mothers. On the advice of Cardinal Jules Mazarin, who was eager to introduce the Baroque style to France, she entrusted the redecoration to the Roman painter Giovanni Romanelli and to Michel Anguier, a sculptor who had worked with the greatest Baroque masters in Rome. Ten years earlier Romanelli had painted

the gallery of Mazarin's palace (today the Galerie Mazarine in the Bibliothèque Nationale). In 1655, at Anne's request, he returned to

France and worked uninterruptedly for four years with Anguier on the decoration of the Salle des Saisons, the Salle de la Paix, and the Large and Small Cabinets. As a result of this sustained effort, these

rooms possess a harmony and unity rare in a building where work was traditionally interrupted at regular intervals and resumed at a much later date. Transformed by Romanelli's soft, subtle palette and Anguier's slender white and gilded stucco, the Greek gods and Roman heroines who run, stride, and fly across these ceilings have shed some of the roughness of antiquity and acquired a distinctly French elegance. The serene beauty of these young Gallic nymphs and youthful godlike musketeers is all

the more moving when one recalls that the beautiful Anne was married to Louis XIII, one of the surliest and most unattractive men in French history – and that for many years she lived in fear of the king's ferocious but brilliant chief minister, Cardinal Richelieu. The refurbished apartments must have been a wonderful consolation for her.

The Rotonde de Mars: the Roman Manner

Between 1655 and 1659, in the aftermath of the Fronde (the aristocratic revolt against the king's advisers), Anne of Austria, regent for her son Louis XIV, redecorated the section of the Louvre housing her residence. Nothing remains of the winter apartment, but the luxurious Baroque summer apartment in the Petite Galerie has survived intact. It comprised an entrance hall (Salle de la Paix), an antechamber (Salle des Saisons), a

grand cabinet, and a bedchamber. Framed by Michel Anguier's white and gold stuccos, the ceilings are a masterpiece of virtuosity by the painter Romanelli. The council apartment – where the king conferred with his ministers – is north of the summer apartment. It was decorated in 1685 by the painter Charles Evrard and the sculptor Thibaut Poissant, a few of whose stuccos can be seen in the Rotonde de Mars.

---

right
Salle des Saisons,
Salle de la Paix
*Columns brought back
from Germany in 1799
by France's
revolutionary armies
have replaced the walls
that once separated the
Salle des Saisons from
the Salle de la Paix.*

left
Ceiling, Queen's
Bedchamber
*This ceiling celebrates
some of history's
outstanding women.
Romanelli painted
Judith and Holofernes,
and Esther and
Ahasuerus. Anguier
carved stucco figures
symbolizing the queen's
virtues: liberality,
majesty, felicity, and
magnificence.*

below
Allegory of Winter,
Salle des Saisons
*Romanelli painted
these cherubic youths.*

below
Faun,
Salle des Saisons
*The Salle des Saisons
evokes the passage of
time: paintings recount
the story of Apollo,*

*and stucco figures like
this white and gilt faun
represent the elements
as divinities.*

center
Studiousness
and Fame
*This allegory was
painted by Peyron in
1799 for the opening of
the Musée des Antiques.*

center left, below
Man Formed by
Prometheus and
Given Life by
Minerva, Jean-
Simon Barthellemy,
Stucco,
Rotonde de Mars
*The Rotonde de Mars
features several 17th-
century stuccos by
Gaspard and Balthazar
Marsy. Others were
added in 1801, when
the Musée des Antiques
was created.
Barthellemy painted
this one in 1802.*

When he reached his majority in 1659, Louis XIV was still unmarried. Seeking to establish an alliance with Spain, Anne and Mazarin looked hopefully to the infanta Marie-Thérèse of Spain as a prospective wife and queen. But their hopes were threatened by the fact that the young king was already in love with Mazarin's niece, Marie Mancini. Marie Mancini lived with her mother and sisters in the attic of the Louvre's Lescot Wing. A lively and spirited girl, Marie opened the young king's mind to poetry and novels. Anne of Austria and Mazarin chose to turn a blind eye to his preferences, persuaded that Louis would eventually put the good of the state before his own happiness. But after Mazarin departed for the south of France to negotiate the terms of the Spanish marriage with envoys from Madrid, Louis dug

in his heels. Seeking to reason with him, Anne invited her recalcitrant son to her apartments. Perhaps she gained inspiration for her lecture from the ringing calls to duty in the works of Pierre Corneille, one of her favorite playwrights, or from the two portraits by Velásquez that recalled the urgency of the need for peace with Spain. Whatever the reason, Louis emerged from this half-hour alone with his mother ready to play his part in the marriage of dynastic convenience.

The next day Marie Mancini left for La Rochelle. As a tearful Louis XIV accompanied her to her carriage, she pronounced these now famous parting words: "You weep, you are the king. And I leave." Much later, Jean Racine echoed her words in his play *Bérénice*: "You are the emperor, my lord, and you weep."

THE SALON CARRÉ

The Salon Carré evokes the Louvre both as palace and as museum. It was the site of Napoleon's marriage to Marie-Louise of Austria in 1810 and the Louvre's first exhibition. From 1692 it housed the Academy of Painting and Sculpture. On August 25, 1699, artists from the Academy displayed their works there. The event met with considerable success and was the forerunner of annual Salons of paint-

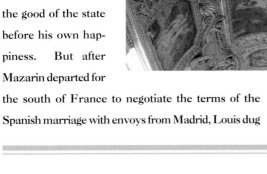

ing and sculpture. The last Salon, held in 1848, presented an impressive number of paintings; the curators decided to put the most beautiful on permanent exhibit. Félix Duban had a sculpted decor executed, commissioning Charles Simart to make large figures, incarnating the four major arts, as well as medallions honoring Goujon, Lescot, Poussin, and Jean Pesne.

THE GALERIE D'APOLLON

After the turmoil of the Fronde rising ended in 1653, the young Louis XIV returned to the Louvre and decided to make the palace a fitting reflection of his personal glory. Since the Petite Galerie had been burned, he had an opportunity to build a larger one with a brand-new decorative scheme. He commissioned Charles Le Brun to paint a ceiling depicting the young Apollo, god of the sun and the Muses, to whom Louis compared himself. The Manufacture de la Savonnerie wove special carpets, and Gucci carved magnificent cabinets for the new building, which would become the showcase for the king's exceptional collection of paintings. This Royal Collection is the richest in the Louvre today.

Later, when Louis XIV left the Louvre to live at Versailles, some of the paintings remained in the palace. But the Petite Galerie soon housed stu-

dents from the Academy of Painting. (They would complete its decoration in the 18th century.)

When the Louvre Museum opened in 1793, the Petite Galerie became the Galerie d'Apollon, displaying a collection of decorative art works. Following the Napoleonic conquests, it temporarily exhibited Michelangelo's *Slaves*. But at the beginning of the 19th century, the gallery, like the rest of the Louvre, was falling into ruin.

After the 1848 Revolution, Félix Duban began a bold program of restoration, commissioning the Romantic painter Delacroix to create a work for this temple of classicism. Delacroix used the Apollo theme, but he did so not to glorify the memory of the Sun King but rather to stage a grand allegory of good and evil, showing the struggle between Apollo and the python.

right
Panel,
Galerie d'Apollon
This gilded panel is in the shape of an urn.

center right
View of the Galerie d'Apollon
In the foreground is a splendid wrought-iron gate forged around 1650 for the Château de Maisons. It was put at the entrance to this gallery at the end of the Revolution, probably by Raymond, the palace's architect at that time.

above
Cabinet, Galerie d'Apollon, detail
In the Galerie d'Apollon the cabinets in which the crown jewels are displayed were made in 1900 and 1990.

below
Apollo Medallion
This medallion features the burnished visage of Apollo, god of the sun and emblem of Louis XIV.

center left, below
Ceiling, King's Bedchamber
Now relocated in the Colonnade, this ceiling was once in the Pavillon du Roi. The gilt-wood oval was carved by Gilles Guérin, one of the two artists who carved the magnificent caryatids of the Pavillon Lemercier. The theme of captivity reflects the influence of Michelangelo.

right
Panel, Galerie d'Apollon
All the paneling and painted shutters of the Galerie d'Apollon were redone by Félix Duban in his renovation around 1850. The fish motif against a wrought-iron background is taken from an 18th-century engraving by Jean Bérain.

THE KING'S BEDCHAMBER

Like the rest of his quarters, the king's bedchamber was at first located in the Pavillon du Roi, in the southwest corner of the Cour Carrée. Its magnificent sculpted ceiling, commissioned in 1657 by Louis XIV, has now been moved to a room in the Colonnade. Like the *putti* in the alcove, the fettered slaves recall those by Jean Goujon on the facade of the Cour Carrée,

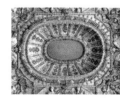

and they reflect Goujon's ongoing influence on the Louvre's sculptors. The paintings by Eustache Le Sueur that once embellished the bedchamber were moved as part of the Grand Louvre project. Le Sueur's twenty-one paintings of the *Life of St. Bruno* are now presented, together for the first time, in the rooms devoted to French painting.

THE GRANDE
GALERIE

When the Grande Galerie was completed in 1608, Henry IV issued several letters expressing his wish to house in it a "great quantity of the best craftsmen, masters of painting and sculpture, silversmiths, and clockmakers." As a result, the mint and the future Gobelins manufactory moved into the Grande Galerie for a time. Starting with the reign of Louis XIII, the Grande Galerie was also the venue for the royal laying on of hands. In the 18th century, after France's kings abandoned the Louvre for Versailles as a residence, the Academy of Painting and Sculpture occupied part of the Grande Galerie, before moving to the Salon Carré.

The Academy's annual Salons elevated the taste of the public, which started calling for the creation of a

museum. As early as 1768 the king approved a project by Marigny to construct a museum in the Louvre. Interrupted by the Revolution, various similar projects were revived in 1792, leading to the opening of the Louvre Museum in November 1793.

Determined to give the museum an exalted image, Napoleon cleared the basement of all its occupants. The drawings and watercolors of Benjamin Zix, especially one showing the wedding procession of Napoleon and Marie-Louise winding across the Grande Galerie, constitute an invaluable record of how Percier and Fontaine originally modeled the great room – and how paintings were hung at that time. Today the Grande Galerie is characterized by a sober style, very close in spirit to that shown in paintings by Hubert Robert, in which the vault has been replaced by large glass apertures.

previous double page
Triumph of Cybele,
Joseph-Benoit
Guichard
Guichard executed the Triumph of Cybele at the northern end of the Galerie d'Apollon, under Félix Duban's direction. Below, the three figures of Fame were sculpted by Gaspard and Balthazar Marsy, who created half the stuccos in the Galerie d'Apollon, under Charles Le Brun's supervision.

below
Wedding Procession

of Napoleon and
Marie-Louise,
Benjamin Zix
A reporter before his time, Zix captured every theatrical nuance of the imperial wedding, as in this watercolor (now on display in the Cabinet of Drawings). The scene is the hanging of Rubens's paintings, which would be repatriated to Flanders after the fall of Napoleon.

above
Project for the
Grande Galerie,
Hubert Robert
This large gallery was intended to house masterpieces from antiquity and paintings of important monuments. The project was brought to fruition under Napoleon.

center left, above
Rotunda,
Grande Galerie
In 1869 Lefuel entrusted the decoration of the two rotundas in the Grande Galerie to the sculptor Albert Carrier-Belleuse. The artist demonstrated great freedom of expression.

right
Imaginary View of
the Grande Galerie
in Ruins,
Hubert Robert
On his return from Italy, Robert brought paintings of ruins – like this work, executed around 1798 – into vogue.

"ROBERT DES RUINES"

The French painter and engraver Hubert Robert (1733-1808) owes his unfortunate nickname to his pre-Romantic penchant for painting ruins. Before being elected a member of the Academy of Painting in 1766 with his *View of Ripetta*, he worked in the studio of the sculptor Michel-Ange Slodtz, then studied in Italy, where he was deeply influenced by Giovanni Paolo Pannini, famed as a painter of the ruins of antiquity. From 1784 to 1792 Robert supervised the accumulation

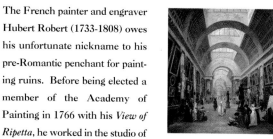

of a collection of paintings for the future museum planned by Louis XVI and the count of Angivillers, superintendent of buildings. After the Revolution and the dramatic events of Thermidor (when Robespierre's Terror was brought to an end) Robert was named curator of the Louvre Museum. He then turned to painting genre scenes, as well as visions of a palace-museum built in his very own architectural style – and even to fantasies of the Louvre in ruins.

Facing the Seine, the Campana Gallery is an exact replica of the Charles X Museum, which overlooks the Cour Carrée. Their histories follow a similar pattern. Like its earlier counterpart, the Campana Gallery (built by Pierre Lescot in the 16th century) was abandoned in the 19th century. Fontaine completed the major part of the work under Napoleon, but the decoration was finished only in 1837, under Louis Philippe.

The nine ceilings depicting landmarks from French history were immensely popular in the 1830. While mythology had slipped somewhat from favor, French historical painting had come into fashion. One of the ceilings represented Egyptian scholars gathered around Bonaparte and a recently discovered mummy. Another depicted Poussin being introduced to the king by Cardinal Richelieu.

For some time these nine rooms housed works by French painters and, later, antique vases. The gallery was finally chosen to display part of a collection that Napoleon III acquired in 1861 from the Marquis Campana. As director of the pawnbroker's office in Rome, Campana had been ideally situated to amass an art collection. He spent all his fortune on works of art and his lavish lifestyle, then "borrowed" considerable sums of money. The pope finally put an end to the growing scandal. Tried and sentenced to the galleys, Campana was released only because of the passionate support of Napoleon III. The emperor's support was justified, for Campana's wife had helped the young Louis-Napoleon escape from an earlier captivity. When the Campana collection was put up for sale in 1861 to benefit the pawnbroker's office, Napoleon III managed to acquire almost the whole of it, with the exception of some artifacts bought by England, Russia, Belgium, and Italy. On August 15, 1863, St. Napoleon's Day, he solemnly inaugurated the Louvre's Campana Gallery.

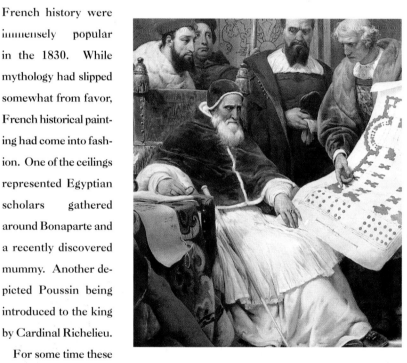

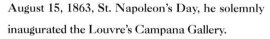

Located on the first floor of the Cour Carrée's south wing, the Charles X Museum shows us how the museum gradually took over areas originally designated as royal apartments. In the 17th century this sweeping space – nine rooms long – housed the queen's apartments as well as the storeroom of the "Menus Plaisirs du Roi," where lavish hangings, costumes, and decorations for royal fetes were kept.

Work on the Cour Carrée was still in progress when Louis XIV decamped from the Louvre. But the palace did not stay empty for long. The Academy of Architecture moved into Marie-Thérèse's apartments, while artists, holders of royal commissions, and members of court turned the neighboring rooms of the old palace into apartments and private town houses, building makeshift roofs where necessary.

Throughout the 18th century pamphleteers denounced the dilapidated state of the Louvre, claiming that it had become an "owl shelter." They called for the establishment of a royal gallery where the king's painting collection could be exhibited. Even the great sage Voltaire pleaded for the Louvre to be rescued from "this shameful condition, which inspires the world's contempt." But not until Bonaparte's reign were those who had made the Louvre their home turned out, leaving the architect Pierre Fontaine free to transform the queen's apartments into museum rooms.

The fall of Bonaparte did not halt the restoration process. Louis XVIII confirmed Fontaine in his post as the Louvre's architect. In August 1819 "Gouty Louis" inaugurated an exhibit entitled "Living Artists and Products of Industry" in the rooms allocated for the Charles X Museum and the future Campana Gallery.

THE ANTIQUE   BRONZES ROOM

The room that now houses antique bronzes was one of the most splendid in the Louvre. Formerly the Salle des Gardes, or guardroom, in the king's apartments, this spacious room was the setting for the memorable balls held by the Valois kings, the masquerades of Henry II, and the ballets of Louis XIV. Abandoned and compartmentalized after the Sun King's departure for Versailles, the Antique Bronzes, Room did not regain its former prestige until 1819, during the Bourbon Restoration, when Fontaine transformed it into the Salle des États (the Estates-General). It was here that the king assembled the two legislative chambers for special sessions. But this function came to end with the July Revolution, when the Bronzes Room finally became part of the museum.

THE STATE COUNCIL ROOMS

THE STATE
COUNCIL ROOMS

This ceiling painting is located in the State Council Rooms.

Like the Charles X Museum and the Campana Gallery, the State Council Rooms were decorated and refurbished under the Restoration – which chose not to further the original "grand design" for the Louvre. Located in the west wing of the Cour Carrée, the rooms had been built by Jacques Lemercier under Louis XIII and were completed twenty years later by Louis Le Vau. Since they were not assigned any precise function, they were divided into apartments and occupied by nobly born courtiers like Madame de Thiange, sister of Louis XIV's mistress, Madame de Montespan; the duchess d'Estrées; and the viscount of Polignac. Between 1825 and 1828 Fontaine converted four of the rooms into State Council offices, forcing the occupants to vacate. The director of the Musée des Beaux-Arts, Sosthène de la Rochefoucauld, selected the themes for the ceilings and commissioned painters to execute them. But he did not show the flair that his successors would later demonstrate (Félix Duban and the count of Forban were to commission works from Ingres, Gros, and Delacroix for the Charles X Museum and the Galerie d'Apollon). Instead, de la Rochefoucauld opted for rigidly academic painters like Merry-Joseph Blondel, who painted *France Victorious at Bouvines,* and *France, Surrounded by Royal Lawgivers and French Jurists, Receiving the Constitutional Charter from Louis XVIII.* Equally uninspiring were Michel-Martin Drölling and Jean-Baptiste Mauzaisse, who chose themes as drearily edifying as Blondel's for the two other ceilings of the State Council Rooms.

THE ROTONDE D'APOLLON: PAEAN TO THE SUN

Glorification of the monarchy began at the Louvre before it reached its apogee at Versailles. Shortly after his coronation in Reims, the young Louis XIV set his personal stamp on the palace of his forefathers. He called upon the architect Louis Le Vau to renovate his apartments. Le Vau remodeled the Salon du Dôme (today's Rotonde d'Apollon) and the Grand Cabinet (which became the Jewel Room). Originally designed to serve as a chapel, the Salon du Dôme had a rotunda similar to the one executed by the architect at the château of Vaux-le-Vicomte. Decorated with stuccos by Francesco Caccia, the Rotonde d'Apollon, which leads to the gallery of the same name, was enhanced between 1818 and 1821 with a fresco by Blondel, *The Fall of Icarus.*

---

above right
Paneling,
Pavillon Beauvais
These luxurious panels in the Pavillon Beauvais are done in the same style as those in the king's bedchamber. They surround The Triumph of Catherine de Médicis, *painted in 1878 by Carolus Duran.*

right
France, Surrounded by Royal Lawgivers and French Jurists, Receiving the Constitutional Charter from Louis XVIII, Merry-Joseph Blondel

above
Louis XVIII's Bedchamber
Originally in the Tuileries palace, this room has been reconstituted in the Department of Decorative Arts.

left bottom
Ceiling,
Rotonde d'Apollon
The architect Louis Le Vau decorated the ceiling of the Rotonde d'Apollon with a work by Poussin, Time Rescuing Truth from the Clutches of Envy and Discord, *which is now displayed in the Department of Paintings. Under the Restoration this canvas was replaced with Blondel's* The Fall of Icarus. *In the various compartments of the cupola, Louis Couder and Blondel painted mythological scenes representing the four elements.*

below and right
Trompe l'Œil,
Jean-Bruno Gassies
In the first State Council Room, Gassies painted these fine trompe l'oeil figures. Inspired by the Carracci brothers and the Italian tradition, the magnificent bodies evoke the statues of antiquity.

THE SALLE DES SEPT CHEMINÉES

right

Stucco Figures, Ceiling, Salle des Sept Cheminées
The gilded stuccos in the corners of the ceiling of the Salle des Sept Cheminées evoke the arts, agriculture, war, and trade. Here, War (left) and Agriculture (right) are executed in strong Neoclassical style. The abundance of gold foreshadows Second Empire opulence.

below

Medallion of Prud'hon
When Duban restored the Salle des Sept Cheminées, he had medallions made of ten artists of the early 19th century. Pierre Prud'hon was known for his portraits and mythological scenes; and

the melancholy of certain of his works anticipated the Romantic age.

right bottom

Apollo Vanquishing the Python, Eugène Delacroix
Commissioned by Duban, Delacroix painted this dazzling work that decorates the ceiling in the Galerie d'Apollon.

Before Louis XIV moved to Versailles, his dressing room, built by Pierre Lescot, formed the heart of the royal apartments. It was here that the body of Henry IV lay in state for several days before being buried at the basilica of Saint-Denis.

After the Sun King left for Versailles, in 1699, he invited the Academy of Sciences to take over his Louvre apartments. As a result his collection of paintings by great masters, tapestries, and beautiful furniture was replaced by a stuffed camel, a dissected elephant, and jars filled with floating entrails, fetuses, and other curious anatomical bits and pieces.

In 1817 Fontaine transformed one of the king's former rooms, the Salle des Sept Cheminées (Room of Seven Fireplaces) into an exhibition room. Its present decor dates from the Second Republic, when the king's former apartments became the "people's museum." In 1851 the architect Félix Duban asked Francisque Duret to carve winged women handing crowns to the painters Gérard, David, Gros, Géricault, and Prud'hon. For a long time the room was devoted to French painting, presenting early-19th-century masterpieces such as David's *Coronation of Napoleon*, Géricault's *Raft of the Medusa*, and Ingres's *Apotheosis of Homer*.

The view over the Cour Napoléon is magnificent, with the Pyramid slightly off-center, the Carrousel, the Rue de Rivoli, the Tuileries gardens, and the long perspective to the Grande Arche at La Défense.

center left, below

Stucco Figures, Ceiling, Salle des Sept Cheminées
The ceiling of the Salle des Sept Cheminées was decorated by Duban just after the 1848 Revolution. The Second Republic wanted to transform the Louvre into a palace of the people and – as Victor Hugo wrote – the "intellectual Mecca." Like the Salon Carré, the Salle des Sept Cheminées is the fruit of this lofty ambition.

right

Paneling, Salle des Sept Cheminées
Like Charles Simart in the Salon Carré, the sculptor Duret was inspired by the Galerie d'Apollon, using large white stuccos on a gold background. The king's rooms became the "people's museum." Masterpieces by David, Géricault, and Ingres were exhibited here until the Second World War.

APOLLO'S CHARIOT

When Louis-Napoleon inaugurated the renovated Galerie d'Apollon and its new ceiling on June 5, 1851, Delacroix was fifty-two years old. His easel painting was still a subject of violent controversy. Painters of the classical school said he painted with a "drunken broom." Fortunately, statesmen were of a different opinion and had already entrusted him with prestigious orders, including frescoes for the Chamber of Deputies, the Senate, and the State Council. Delacroix spent two years painting *Apollo Vanquishing the Python*. The wealth of the yellows – ranging from the palest hues for the luminous figure of Apollo to the deepest for the darkness of the snake – is superb. Preempting critics, Delacroix wrote: "I care little for the opinion of the majority of people who will see this. In this day and age, it is not such a bad sign not to please many people: turgidity, pathos, and poor taste are the general norm."

Like the rest of the Denon Wing, the Michelangelo and Donatello rooms were built by Hector Lefuel between 1852 and 1857. Inspired by the Caryatid Room, the Michelangelo Room is sober in style, its decor confined to carvings on its double arches and colored marble flooring. The Donatello Room, which once housed the imperial stables, preserves the same simplicity. Its decoration relies on the alternating use of brick and stone, arches and pillars. These galleries were only recently transformed into exhibition rooms. Before the construction of the Pei Pyramid, the Michelangelo Room (formerly the Mollien Room) served as the museum's main entrance, while the Donatello Room was a staff restaurant.

Michelangelo's *Slaves* and Italian Renaissance sculpture are displayed in the

Michelangelo Room, a gallery flooded with light. In the Donatello Room, the rustic decor of the former imperial stables now serves as a backdrop for displays of Italian, Flemish, and Northern sculpture.

Catherine Bizouard and François Pin, the two architects who remodeled these rooms, respected their original character. They linked the rooms with a double spiral staircase that extends the Mollien Staircase; built of stone and white concrete, it is so perfectly integrated into its surroundings, it seems timeless.

The Michelangelo Room overlooks the Cour Lefuel and its double helical stairway, inspired by the one in the Cour des Adieux at Fontainebleau. At the base of the banister, above the Porte du Manège, are animal sculptures by Pierre Rouillard.

HECTOR-MARTIN LEFUEL

Born in Versailles in 1810, Hector-Martin Lefuel won the Grand Prix de Rome, awarded for artistic excellence. He was the architect of the Château de Meudon, and following Ludovico Visconti's death in 1853, he was appointed chief architect of the Louvre, a position he held for more than twenty years.

The large-scale works he undertook at the Louvre matched the enormous sums the emperor devoted

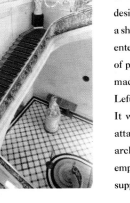

to realizing the original "grand design" and to making the Louvre a showcase of his empire. The giant enterprise included the destruction of part of the Grande Galerie and made generous allowance for Lefuel's love of overcrowded decor. It was sharply criticized, but the attacks were without effect. The architect, alert to the tastes of the emperor and empress, enjoyed their support to the very end.

THE MOLLIEN STAIRCASE

right

The Nymph of
Fontainebleau,
Mollien Staircase,
Benvenuto Cellini
The Nymph of
Fontainebleau,
*sculpted in 1543
during the artist's five-
year stay in France, is
Cellini's most famous
bas-relief.*

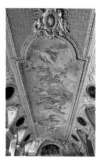

above
Gathering of the
Gods, Louis Matout
*The ceiling of the Salle
des Empereurs was
painted by Matout at
Lefuel's request during
the Second Empire.
Inspired by Anne of
Austria's Apartments,
it has a distinctly 17th-
century spirit.*

right
The Roman Empire,
Victor Biennoury
Painted in 1860, this
Roman Empire
*decorates the
tympanum of the Salle
des Empereurs.*

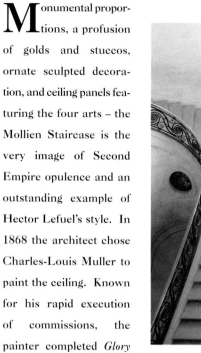

Monumental propor-
tions, a profusion
of golds and stuccos,
ornate sculpted decora-
tion, and ceiling panels fea-
turing the four arts – the
Mollien Staircase is the
very image of Second
Empire opulence and an
outstanding example of
Hector Lefuel's style. In
1868 the architect chose
Charles-Louis Muller to
paint the ceiling. Known
for his rapid execution
of commissions, the
painter completed *Glory
Distributing Crowns to the Arts* a few months before
the beginning of the disastrous Franco-Prussian War

in 1870. The banister and
the vault leading to the
painting rooms, however,
were not completed until
1914.

Benvenuto Cellini's
Nymph of Fontainebleau
stands out gracefully in the
vast sweep of the stair-
case. From the landing,
visitors can look out
onto the Cour Napoléon
at Bernini's statue of
Louis XIV, then enter the
Mollien Gallery, where
Delacroix's most beautiful
works are on display. The
gallery's Pompei-red walls and arches decorated with
wreaths reflect another facet of Lefuel's talent.

left center
Imperial Eagle and
Atlantes, Pierre-
Jules Cavelier
*A teacher at the École
des Beaux-Arts,
Cavelier participated
in several large-scale
projects of the Second
Empire and Third
Republic: the Palais
Longchamp in
Marseilles, as well as
Paris's Saint-Augustin
church and the Gare
du Nord railway
station.*

VICTOR BIENNOURY

In the Salle d'Auguste, Victor Biennoury painted
two tympana in a range of grays against a red background: *The French Empire* and *The Roman Empire.*
As an official painter, Biennoury worked on a number of decorative projects for
Napoleon III. At the Louvre
he painted the corner medallions in the Finance Ministry's
spacious state salon, several
works in Anne of Austria's
Apartments (*Roman Sculpture,
Greek Sculpture,* and *French*

Sculpture), and on the ceilings *Sacred History* and
Profane History. Biennoury also placed his talents at
the service of official discourse. Whether they
depict allegories of the Renaissance monarchs,
the Sun King's 17th-century
glory, the emperor's victories,
or the Restoration monarchy's
virtues, the Louvre's frescoes
give voice to the dreams, political philosophies, and even the
propaganda of the palace's
royal denizens.

right
Glory Distributing
Crowns to the Arts,
Charles-Louis
Muller
*In 1869 Lefuel chose
Muller to paint the
central ceiling panel
for the Mollien
Staircase. The artist
had already worked on
large decorative
schemes in the Salle des
États and the Pavillon
Denon, and Lefuel
appreciated his quick
pace. Glory, a winged
woman wearing
Apollo's crown, is
surrounded by small
putti and streamers
bearing the names of
Velásquez, Rembrandt,
Le Sueur, Raphael,
and Claude. This
landing leads into the
paintings rooms.*

right

Dining Room with
Hunting Scenes,
Louis-Godefroy
Jadin
*The furniture is
decorated with gilt
bronze by Charles
Cristofle and Charles
Barbedienne. Most of
it looks like heavy
pastiches of Louis XV
furniture.*

center (left)

Painted Stucco,
Salon de Famille
*In the Salon de
Famille of Napoleon
III's apartments, the
ceiling and medallion
are by Émile Levy and
the sculpted decor by
Émile Knecht. These
rooms display
collections (notably
exquisite 18th-century
porcelains) acquired by
the Second Empire
statesman Louis-
Adolphe Thiers and his
wife.*

center (right)

Painted Stucco,
Grand Salon
*Painted stuccos in the
Grand Salon are
placed beneath
medallions of the arts,
painted by Victor
Biennoury. The
sculpted decor is by
Louis-Alphonse
Tranchant.*

This wing of the Louvre –
a unique example of
interior architecture under
Napoleon III – still has the
exquisite tang of forbidden
fruit, for the Ministry of
Finance occupied it until 1989.
Pastiche is the ruling design
concept in these immense
rooms, with their ornate gilt-
work, chandeliers, and profu-
sions of red silk, statues, stuccos, and frescoes. There are
simply too many columns, too
much gold and crystal, too
many angels, and too many
copies of artworks from every
century. The apartments feel
invaded by excess: the eye
finds no empty space for
repose, not even the ceiling,
which triumphantly celebrates
Napoleon III and Empress

Eugénie, seated on a fluffy
cloud, receiving the plans for
the completed Louvre.

After so many centuries of
enduring beauty, why did late
19th-century French architecture collapse into overcrowded plagiarism – at a time
when French painting was
enjoying its period of greatest
brilliance, with Daumier,
Ingres, Courbet, Manet,
Corot, and Degas? It was
Empress Eugénie who
(despite her infatuation
with Louis XVI elegance)
requested this confectioner's
cornucopia. Eager to please
her and handsomely paid to
satisfy her questionable over-
ripe taste, the imperial architects (supervised by Lefuel)
vied to outdo one another.

right

Arch and Ceiling,
Salon de Famille
*The paintings on the
ceiling and archways
of the Salon de
Famille are the work
of Émile Levy. This
apartment, maintained
in its original state,
provides a striking
glimpse of wealthy
bourgeois life during
the Second Empire.
The Ministry of
Finance occupied the
apartment from 1871
to 1989 – but never
altered its decor.*

bottom left

Grand Salon
*Like all interiors of
other public buildings
during the Second
Empire, the Grand
Salon is decorated in
Louis XIV style. A few
of the furniture pieces
are by the wood
sculptor Degueil and
the furniture-maker
Ramillon. Gilt wood
predominates in the
salon, while a darker
wood decorated with
gilt bronze in Bouille
style was chosen for the
dining room. Although
the room's velvet sofas
and light armchairs
are not pure Louis XIV
in style, they reflect a
concern for comfort
first expressed under
the Sun King.*

Ceiling,
Grand Salon,
Maréchal
The four lateral
compartments
represent the four kings
who built the Louvre;
the one in the center
shows Napoleon III
and the empress
Eugénie receiving the
plans of the completed
Louvre. The ceiling
has been completely
restored to repair
infiltrations and the
consequences of rough
handling during
cleaning at the turn of
the century.

While Charles Garnier, the Beaux-Arts architect, was discussing his project for the Paris Opera House with the empress, she asked him: "But what style is this? It's not a style: it's not Louis XIV, nor Louis XV, nor Louis XVI!" Garnier is said to have replied: "Madam, the style is Napoleon III. How can you complain?" In one room Franz Xaver Winterhalter's beautiful portrait of the empress shows off her magnificent dress and diadem but also captures her lovely, melancholy eyes; they seem already to see the day in September 1870 when she would dash across the Pavillon de Flore and the Grande Galerie into a coach waiting at the foot of the Colonnade to carry her – incognito – to safety.

For a long time these apartments were erroneously attributed to the duke of Morny, half-brother of Napoleon III, but in fact he never lived in them. It was Achille Fould, eager to make the Ministry of State into the showcase of Second

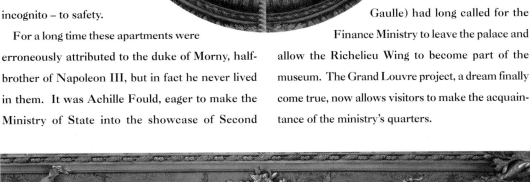

Empire prosperity, who commissioned the decor. Alexandre Walewski, Fould's successor and the illegitimate son of Napoleon Bonaparte and the countess Maria Walewska, inaugurated the move. Fould, by now minister of finance, sought vainly to limit the costs.

To celebrate the Louvre's bicentennial in November 1993, François Mitterrand solemnly inaugurated the Ministry of State Apartments, at long last "recovered" by the museum. His sense of pride was legitimate. If kings and emperors had dreamed over the centuries of linking the Louvre to the Tuileries, the museum's more recent curators (as well as President Charles de Gaulle) had long called for the Finance Ministry to leave the palace and allow the Richelieu Wing to become part of the museum. The Grand Louvre project, a dream finally come true, now allows visitors to make the acquaintance of the ministry's quarters.

Ceiling,
Family Apartment,
Émile Levy
While the Finance
Ministry offices in the
Richelieu Wing were
being demolished, every
one of Napoleon III's
lavish apartments
required protection.
The architects of the
Grand Louvre sealed
them off to protect them
from theft, dust, and
strong vibrations.

Stucco Atlantes,
Grand Salon,
Louis-Alphonse
Tranchant
Thousands of stuccos
like these decorate the
Louvre. This Italian
technique was first
used in France in the
King's Gallery at
Fontainebleau. A mix
of marble powder, glue,
and plaster, stucco is
more malleable than
earth and lighter than
stone and marble,
allowing the artist to
give figures less
"posed" attitudes.

Decor,
Théophile Murgey
This sculpted decor by
Murgey is located
between the Grand
Salon and the Salon
de Théâtre. As with
the other stuccos in this
apartment, the artist
used gold lavishly to
create an effect of
luxury.

THE MODERN ROOMS

As the outwardly visible part of the Grand Louvre, the Pyramid symbolizes an edifice that has survived for centuries. The Grand Louvre project, led by I. M. Pei over a period of more than ten years, can be encompassed in two very simple ideas: first, creating a vast entrance hall and accommodation for technical facilities at the heart of the Louvre, under the Cour Napoléon; second, using the space vacated by the Ministry of Finance to enhance and rearrange the museum's various collections, displaying them in more effective and accessible fashion.

It was high time the country realized that the Louvre was still living in the 19th century. The list of the museum's shortcomings was long: a poorly signposted, narrow entrance that forced visitors to stand in crowded lines; a baggage-deposit area located a couple of miles away at the Gare Saint-Lazare station; a confusing and discouraging visitors' itinerary as complex as King Minos' labyrinth; rooms frequently closed due to staff shortages or strikes; poor natural lighting; research lab-oratories and restoration workshops cramped under the eaves and scattered through the palace's least accessible areas; and storage rooms crowded with homeless masterpieces and collections in search of display space. Not surprisingly, the Georges Pompidou National Center of Art and Culture, just north of the Île de la Cité, was attracting more visitors each year than the world's most illustrious museum. Such was the dismal picture before Pei set to work. The first step was to enumerate the symptoms and compile a report on the health of this historic patient. Starting in March 1983, planning experts spent a year conducting a detailed study on the public's behavior, the requests of curators, and staff demands. This resulted in a draft program that Pei and his team – establishing themselves as distant successors of Visconti and Lefuel – went over point by point.

In its goals and in the breadth of the changes it brought about, today's Grand Louvre stands comparison only with Napoleon III's "new" 19th-century Louvre, a project that lasted more than ten years

THE NAPLEON ENTRANCE HALL

From the outset the Napoleon Hall was the heart and center-piece of the Grand Louvre project, For one thing, it gave the Louvre a space large and light enough to welcome several thousand visitors a day. Moreover, the project grouped the museum's reorganized departments around this central entrance. And finally, for a modern museum to function smoothly, technical communications corridors as extensive as its display areas are essential. I. M. Pei there-fore set out to give the Lou-vre more than fifty thousand square yards of underground space for laboratories, storage, a computer center, and so on.

To meet all these needs, it was necessary to excavate the subsoil - but the level of the nearby Seine prohibited digging deeper than twenty-five feet. It was therefore essential that the summit of the complex stand out among the surrounding palace buildings. Pei's solution: the translucent Pyramid.

and involved thousands of workers. Once stretched out in the shape of a long letter I along the Seine, today's museum, shaped like a compact U, is more "compressed" and symmetrical. The collections are grouped around three poles: the Richelieu Wing, the Cour Carrée, and the Pavillon Denon, all of which can be reached from the central point, the Pyramid.

The opening of the Richelieu passage has linked the Louvre to the Palais-Royal area. The museum, no longer standing like a long barrier between the banks of the Seine and the Rue de Rivoli, is now better integrated into the surrounding city.

Everything necessary for making the Louvre a more welcoming museum is located under the light-trap of the Pyramid, including the I. M. Pei Auditorium and the temporary exhibition rooms, bookshops, and restaurants. Radiating out from the Pyramid, the

Louvre has been endowed with a brand-new circulatory system of corridors, stairways, and escalators, some of them mere capillaries, others great arteries, like the passage in the Richelieu Wing with its giant oculi. All these passageways bring visitors closer to the museum's seven departments, which all boast greater exhibition space.

The Department of Sculpture doubled its surface area and now occupies the Marly and Puget courtyards. Glassed over and modified by Pei and Peter Rice, the two courtyards enable the huge *Horses of Marly* (which once stood guard at the eastern end of the Champs-Élysées) and several other large outdoor sculptures to be exhibited for the first time. The Department of Near Eastern Antiquities was reorganized around a closed court-yard where Pei and Stephen Rustow have recon-structed the Khorsabad palace of King Sargon II. On the second floor of the Cour Carrée, Italo Rota has

previous double page
(from left to right)
Justice of Cambyse;
Zaleueus; Sacrificer;
Prisoner Breast-Fed
by His Daughter,
Bas-relief,
Jean Goujon,
ca. 1560-1564
The Hall of the Pyramid is like a white stone showcase for Goujon's antique figures. Nothing distracts the eye from their ample, powerful bodies and magnificent hands.

left
Burgundian Tomb,
Philippe Pot
The neutral decor of room ten in the Richelieu Wing is ideal for the display of sculpture from Burgundy, like these from Pot's imposing tomb.

above
Antique Bronzes
Room
Once the Salle des Gardes in the king's apartments, the Antique Bronzes Room is one of the Louvre's most splendid chambers. Greek and Roman bronzes are now exhibited here.

left, and below
The Foreign
Painting Rooms
These new rooms, located under the roofs, benefit from natural top lighting. Pei, an expert in the field since his work on the East Wing of the National Gallery in Washington,

D.C., created a sophisticated system of computer-controlled grids to monitor the sunlight.

above
18th-century Bas-reliefs and Bronzes
Bas-reliefs of white marble from the 18th century stand out against the room's ocher walls, while a highly kinetic bronze appears to show visitors the way.

center left, below
View of the
Cour Marly

HORSES IN THE COURTYARD

The third stage of the Grand Louvre project was the 1993 recasting of the Richelieu Wing by I. M. Pei, assisted by Michel Macary for the Department of Sculptures, Jean-Michel Wilmotte for the Decorative Arts Department, and Stephen Rustow for Antiquities. The far-reaching changes they effected made it possible to reclaim two long-suffering court-yards formerly used as parking lots by staff of the Finance Ministry. Glassed over, and with staggered floor levels that enhance the effects of perspec-

tive, the Cour Marly is now home to the monumen-tal works of French sculpture that originally adorned the grounds of the château at Marly. Featured prominently among them are the equestrian groups by Antoine Coysevox, *Mercury Riding Pegasus*, and Guillaume Coustou, *Escaped Horses Recaptured by a Groom*. Carved from Carrara marble, the horses are of striking size and power; their energies have been unleashed by the daylight flood-ing through the glass roof of the courtyard.

created an series of thirty-nine new rooms dedicated to French painting. Paintings from the Northern Schools, previously dispersed and poorly displayed, are now also grouped in thirty-nine rooms and small cabinets on the top floor of the Cour Carrée, where they benefit from ideal natural top lighting.

The twenty-four canvases commissioned for the Luxembourg palace by Marie de Médicis from Rubens are displayed for the first time in the Salle Médicis, specially designed by Pei for their presentation.

Drawings are exhibited in galleries throughout the palace, near the rooms where paintings are displayed in the Richelieu and Denon wings, as well as in the Cour Carrée. Technical and computer facilities, indispensable to any modern museum, along with the Musées de France research labs and the restoration workshops,

have moved from their cramped quarters into specially designed rooms occupying several thousand square yards under the Cour Napoléon and the Carrousel.

Given the scale of these extensions, and the improvements brought to every department, the curators' wholehearted support for the project is readily understandable. Although some rooms (like those in the Colonnade, earmarked for the Department of Egyptian Antiquities) are not yet complete, the Grand Louvre project can already be considered a success. Modern architecture has given the Louvre's rich history and collections new life. Just as in the past, the Grand Louvre still conquers the beholder with its magical arrangement of volumes, the beauty of the materials used in its construction, the perfection of every detail, and the harmonious proportions of the whole complex.

above right
The Richelieu Café
Boasting terraces looking out over the Cour Napoléon, the café was designed and decorated by Jean-Michel Wilmotte. A compression by César, stripes painted by Buren, and photos of great men on the walls, computer-treated by Francis Giacobetti, have turned this inner sanctum of France's finance ministers into a highly contemporary space.

right center and below center
A room in the Islamic Arts Department
Like the rest of the Islamic Arts Department, this room was redesigned by architect Jean-Paul Boulanger and master builder Denis Cajet. The ocher stucco of the walls evokes the sands of eastern deserts. The fiber-optic lighting of the showcases was designed by Wilmotte and installed by Boulanger, who blended wall-washer spots, which spread natural light, with spots directly trained on the objects displayed.

right
Ceiling, Department of Near Eastern Antiquities
The ceiling of this room is a modern interpretation of a coffer ceiling, in which the magic of electricity (in the form of low-tension spots) complements natural light.

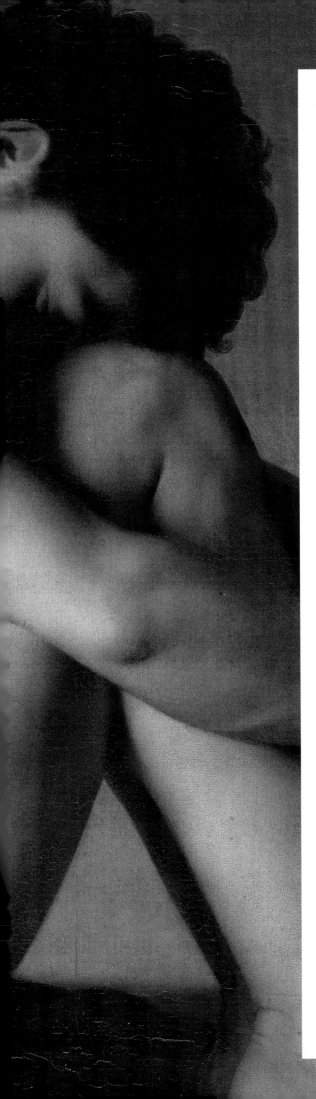

Department of Painting

*Where else but in the Louvre can one find
such a vast and historically comprehensive range of European paintings – and
more specifically, French paintings?
Where else can one find such diversity of
format, from miniatures by François
Clouet and Corneille de Lyon to such
gigantic canvases as Paolo Veronese's*
Marriage at Cana, *Charles Le Brun's*
Battles of Alexander, *or Théodore
Géricault's* The Raft of the Medusa *?
It is hard to imagine a more fabulous
visual feast of schools and styles than the
six thousand paintings in the Louvre collections. Painted from the late 13th to the
middle of the 18th century (works executed between 1850 and 1910 are displayed
at the Musée d'Orsay), the thousands of
canvases reflect the wildly different styles
and interests that prevailed through those
centuries. But they are also linked to the
history of France itself, since the collections were originally dependent on the
patronage of the country's leaders, from
Francis I in the 16th century to Louis
Philippe and Napoleon III. Moreover,
the Louvre benefited from the enthusiasm
and generosity of private donors, from Dr.
Lacaze to Etienne Moreau Nélatons, who
bequeathed to the museum the fruits of
their lifelong passion for art collecting.*

FROM THE PRIMITIVES
TO THE RENAISSANCE:
1350-1570

For medieval man, visual expression was essential. It was through images that the faith, philosophy, and ideals of his time were transmitted. The demand for works of art was much greater than today: churches and convents commissioned many of them. So did kings, princes, and great lords, whose idea of patronage far exceeded that of contemporary sponsors of the arts. Religious ceremonies, weddings, and tournaments were all perfect occasions for the common people to admire the work of artists and craftsmen.

From the early Middle Ages (ca. the 8th century) to the late Gothic period in the 15th century, French painting was closely linked to the arts of illuminated manuscripts, frescoes, and stained glass – media that favored a symbolic and stylized vision of the world, with no concern for realism or spatial representation. All the craftsmen of Europe were engaged in these shared occupations. But toward the end of the 14th century, France – ensnared in the Hundred Years' War – became more isolated from outside currents. Craftsmen drew themes and inspiration from

ordinary daily life. This new sensibility was first expressed in painting, which broke free of the rigid constraints of the stained-glass window and the church or palace wall to find a home on canvases and easily transportable wooden panels. Thus began the era of so-called easel painting.

While the Hundred Years' War raged in France, schools of painting also flourished under the patronage of distant princely courts. The dukes of the Burgundian court, from Philip the Bold to Charles the Bold, hired the greatest Flemish painters – the van Eyck brothers, Rogier van der Weyden, and Hans Memling. The duke of Berry, an enthusiastic collector, was a strong supporter of such artists as the Limburg brothers (creators of the duke's famous Book of Hours), who represented the French International Gothic style. King René of Provence surrounded himself with Flemish artists as well as painters from the School of Avignon, who included Nicolas Froment and Enguerrand Quarton.

When the war finally ended in 1453, France's

INTERNATIONAL GOTHIC

From 1380 to about 1450, an independent artistic movement spread across much of Europe. Art historians have called it the International Gothic style, because of its affinities with Gothic and because it crossed political borders. It flourished, in fact, in France, Italy, Germany, and Bohemia. An elegant, decorative, and lavish court art, the style transfigured reality into enchanting and meticulously detailed paintings. These works, such as the duke of Berry's *Very*

Rich Hours (illuminated by the Limburg brothers), were usually small in size and therefore portable. Yet such artists as Antonio Pisanello and Lorenzo Ghiberti also created monumental works, in this style, including the fresco of *Saint George and the Princess* in Verona. The swan song of a courtly and chivalrous civilization, the International Gothic style disappeared when states, republics, and townships wrested power from the great feudal lords.

Valois kings were delighted to return to their Loire Valley châteaux, where they once again began to commission artwork. Jean Fouquet, Louis XI's "painter and illuminator," incarnated the pictorial spirit of the late Middle Ages, creating perhaps the purest expression of a truly French art. This art would reach its peak – after the interlude of the Italian-dominated Renaissance – in the classicism of the 17th century. But a hundred years earlier, beginning with Francis I, French kings returned from military campaigns in Italy with the light of a Renaissance ideal glittering in their eyes.

MANNERISM AND THE SCHOOL OF FONTAINEBLEAU

In the late 16th century, during the moral crisis that contributed to the Reformation, Italian artists turned away from Renaissance values to express an unusual ideal of Beauty. Begun by Andrea del Sarto in Florence, this new style, Mannerism, was embraced by such great artists as Jacopo Pontormo, Bronzino, Girolamo Parmigianino, and Il Rosso Fiorentino. But this style bloomed most strongly in France with the School of Fontainebleau, whose artists – Rosso and Primaticcio – were invited by Francis I to decorate the chateau of Fontainebleau. Their favorite subjects were mythological and allegorical themes from antiquity and elegantly rendered nudes. Later, French and Flemish artists formed a second School of Fontainebleau, devoted to the celebration of feminine beauty.

(It was an ideal far removed from the national artistic tradition, which now retreated into portraiture, best illustrated by the realism and psychological acuity of the Clouet family and Corneille de Lyon.) With the Italian painters Primaticcio, Il Rosso Fiorentino, and other artists of the School of Fontainebleau, French painting now exalted profane and sensual pleasures and glorified pagan and antique mythology. It aimed to please the senses rather than the spirit. If the art of the Middle Ages had celebrated the glory of God, that of the Renaissance reflected man's Promethean dream.

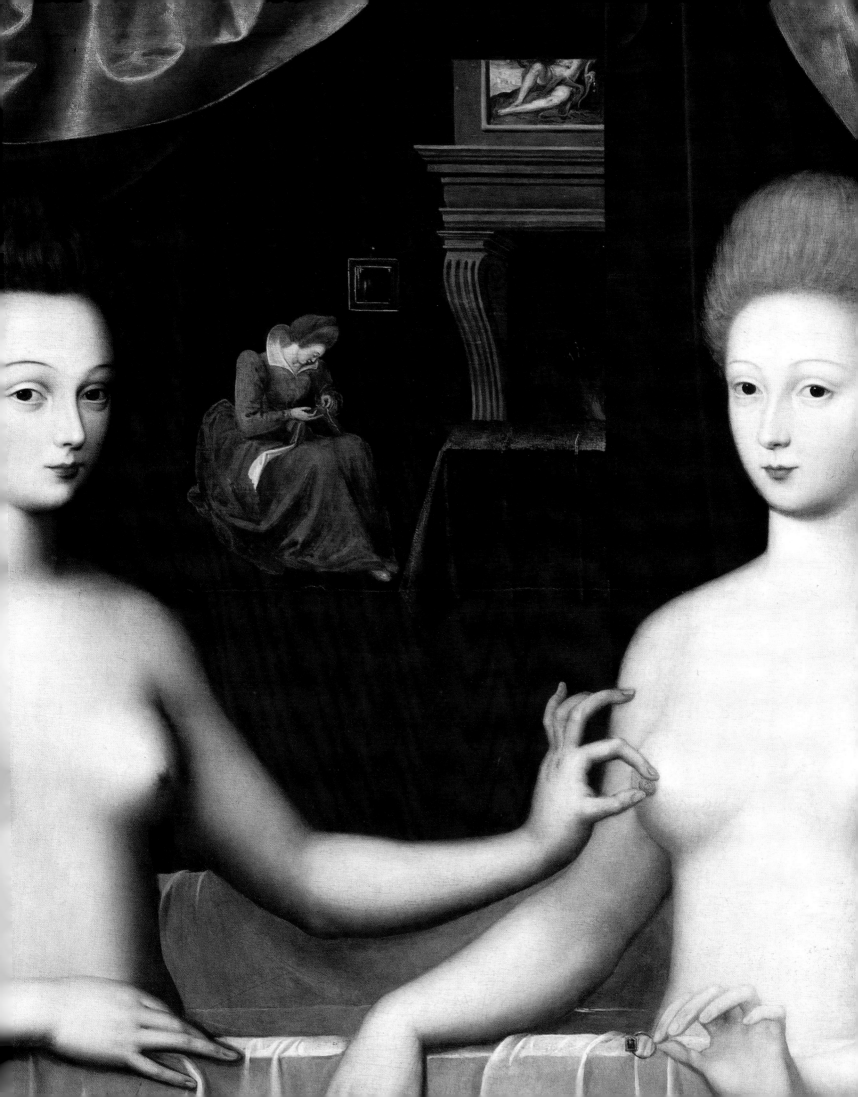

In the 16th century, it was primarily influences from abroad that guided French art. In the 17th century, however, France created and exported its style – classicism – to other countries. The notion that ideal beauty requires strict discipline and adherence to universal rules had begun to take form. Perhaps institutions that the king's advisers conceived for them. Despite its very diverse facets, the French spirit ever since the Middle Ages has leaned toward rigorous, harmonious, rational, and simple forms. After the Mannerist excesses of the Renaissance, French taste returned to this natural state. It was under the reign of Louis

right

The Pilgrims of Emmaus, Mathieu, Louis, and Antoine Le Nain
Paintings by the Le Nain brothers were usually collective endeavors, signed simply "Le Nain." Their works reflect the abiding importance of workshops in the 17th century, when painters worked for one or several master artists. Like most of their religious works, this painting is attributed to Mathieu. Its freshness and naïveté are far removed from the enigmatic poetry of works by his brother Louis.

right

Saint Thomas, Georges de La Tour
This is among the most striking of the "daylight period" paintings of Georges de La Tour (1593-1652). He spent his last years painting almost exclusively nocturnal scenes with luminous effects inspired by Caravaggio. The pike is the traditional attribute of Saint Thomas, who was apparently beaten to death by pagan priests while preaching the gospel in India. It may also refer to the New Testament story of "Doubting Thomas," who refused to believe in Christ's resurrection until he had touched Jesus' wound.

as a consequence of the horrors of the Wars of Religion, a desire for order filtered into the political realm between the reigns of Henry IV and Louis XIV and soon it also conquered the arts. By 1661, when the young Louis XIV freed himself from Mazarin's tutelage and took the reins of the kingdom into his own hands, artists were ready to accept the XIII that French classicism was born. Yet it had a strong Italian flavor: for the majority of painters at that time – such as Simon Vouet, Nicolas Poussin, Claude Lorrain, and Charles Le Brun – a pilgrimage to Italy was a mandatory step in their career.

As French painters discovered the work of their transalpine counterparts, they began to distance themselves from the

left center, below

Ex-Voto of 1662, Philippe de Champaigne
As indicated by the Latin text on the left-hand side of the painting, this ex-voto by Philippe de Champaigne (1602-1674) gives thanks for the miraculous recovery of his daughter, Sister Catherine de Sainte-Suzanne. De Champaigne was Louis XIII's and Cardinal Richelieu's favorite painter.

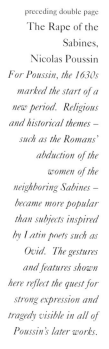

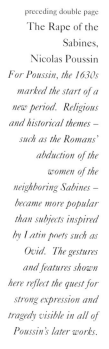

preceding double page
The Rape of the
Sabines,
Nicolas Poussin
*For Poussin, the 1630s
marked the start of a
new period. Religious
and historical themes –
such as the Romans'
abduction of the
women of the
neighboring Sabines –
became more popular
than subjects inspired
by Latin poets such as
Ovid. The gestures
and features shown
here reflect the quest for
strong expression and
tragedy visible in all of
Poussin's later works.*

left
Cleopatra's Landing
at Tarsis,
Claude Lorrain
*In most of his
paintings, Claude
Gellée (known as
Claude, or Le
Lorrain) used anecdote
– in this case the
arrival at the port of
Tarsis of Cleopatra,
Queen of Egypt – as a
pretext for creating an
imaginary landscape.
The planes of the
temples echo the oblique
lines of the ships'
rigging. Claude's
highly skilled use of
perspective draws the
viewer's eye to the
horizon, where the
setting sun bathes the
sea in gold.*

Mannerism prevailing in France and took sides in the quarrel between the followers of the Carracci and those of Caravaggio. On the one side, Poussin was eager to pursue the classical lessons of the Carracci; on the other, Vouet, Georges de La Tour, and a swarm of less famous artists adopted Caravaggio's exacerbated realism and dramatic chiaroscuro effects.

French artists in Rome were also struck by their encounter with the Baroque style, which was encouraged by the Jesuits and the Counter-Reformation. Both the Baroque style and Italian realism were to spread throughout Europe, but the Baroque encountered determined opposition in France. From its clash with realism, the two styles merged in the birth of French classicism, which drew its inspiration more from ancient than from contemporary Rome.

Like the spirit of the Renaissance, classicism called for a return to antiquity yet extolled realism and the

center right, below
Self-Portrait,
Nicolas Poussin
*One of two self-
portraits completed by
Poussin, this one was
painted in 1650 for the
collector Paul Fréart
de Chantelou, who was
executor of the artist's
estate. The assurance
and majesty of this
painting reflect the
artist's confidence in
his own talent.*

POUSSIN: A FRENCHMAN IN ITALY

Ironically, Nicolas Poussin (1594-1665), the most French of all painters and a symbol of 17th-century French classicism, spent his entire adult life in Italy. In 1624 he left France for Rome. There, thanks to commissions from collectors such as Cardinal Francesco Barberini and his secretary Cassiano del Pozzo, he became famous for his large religious and mythological compositions, which earned him a reputation as a "philosopher-painter." The Baroque character of his early canvases gradually gave way to a more intimate and more complex style. Richelieu gave him commissions and in 1641-42 brought him back to Paris. But the work Poussin was asked to do – altarpieces and vast allegorical paintings – did not suit his temperament, and he never completed the decoration of the Grande Galerie in the Louvre. As his work met with hostility in France, Poussin returned to his beloved Italy. After his death, his influence endured over subsequent centuries, perhaps justifying the audacious statement he made at the end of his life: "There is nothing I have not attempted."

Alexander and
Porus, Charles Le
Brun
First planned in 1661,
this series of four
paintings by Le Brun
reveal the ambition of
the young King Louis
XIV, who had himself
represented as
Alexander – and of Le
Brun, who hoped to
rival Raphael. This
canvas evokes a
famous example of
Alexander's
magnanimity: after
defeating the Indian
prince Porus, the
Macedonian conqueror
asked his captive how
he wished to be treated.
"As a king," was the
reply. Impressed,
Alexander allowed
Porus to keep his
kingdom.

natural order. It set the virtues of reason high above the extravagances of the imagination, which was described by Descartes as "the madwoman in the attic."

Classicism rejected facility, demanding of artists long years of effort and study and a wide-ranging knowledge of culture. It preferred noble themes, inspired by mythology and antiquity, to themes drawn from everyday life, which it considered trivial. All of this created an art more elitist than popular, yet this royal art did not shut itself off from the people. When the French saw it (particularly in its "showcase" of Versailles), they associated its abundance with the crown's wealth. It seemed less a discouraging imi-

of the Academy and the triumphant early years of Louis's reign, the arts were organized as a function of absolute monarchy. It was the era of the "royal style": the king believed that the arts should contribute to his own and the State's aggrandizement. Charles Le Brun, first painter to the king and director of the Academy of Painting and Sculpture and the Gobelins manufactory, performed this role to perfection. This great decorator, who oversaw the design of the interiors at Versailles, is considered to have created the Louis XIV style. When his influence waned, ca. 1680, Pierre Mignard followed in his footsteps. By the late 17th century, France could rival Italy as a great culture: with close to 20 million subjects, it was the richest, most pop-

The Chancellor
Séguier,
Le Brun
The Chancellor Pierre
Séguier (1588-1672),
a powerful and
somewhat
unscrupulous man,
worked for Cardinals
Richelieu and
Mazarin, Anne of
Austria, and Louis
XIV, all the while
keeping a clear eye on
his own interests. Yet
he was also a
bibliophile and art
collector, and a patron
to academies and
artists (including Le
Brun). He sent Le
Brun to Rome in
1642 and later
commissioned his
portrait. In 1660 Le
Brun made this second
portrait, showing the
chancellor's sumptuous
appearance on the
occasion of Queen
Maria Theresa's entry
into Paris.

tation of life than a reassuring vision of a perfect world.

Toward the middle of the century, with the creation

ulous, most civilized country in Europe. From this time on, France was the center of style, and its influence radiated throughout Europe and beyond.

LE BRUN: MANAGING DIRECTOR OF FRENCH ART

The art critic Pierre du Colombier wryly nicknamed Charles Le Brun (1619-1690) the "managing director" of French art. Other 19th-century writers, however, called him the "dictator" of the art world. An epic painter and ostentatious decorator, Le Brun traveled to Rome, then worked for Cardinal Jean Mazarin, who introduced him to the young Louis XIV. The king gave him the responsibility of reorganizing the arts in France. Founder and first director of the

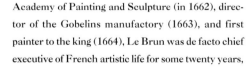

Academy of Painting and Sculpture (in 1662), director of the Gobelins manufactory (1663), and first painter to the king (1664), Le Brun was de facto chief executive of French artistic life for some twenty years, a position he maintained up to the death of the king's chief minister, Colbert. After that, he was replaced by his rival Pierre Mignard. Le Brun's influence was great. But he was not so all-powerful as has been claimed, nor was his "dictatorship" so ruthless.

THE TRIUMPH OF FRIVOLITY: 1715–1760

left

The Embarkation for Cythera, Jean-Antoine Watteau, 1717
Watteau, a society painter eager to leave behind the moralism and austerity of the last years of Louis XIV's reign, elevated the status of the fête galante *genre that characterized life during the regency of Philippe d'Orléans. His paintings celebrated a way of life devoted to amorous gallantry; his subjects were leisure, masked balls, elegant manners and costumes, games, and the theater. This canvas, which he reworked many times, is Watteau's most successful painting in the genre. A spirited group of lovers is shown unfurling in an elegiac landscape before a statue of Venus, before departing for the island of Cythera – the mythological cradle of amorous delights.*

On September 1, 1715, Europe and France began to breathe again. After seventy-two years, the reign of Louis XIV was over. Political absolutism, wars, taxes, and moral austerity had made his rule increasingly unpopular. French supremacy on the Continent was coming to an end. A new society emerged, breaking free of the Sun King's "glorious century." The nobility, reduced to a life of gilded captivity at Versailles, surrendered its influence

by quite different values – pleasure, happiness, and comfort.

Louis XIV's grand style had glorified royal sovereignty, but it had also imposed unbearable constraints. Late in his life the monarch had become aware of this: when asked for his opinion on the decoration of the Menagerie at Versailles, he answered: "Spread childhood everywhere."

No sooner did he die than his wish was granted. Artists became more free, shaking off the grandiose

left center

Two Views of the Artist's Mother, Hyacinthe Rigaud
This portrait of Madame Rigaud, painted in 1695, was bequeathed by her son to the Royal Academy of Painting and entered the Louvre during the Revolution. It is one of the more intimate works by Rigaud, who was better known for his large and decidedly solemn official portraits. The influence of Van Dyck and of the early Rembrandt is visible in this work.

to a new class of middle-class financiers and merchants who were only too eager to assert their energy and ambitions. Christian ideals, which under Jansenist influence had assumed somber tones, were replaced

manner and devoting themselves to the creation of a gentle, lighthearted art aimed to please the senses – gone was the concern to edify or overawe. Increasingly drawn to intimacy and well-being, art lovers now dec-

left, bottom

Pierrot, Jean-Antoine Watteau
The Pierrot, *also known as* Gilles, *painted in 1718-19, clearly illustrates Watteau's debt to the stock characters of the Italian commedia dell'arte and is infused with the faint but distinct melancholy of the* fête galante *genre. Pierrot, the only full-length, life-size figure in Watteau's paintings, appears even larger because of the figures – the doctor on his mule, Leander, Isabelle, and the Captain – at his feet.*

THE INIMITABLE WATTEAU

This 18th-century prince charming started life as the son of a poor roofer. The painter who celebrated joie de vivre and sophisticated fêtes was actually of chronically poor health and was haunted by the presentiment of the early death that would take him. Jean-Antoine Watteau (1684-1721), therefore, did not truly identify with the spirit of his own paintings, which Delacroix described as "Venice and Flanders combined." In Paris, he studied under

Claude Gillot and Claude Audran, who introduced him to the Italian commedia dell'arte and the Rococo style. Despite his early death, Watteau worked in every genre, although he is most often identified with *fêtes galantes*, Italian theater, and military scenes. At his death, the "inimitable Watteau," as he was described by the Venetian artist Rosalba Carriera, left behind two hundred paintings and innumerable drawings.

orated their homes with brightly painted works of entertaining subjects. Le Brun's large allegorical compositions, not to speak of frozen, starched, and bewigged portraits, were finally out of fashion. They were replaced by graceful themes in which Sentiment triumphed over Reason, and Venus, goddess of love, dismissed Mars, god of war.

One man embodied this new spirit: Philippe d'Orléans, the nephew of Louis XIV who became regent until the future Louis XV came of age. Inquisitive and impatient, he was also a discerning connoisseur. He collected both women and works of art, supporting such painters as Jean-Antoine Watteau and Jean-Baptiste-Joseph Pater, as well as the cabinetmaker Charles Cessent. Indeed, it was Philippe who christened the style of the day as Régence – but

because of its predilection for complex and intricate forms, it was also known as Rococo. Under his tutelage, court life yielded to a more sociable style that favored individualism, fantasy, games for the mind and the senses, and the quest for pleasure.

In painting, Watteau (1684-1721) was the leading proponent of the new amourous *galante* style. His canvases, fascinating blends of charming decors, subtle and luminous colors, and gentle melancholy, were meant not for the mind but the heart.

Following in his footsteps were such lesser masters as Pater and Nicolas Lancret, who brought a more realistic and less poetic eye to this fantasy world of pleasure and sentiment. Their works prefigure the celebrations of the senses later painted by François Boucher and Jean-Honoré Fragonard.

D. CÆSARE BENVE:
NVTI ABBAS GENLIS.

Although Louis XV far preferred hunting to the muses, his mistress, the marquise de Pompadour, was an excellent "Secretary for the Arts." During Louis's reign, painting became increasingly sensual, elegant, and stylized. More than any other genre, Rococo was the defining style of the century.

François Boucher (1703-1770), named first painter to the king in 1765, explored mythological and pastoral themes with licentious intent. He loved to paint Eros, lavishing a luminous and blissful sensuality on his Venuses, Dianas, and other bathers. The younger Honoré Fragonard (1732-1806) began as a history painter, but collectors were soon drawn to his own representations of love, in which he veiled his daring with allusion and with subtle brushstrokes. The marquis de Marigny, brother of Madame de Pompadour, and the comte d'Angivillers, who both held the title of superin-

tendent of buildings, pursued an active commissioning policy. The Salons organized by the Academy also encouraged new and talented artists, including François Le Moyne, the greatest decorator of the period; Jean-François de Troy; Jean-Baptiste and Carle Van Loo; and Charles Parrocel, who specialized in the equestrian paintings and battle scenes beloved of Louis XV.

Although genre scenes, still lifes, and animal paintings ranked low in the hierarchy established by the Academy, the public liked them. The undisputed master of the still life, Jean-Baptiste-Siméon Chardin (1699-1779), was widely admired. Spontaneity and a natural approach also infiltrated the art of the portrait. With Jean-Marc Nattier and Maurice Quentin de La Tour, portraiture relinquished the stiff poses of the previous century in favor of psychological reality.

"ROBERT DES RUINES"

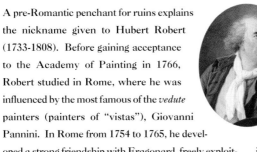

A pre-Romantic penchant for ruins explains the nickname given to Hubert Robert (1733-1808). Before gaining acceptance to the Academy of Painting in 1766, Robert studied in Rome, where he was influenced by the most famous of the *vedute* painters (painters of "vistas"), Giovanni Pannini. In Rome from 1754 to 1765, he developed a strong friendship with Fragonard, freely exploiting their shared love of landscape painting. Unlike Fragonard, however, Robert was drawn to unusual sites and delighted in painting imaginary buildings. From 1784 to 1792, he was director of the future Louvre's painting collection. After Thermidor (late July 1794, when Robespierre's "Terror" was brought to an end), he was appointed curator of the Louvre. He alternated between painting scenes of everyday life and visionary views illustrating his proposals for improving the Louvre.

The Paternal Curse, or the Ungrateful Son, Jean-Baptiste Greuze
Greuze (1725-1805) abandoned allegorical and mythological scenes early in his career to devote himself to sentimental and rhetorical genre scenes, much praised by the philosopher Diderot.

below right

The Silver Goblet, Jean-Baptiste-Siméon Chardin
"Oh, Chardin," exclaimed Diderot, "it is not white, red, or black that you grind on your palette. No, it is the very substance of things, it is the azure and the light you transfix on your brushpoint and transfer to the canvas." This still life is certainly one of Chardin's finest and most luminous.

But in the final decades of the 18th century, the public tired of all these diversions, celebrations, and license. The popularity of Louis XV (hitherto known as the "Well-Beloved") evaporated as the country's problems mounted; optimism withered; social criticism grew increasingly severe.

After the reign of frivolity and cynicism came a return to virtue. The philosopher Denis Diderot (who, with Jean-Jacques Rousseau, was a leading advocate of this reforming movement, whose moral beacons were nature and sincere sentiment) violently attacked Boucher, calling for a revival of virtuous, "moral painting": "What

DIDEROT AND PAINTING

Theatrical producer, stage director, editor in chief of the *Encyclopedia*, author of *Rameau's Nephew* and *Jacques le Fataliste*, Denis Diderot (1713-1784) was also the first writer to undertake systematic art criticism. Between 1759 and 1781, he commented on the exhibits at nine successive Salons, formulating one of the world's first theories of aesthetics. But he remained a staunch social philosopher, quick to condemn any picture, however flawless, that did not conform to his own conception of what was "noble" and "true."

Unlike later critics, Diderot saw evidence of vulgar taste in the "galante" paintings of Boucher and Van Loo. He was full of praise for artists like Chardin and Horace Vernet – who had "stolen her secrets from Nature" – and above all for Greuze. It must be admitted that Diderot's canon left him open to charges of preaching, and of the hypocrisy inseparable from it.

would you have this artist hurl at the canvas? What he has in his imagination? And what could be in the imagination of a man who spends his life with prostitutes?"

Then came Jean-Baptiste Greuze (1725-1805), who infused his anecdotal scenes (*The Village Bride, The Broken Jug*) with a mixture of deep feeling and sentimentalism. As the century neared its end, the rehabilitation of the straight line (the Louis XVI style) in figurative art, growing moral rigidity, and increasing reverence for pure feeling prefigured the explosion of Neoclassicism that marked the transition between the ancien régime and post-Revolutionary France.

Portrait of Chardin Wearing an Eyeshade, Jean-Baptiste-Siméon Chardin
By 1775 Chardin was nearing the end of his life, had abandoned oil for pastels, and had fallen from public favor. Yet it was now that he created some of his most moving paintings. His gift of observation, and the simplicity of a style he constantly pared and purified, brought him new acclaim. Diderot described Chardin's work as "magical" and wrote that "we could say of Monsieur Chardin and Monsieur Bouffon [the naturalist] that they had "stolen her secrets fram Nature."

THE INFLUENCE OF THE SALONS

The annual Salons held by the Academy of Painting guided the entire artistic life of the 18th and 19th centuries. Inaugurated by Colbert, the first exhibition of the Royal Academy of Painting was held in 1667. It was renamed the "Salon" after the square *salon* (or room) in the Louvre in which it was held. Participation in the Salon was initially restricted to academicians and to painters approved by the Academy, but during the Revolution – between 1791 and 1798 – it was placed under the control of a jury of administrators selected by the government, and every-

one was admitted. From that time until the Second Empire, in the third quarter of the 19th century, its influence was great. In 1881 Jules Ferry decided to create a committee of twenty members elected by previously admitted artists. But as a result of the gulf separating official art from the innovative work of the 19th century, the Salon had already become a refuge for academic artists. Competing exhibitions were multiplying (the famous Salon des Refusés in 1863, and the Salon des Indépendants in 1884) and gradually undermining the Salon's importance.

FROM NEOCLASSICISM TO PRE-ROMANTICISM

Under Louis XVI, French painting moved away from the sensuality of Boucher and Fragonard to embrace the lessons of the masters of classical antiquity. A new ideal of beauty arose, based on the purity and balance of classicism and antiquity, rather than on the fluid, capricious forms recently in fashion. The classical ideal, given new life by the excavations at Pompeii and Herculaneum in the 1740s, now came to the artistic forefront. The many archaeological and historical publications of the day gave artists the elements of a new stylistic grammar that inspired furniture designers and decorators during Louis XVI's reign. The Italian

PRUD'HON THE RHAPSODIC

The tenth child of a stonecutter, Pierre-Paul Prud'hon (1758-1823) received his early training at the studio of the painter Devosge at Dijon. After winning the Prix de Rome, awarded to painters and sculptors, he traveled to Italy in 1785, meeting the sculptor Antonio Canova. He returned to France during the Revolution and painted several portraits, including one of the revolutionary leader Saint-Just. Primarily a historical painter, he also tackled large genre works. But he was best known as a painter of love scenes and of women. His models, subtly defined by his *sfumato* technique, blend into misty backgrounds. The style was a great success with Napoleon's two empresses, Josephine and Marie-Louise. Prud'hon is considered one of the greatest Neoclassical artists. The lyricism and open feeling in his paintings already prefigured the Romantic sensibility.

artist Giambattista Piranesi's *Vedute di Roma* (*Views of Rome*) revived interest in Roman monuments, as did the work of the Frenchman Hubert Robert. At the same time, the German art historian Johann Winckelmann was elaborating his theory of Neoclassicism.

Winckelmann never called for artists to imitate ancient or Renaissance themes; rather he laid down new rules for artists, inspired

DAVID
REVOLUTIONARY CLASSICIST

Few painters are so strongly identified with a single historical period as Jacques-Louis David (1748-1825) is with the Revolution and Empire. By the time the ancien régime disappeared, he had already defined his own theory of aesthetics and was famous for his large historical canvases. He sided wholeheartedly with the Revolution, becoming one of its strongest chroniclers and participants, voting for the death of the king and working strenuously at the reorganization of French cultural life. Imprisoned after the fall of Maximilien Robespierre, he emerged to become the official painter of the reign of Napoleon. After the restoration of the monarchy he went into exile in Brussels, where he returned to the large historical and mythological subjects of his youth. A revolutionary in politics, David was also a revolutionary in the arts. He trained innumerable students and was the leader of the Neoclassical movement.

in part by Enlightenment rationalism.

The forerunner of this style in France was Joseph-Marie Vien, who returned from Rome in 1750 to lead the revival of the antique style. But the driving force was his student, Jacques-Louis David, who glorified the supposedly antique virtues of heroism, virility, patriotism, honor, justice, and an almost suicidal readiness for self-sacrifice. With his *Oath of the Horatii, Intervention of the Sabine Women,* and *Brutus,* David quickly became the leading proponent of Neoclassicism.

In 1815 the Napoleonic Empire ended on the fateful field of Waterloo. The Bourbons regained their throne but were unable to revive the values of the ancien régime. The upheavals of Revolution and Empire had replaced court society with a middle-class elite whose relationship to art would be completely different. For centuries, artists had depended on royal and aristocratic patronage and been supported by guilds and academies. In post-Revolutionary and post-Imperial France, they were free of tutelage and outside constraints. But they now faced more ruthless masters – the laws of supply and demand, and the whims of fashion.

Reared under the Empire to the rattle of drums and cannonfire, the generation that came of age during the Bourbon Restoration was disenchanted with the drab future it faced. This early "identity crisis" was given a name by the young poet Alfred de Musset: the *mal du siècle*. Members of this "lost generation" challenged the reigning mediocrity with a revolt based on the cult of strong passions and a glorification of the irrational, laying the foundations for the Romantic movement, which would influence literature, music, sculpture, and painting.

Unlike Neoclassical painters, the Romantics preferred fleeting feeling and personal passion to universal, unchangeable truths. They turned away from mythological themes and moralizing in order to grapple directly with the tragic and sordid realities of their day. In painting, this meant that they favored color over line.

Romanticism was not accepted in France without a struggle. The Neoclassicism of David and his students remained a powerful foe. At every Salon held between 1817 and 1827, the new artistic movement locked horns with the old. This battle was symbolized by the dispute that pitted Eugène Delacroix (1798-1863), champion of Romanticism, against Jean-Auguste-Dominique Ingres (1780-1867), standard-bearer of classicism.

Delacroix's imagination, his brilliance as a colorist, and his love of violence and exoticism made him the leading painter of French Romanticism. Attracted to extremes, he poured his energetic talents into the

left
The Toilet of Esther, Théodore Chassériau
Initially a follower of his teacher Ingres, Chassériau (1819-1856) was later influenced by Delacroix and by Orientalism, as can be seen in this work, painted in 1841. Orientalism, which began with the French conquest of Algeria in the 1830s, was an enduring theme in 19th-century France.

left center
Achille Devéria, Louis Boulanger
A painter of everyday life, Devéria (1800-1857) became successful by making innumerable lithographs dealing with social issues of the day. This portrait was painted by his student Boulanger (1806-1867), a friend of the poet Victor Hugo. Boulanger also made a series of engravings inspired by Hugo's writings.

below left
The Shades of Francesca da Rimini and Paolo, Ary Scheffer
Born in Holland of German parents, Scheffer (1795-1858) here shows the ghosts of two characters from Dante's Divine Comedy *– a work "rediscovered" by the Romantic movement – appearing to the poet.*

GÉRICAULT THE SUBVERSIVE

right

The Derby at Epsom in 1821, Théodore Géricault *During a trip to England in 1821, Géricault painted this famous race – with a treatment very different from contemporary English engravings of the same event. He has represented the galloping horses as if suspended in midair. It was only after the camera captured the actual sequence that Edgar Degas – the first to do so – correctly depicted a galloping horse.*

Just before he died at the age of thirty-three, after a fall from a horse, Théodore Géricault made this terrible declaration: "If only I had made five paintings! But I've done nothing, absolutely nothing."

Later generations were less severe. Along with Delacroix, the painter of *The Raft of the Medusa* (above) is justifiably considered one of the major figures of 19th-century painting. Horses were one of his great passions, and they remained a source of inspiration throughout his life. Looking for new pictorial themes in current history, Géricault seized on a contemporary drama, the shipwreck of the frigate *Medusa* on a shoal off the West African coast. The captain and officers managed to survive by claiming the lifeboats, while most of the crew and passengers perished in the course of an endless ordeal as they clung to life aboard a makeshift raft. Only fifteen men survived the disaster brought on by the incompetence of the captain – a former émigré who had only recently returned to France's Royal Navy.

This gigantic canvas – for which the painter made forty-nine preliminary studies – is the fruit of Géricault's search for his own path between classicism and Romanticism. It created a scandal at the Salon of 1819. The press saw it as an allegory of the inefficiency of royal government and the misfortunes of France. Some people were offended by its unacademic treatment of a mere "current event." Despite its provocative impact, the painting received a gold medal, and the artist a commission for a religious work.

below

The Wounded Officer of the Imperial Guard Leaving the Battlefield, Théodore Géricault *After painting* An Officer of the Imperial Horse Guards Charging *in 1812, Géricault took a new direction in his work. He switched his focus from heroism to suffering, from victors to victims – a theme he explored in his late works.*

service of his liberal political views. After traveling to Morocco and Algeria, he became one of the pioneers of French Orientalism. Escape to "the Orient" was valued as flight from an era artists considered unpromising, meager, and sterile. Artists also sought refuge in earlier historical eras: the Gothic, Renaissance, Henry II, Louis XIV, Louis XV, and Louis XVI styles were freely reinterpreted throughout the 19th century.

After Delacroix, Théodore Géricault (1791-1824) was the second champion of Romanticism. He died young in a fall from a horse, but he had already explored new themes and possibilities by representing such contemporary events as a shipwreck in his *Raft of the Medusa*, exhibited at the 1819 Salon as the manifesto of Romanticism. He also glorified the Imperial era in works like *The Officer of the Imperial Guard* and *The Wounded Cuirassier*. Around these two stars

Two Men,
Two Aesthetic Ideals

A contemporary caricature shows Delacroix fighting a duel with Ingres, the former armed with a brush, the latter a pencil. Their debate was over aesthetic principles rather than philosophies. Ingres (1780-1867), one of David's students in the late 18th century, considered himself a disciple of Raphael.

In his major works, such as the *Grande Odalisque*, *The Valpinçon Bather*, and *The Turkish Bath*, Ingres invented a personal style in which strong line contrasted with yielding, voluptuous subject matter. A

staunch defender of the "purity" of line against the "excesses" of color, Ingres adamantly opposed Delacroix.

Eugène Delacroix (1798-1863), leader of the French Romantic movement, studied at the Beaux-Arts School under Pierre-Narcisse Guérin. Although he was initially drawn to historical themes, he quickly abandoned the Academic style to give free rein to his use of color. *The Death of Sardanapalus* of 1828, painted as a manifesto of Romantic art, combines both violence and sensuality.

preceding double page
Race of Wild Horses
at Rome,
Théodore Géricault
*In this study for a
studio composition,
inspired by a race of
wild horses in the
Corso in Rome,
Géricault came close to
matching Delacroix's
passionate energy and
violence.*

above
The Colosseum
Seen through the
Arcades of the
Basilica of
Constantine,
Camille Corot
*The pale, powerful
light of his beloved
Italy, evident in this
view of the Roman
Colosseum, would
remain with Corot
even as he turned to
painting the landscapes
of his native France.*

orbited a throng of lesser masters: Octave Tassaert, Eugène Lami, Hippolyte Gavarni, Louis Boulanger, Achille Devéria, and Rosa Bonheur, all of whom explored Romantic themes.

The opposition to Romanticism was represented by Jean Auguste-Dominique Ingres, one of David's students and a champion of the purity of line and the "integrity of the drawing," against the perceived excesses of color. The disturbing effects of his major works – the *Grande Odalisque*, *The Valpinçon Bather*, and *Roger and Angelica* – result from the contrast between rigorous line and sensuality of subject.

Landscape painting, once ranked as a minor genre in the Academy's pecking order, gradually moved to center stage in the hands of a group that came to be

In 19th-century France, landscape finally escaped from the confines of historical and mythological canvases. Painters like Valenciennes, Demarne, Bertin, and Granet broke free of the Academic traditions established by Poussin and Lorrain. Yet it is only with the formation of the Barbazon School that it became a full-fledged subject in its own right. After Corot, the ritual trip to Italy was slowly replaced by excursions to the Normandy coast or to regions of the Ile-de-France. At Barbizon, a group of artists (they included Rousseau, Daubigny, Millet, and Diaz) gathered around Corot and painted on the spot, working with a wider range of colors to capture the effects of light and of climatic change. Aware that sketches made on site were closer to reality than the finished studio work, these painters were blazing a trail for Impressionism.

known as the Barbizon School. It included a handful of artists who painted with poetic realism, which Camille Corot (1780-1867), one of the greatest landscape painters of all time, also expressed in his portraits. This realism, also pursued by Jean-François Millet (1814-1875) and Gustave Courbet (1819-1877), can be viewed as a reaction to the rising popularity of photography, an innovation that provoked Delacroix's famous observation: "From this day on, painting is dead."

But it was not until the end of the century that photography began to change attitudes in art, forcing painters to find a new, more abstract form of expression – a new direction that began with Impressionism.

above left
Venice, the
Piazzetta,
Camille Corot
*For Corot, a painting
of a historical site, such
as this view of Venice,
(1834), was always a
testing ground for his
experiments with light.*

right
Ischia,
Camille Corot
*A student of the
Neoclassical painter
Achille-Etna
Michallon, Corot
returned from his first
trip to Italy in 1825
with numerous
paintings that were
masterpieces of
composition and color.
One such work is this
view of Ischia, painted
from the hills above
Vesuvius.*

below left
The Cascades,
Tivoli,
Camille Corot
*Corot returned twice to
Italy (in 1834 and
1843) after his first
journey there. It was
during his first visit
that he painted this
landscape, which
reveals his progress in
handling color and
spatial composition.
He painted landscapes
on the spot, always
carefully observing
the infinite variations
in light.*

FROM GIOTTO TO THE RENAISSANCE (13TH TO 15TH CENTURIES)

The 14th century was a particularly turbulent period in European history. France and England were locked in the endless struggle of the Hundred Years' War, the conflict that put an end to France's long-standing supremacy in Europe. But the French kingdom's misfortunes proved beneficial to Italy. From the first years of the century, Italy was finally spared the struggles of larger, more united powers to extend their influence over its fragmented territory.

For Italy, birthplace of beauty, was an entity in geographical terms only, its territory broken up into a colorful mosaic of small independent dominions and city-states. The north was parceled out among the republics of Venice, Genoa, Florence, and Siena, the duchies of Savoy, Milan, Modena, and Ferrara, and the mar-quisates of Saluzzo, Monferrato, and Mantua. The Papal States occupied the center, the kingdoms of Sicily and Naples the south.

This division had long made Italy a tempting prey for her rapacious neighbors, for these prosperous kingdoms and duchies were active manufacturing and commercial centers. Moreover, they offered an environment in which the arts flourished. Now far removed from war and looting armies, Italy was free to devote herself to aesthetic pursuits. These scattered Italian territories were like a vast construction site in which 14th-century craftsmen were on the verge of developing new techniques for handling light and shadow and rendering volumes and perspective.

Italian scholars were the first to rediscover classical antiquity, and Italian painters were the first to

BOTTICELLI: FROM IDYLL TO ANGUISH

Because of his fragile health, Sandro di Mariano Filipepi (1445-1510) was apprenticed to his brother, a broker nicknamed Botticello (barrel), hence the name by which he is known. Except for a brief stay in Rome, he never left Florence, where he was the favorite painter of the Medici family. Toward the end of the 15th century, however, the downfall of the Medici dynasty ushered in a theocratic republic (1494-1498) led by the Dominican monk Savonarola, a violent critic of corrupt secular and clerical power. Thereafter, Botticelli's idyllic art turned tragic, and his paintings expressed only a sorrowful, anguished spirituality. Botticelli was the last of the great 15th-century Florentine masters.

break away from the tyranny of medieval artistic dogma. As they worked to grasp proportions and the principles of perspective, they were looking beyond appearances and seeking out the laws of an ideal world.

As early as the mid-13th century, Tuscan painters began to distance themselves from the traditions of Byzantine art, whose brightly colored figures, standing stiff, stylized, and flat against gold backgrounds, had been a model for all medieval Europe. Under the influence of Saint Francis of Assisi and the spiritual reformation associated with his name, Italian art became more realistic and humane. The wooden, staring human figures of medieval frescoes slowly gave way to flesh-and-blood creatures able to feel joy and sorrow. Artists stopped painting symbols and conventions; they sought to show the real world, with its beauty and blemishes, shadows and light, depth and three-dimensional space.

Three masters were responsible for the birth of Italian painting: the Florentine artist Bencivieni di Pepo, called Cimabue (1240-1302), the Sienese painter Agostino di Duccio, and the Roman Pietro Cavallini. Cimabue brought an end to the Byzantine

tradition of rigid, static human figures. Duccio humanized the faces of his madonnas and gave birth to the Sienese school. And Cavallini, seeking freedom from the two-dimensional image, laid out the rudiments of perspective. So great was the impact of their discoveries that the citizens of Siena, urged on by the ringing of the town's bells, carried a painting by Duccio in triumph to their cathedral. To Cimabue's pupil Giotto di Bondone, better known as Giotto, fell the honor of combining all these discoveries to make painting a mirror of life and emotion. In the true spirit of Saint Francis, Giotto gazed upon nature: his rendition of the smile perfectly translated the Franciscan ideal of love into pictorial terms. Among Duccio's pupils were Simone Martini (who followed Pope Benedict XII into exile in Avignon), a painter who combined the preciosity of Gothic art with a passion for rendering depth and detail; and the Lorenzetti brothers, who laid the groundwork for a realism so audacious that it shocked their contemporaries.

It was in Florence, however, that Italian painting really came into its own and the greatest advances were made. In the next century, Giorgio Vasari, not

THE INVENTION OF PERSPECTIVE

How can distance be suggested on a flat surface? Using geometry, Florentine painters proved that it was possible for a drawing to simulate three optical effects: the diminished scale of objects observed from a distance; the seeming convergence of parallel lines meeting in infinity; and the apparent shortening of equal distances as the eye approaches the hori-

zon. These principles were set forth in Alberti's *On Painting* (1436) and in Piero della Francesca's *De Prospectiva Pingendi*. Passionate feelings were aroused by such experimenting; Vasari claimed that Uccello's wife, tired of his spending nights tackling the problems of perspective, begged him to come to bed. His reply: "What a sweet perspective!"

*Jacopo di Arcangelo,
called Jacopo del
Sellajo, was born and
died in Florence where
he was influenced by
Botticelli and
by Domenico
Ghirlandaio. This
painting (which entered
the Louvre in 1863)
evokes Italian and
Flemish landscapes
rather than those of the
Middle East. Saint
Jerome, shown either in
the wilderness or in his
study, is a frequent
theme in 15th- and
16th-century painting,*

The Virgin and
Child between Saint
John the Baptist and
Saint Anthony
Abbot; known as the
Virgin at the
Fountain, Jacopo
de'Barbari
*The Venetian painter
Jacopo de'Barbari (ca.
1450-1515) worked in
Germany for the
emperor Maximilian.
After a period in the
Netherlands, he was
appointed court
painter to Margaret of
Austria in 1511. He
knew and was
influenced by Albrecht
Dürer.*

*reflecting the spiritual
and intellectual
authority of this father
of the early Church.*

only a painter but the world's first art historian, was to stress the spirit of competition that characterized the arts in the Tuscan capital.

The wealth of Florentine bankers and merchants, and the proliferation of local guilds and brotherhoods, brought about a tremendous increase in private and public patronage. Well-to-do citizens considered it their duty to commission artworks and buildings. Donating these to the Church was away to obtain remission for one's sins, especially the direst of them, usury. But atonement was not the only motive for artistic patronage. As one wealthy Florentine patron, Giovanni Rucellai, explained, patronage had three goals: glorifying God, honoring the city, and perpetuating the patron's memory.

It was an age when men and women were becoming aware of an individuality independent of the collective framework of guild and city. Modern individualism was born in Italy. With Paolo Uccello, Tomasso Guidi, known as Masaccio, Fra Angelico, Piero della Francesca, and Sandro Botticelli, Florentine art turned to the new scientific and experimental practices that heralded the Renaissance.

Artists, who regarded themselves as only a notch above craftsmen, began to depict individuals; religious paintings increasingly included actual portraits; and human anatomy was studied in all its details. Settings were no longer merely symbolic but represented actual landscapes, while the architectural components of pictures indicated vanishing points and converging planes. The size of figures varied with their distance from the foreground. With Paolo Uccello and Filippo Brunelleschi, perspective became a science.

Receptive to the new humanism, which gave pride of place to ancient Rome, artists such as Fra Angelico, Giovanni Bellini, and Andrea Mantegna adorned their scenes with triumphal arches, columns, and capitals. They even went so far as to populate them with the gods and goddesses of the classical pantheon.

Botticelli envisioned the birth of Venus, and Mantegna depicted Mount Parnassus. Medieval man and woman, obsessed with salvation and fear of the Last Judgment, gradually yielded to a figure closer to Prometheus. Avid for glory and power, artists wanted art not to venerate the divine but to celebrate the cult of beauty. The Renaissance was knocking at the door.

THE RENAISSANCE, OR THE AGE OF GENIUS

The Marriage at Cana, Paolo Caliari, called Veronese

The largest picture in the Louvre (22 × 32'), The Marriage at Cana was painted in 1562–1563 for the refectory of the Benedictine monastery at San Giorgio Maggiore in Rome. It was removed by French troops in 1798. Cut in half, then remounted in Paris, the canvas was so large that France was not even asked to return it in 1814, along with other works stolen from Italy. Veronese depicted artists and princes of his time among the guests at the wedding feast. Veronese himself, along with Tintoretto, Jacopo Bassano, Andrea Palladio, and his own brother Benedetto, figures among the musicians in the foreground.

At the dawn of the 16th century, a new era was born in Italy, one that would radiate from Rome and Florence to almost all of Europe. Its way had been paved over the previous two centuries by an uninterrupted succession of artistic geniuses. But the distinctive character of the Renaissance came from the conjunction of several crucial events.

Thanks to Byzantine scholars, who had remained familiar with the ancient Greek and Roman authors and who had sought refuge in Italy after the Turkish capture of Constantinople, classical studies enjoyed a powerful revival. Concurrently, the invention of the printing press had contributed by the middle of the century to the spread of Greek and Roman literature and to growing interest in the ancient world. A philosophical and scientific revolution followed in the wake of this scholarly and literary movement.

In 1492, the Genoese navigator Christopher Columbus discovered America. A new map of the world suddenly appeared, replacing the old medieval charts. Scientists, chiefly astronomers like Copernicus, Tycho Brahe, Kepler, and Galileo, developed a theory of the universe that swept away the ideas of the Middle Ages.

Apparently, the earth was not flat at all. Nor was it a fixed

THE MONA LISA

Undoubtedly it is the most famous portrait ever painted. According to Vasari, Leonardo da Vinci's model was Monna Lisa Gherardini, who was married to Francesco del Giocondo, a Florentine nobleman. However, the subject of the *Mona Lisa*, probably painted between 1503 and 1506, has also been identified as two other famous Italian women: Isabella d'Este and Constanza d'Avalos. According to a drawing by Raphael, the canvas was once slightly larger, and the painting was bordered on both sides by the columns of a loggia, perhaps explaining why she now seems to sit before such an improbable landscape. More than the portrait of an individual, the *Mona Lisa* represents the ideal figure in harmony with the universe. Da Vinci's use of *sfumato* (a gradation of tone that blurs the outlines of forms) gave his sitter a kind of willful imprecision, particularly visible in her eyes and the corners of her mouth – source of the *Mona Lisa's* mysterious half-smile. Without this feature, her power to fascinate might not have been so universally recognized.

The Virgin and Child with Saint Anne, Leonardo da Vinci, ca. 1508-1510

Commissioned for the main altar of the church of the Annunziata in Florence, this unfinished work by Leonardo depicts the spiritual and physical bond between mother and child, as well as the continuity of the generations.

point in space: it was an orb circling dizzyingly around the sun. This view flew in the face of religious beliefs and raised perplexing questions. That caused the Age of Faith to retreat before the Age of Reason. The future no longer seemed to lie in the lap of the gods but in human hands.

Inevitably, developments in the arts echoed these changes. Between 1500 and 1600, Italy was gripped by a mighty intellectual and artistic ferment. Brilliant artists executed the finest easel paintings and frescoes in Europe, in an unprecedented variety of styles.

The peninsula's artistic center was no longer Florence but Rome, where the papacy was a particularly active patron. Artists from all over Italy hastened to the Eternal City to enjoy the pope's munificence. Donato d'Agnolo, called Bramante, designed the plans of Saint Peter's; Michelangelo painted the Sistine Chapel's ceiling; and Raphael decorated the Vatican apartments. Leonardo da Vinci developed his famous sfumato technique, while Antonio Allegri, known as Correggio, drew on classical mythology to celebrate the beauty of the human body.

From the tranquillity of its lagoon, Venice also contributed to Renaissance art. Captivated by its peerless light, Titian, Tintoretto, Paolo Veronese, and Giorgione handled color as it had never been rendered before.

The intensity and stylistic perfection of Renaissance art were such that it could not long maintain itself on the heights it had scaled, and the turbulence of the early 16th century eventually put an end to the serene and eminently rational order it had installed.

A new generation of artists – Girolamo Mazzola, or Parmigianino, Jacopo Carrucci (Pontormo), and Agnolo di Cosimo, called Bronzino – began to rebel against Renaissance values. Reflecting the upheavals of their age, their art dwelt on bizarre and violent images, on powerful emotions that distorted lines and features. Toward the end of the century, Mannerism ushered in a new style: the Baroque.

THE RENAISSANCE: ARTISTS COME INTO THEIR OWN

In the Middle Ages, human activities were divided into two categories: the "mechanical arts" and the "liberal arts."

The first were regarded as menial, the second as suitable for free citizens educated in the so-called noble disciplines: grammar, rhetoric, arithmetic, astronomy, and music. Up to the early 16th century, painting, sculpture, drawing, and architecture were considered

mechanical arts, and the artists who practiced them were viewed as craftsmen.

Only in the High Renaissance, with Leonardo da Vinci, Giorgio Vasari, and Michelangelo Buonarroti, did artists begin to gain a social status equal to that of poets and writers. To break their association with the manual trades, Renaissance painters and sculptors banded together in academies rather than guilds.

preceding double page

Esther before
Ahasuerus,
Paolo Veronese
*"We painters take the
same liberties as poets
and court jesters,"
Veronese exclaimed to
justify his creative
inventiveness. The
figure of King
Ahasuerus's wife
Esther, who saved the
Jews, is a relatively
insignificant element in
the swirl of rich
materials, crystals,
and jewels dear to
Veronese's opulent
vision.*

left

The Doge of Venice
Goes to the Salute
on 21 November to
Commemorate the
End of the Plague
of 1630,
Francesco Guardi
*Drawing on a series of
engravings by
Canaletto, Guardi
painted a dozen
pictures representing
different episodes in the
election of the Doge
Alvise Mocenigo.
Executed between 1766
and 1770, his
picturesque reportage
distills the melancholy
of the last Venetian
celebrations at the end
of the 18th century, at
a time when the Most
Serene Republic had
become a favored
resort for the elite of
Europe.*

CARAVAGGIO TO CANALETTO (17TH TO 18TH CENTURIES)

In the late 16th century a new Michelangelo sprang from Italian soil. Michelangelo Merisi, more commonly known as Caravaggio, revolutionized painting once again. Just as van Eyck had shattered the mold of the Gothic style to observe nature as it really was and bring realism into art, Caravaggio swept away Renaissance proprieties and idealism, introducing a brand of realism that provoked passionate reactions among his contemporaries. This new naturalism did not merely imitate reality. By exploiting shadows and light in a completely new way, Caravaggio brought drama to his themes and imparted a singular emotional eloquence to them.

The upheaval that Caravaggism produced in 17th-century art was paralleled in religion and science. The Catholic Counter-Reformation expressed the

above

The Fortune-Teller,
Caravaggio
*A foppish and gullible
young nobleman has his
palm read by a crafty
gypsy woman who
deftly relieves him of a
precious ring. Fond of
realistic details not
much to the liking of
his ecclesiastical and
aristocratic clients,
Caravaggio here paints
a street scene very
similar to those he
must have seen when
walking around Rome.*

CARAVAGGIO

Unbalanced, a streetfighter, an assassin, Michelangelo Merisi, known as Caravaggio (1571-1610), seems to have been a delinquent of genius. In Rome, he painted genre scenes of humble neighborhoods thronging with musicians and fortune-tellers. His works offended the sensibilities of art lovers and clients. But in Cardinal del Monte of Rome and, later, in the Grand Master of Naples, he finally found understanding patrons.

His paintings were responsible for two revolutionary innovations. Caravaggio shattered the traditional division between the sacred and the profane: when he painted the Virgin or saints, his models were women from everyday life or dockhands. He also used *chiaroscuro* by projecting side-lighting onto pictorial masses, which then stood out from their dark backgrounds. Despite his short life, Caravaggio was immensely influential in Italy and throughout Europe.

bottom left

The Death of
the Virgin,
Caravaggio
*Like a number of other
religious pictures
Caravaggio was
commissioned to paint,
this picture was
considered irreverent
and was rejected by the
artist's patrons. Small
wonder, for the Virgin
is here realistically
depicted as an
ordinary woman dying
in a poverty-stricken
setting.*

Church's reaction to the expansion of Protestant influence. The Council of Trent, which convened in 1542 and concluded its deliberations in 1563, gave voice to a new religious sensibility, one that was more internalized and less subject to formalism and liturgy. It contributed significantly to the rise of the Baroque movement, which first developed in Rome. An art of illusion, of dynamic movement, Baroque spread throughout Europe, even to non-Catholic countries.

A scientific and philosophical revolution was also under way, with the advent of the experimental method and of Cartesian rationality in scientific inquiry. Politically, the European nation-states triumphed over smaller independent territories, adopting the system of absolute monarchy, efficiently administered by royal magistrates and officers. Germany and Italy alone remained divided and hence vulnerable to the covetous ambitions of the new large states. In Italy, the contrast between

Baroque art and the classicism inherited from the Renaissance was embodied in the split between Caravaggio and his disciples on the one hand, and the Carracci brothers on the other.

After Caravaggio, the energies of Italian art were dissipated by this aesthetic controversy. The artists of the peninsula, unable to draw either on religious faith or on a celebration of life, seemed to lose their creative impulse.

In the 18th century, Venice alone – stripped of political prestige and economic power, but a favorite gathering place for connoisseurs of art and pleasure-seekers – still exerted influence through the brilliance of its artists. Giambattista Tiepolo perpetuated the Venetian tradition of aristocratic fetes, exporting his opulent architectural settings and vast theatrical compositions to Spain and Germany, while the last lights of Venice's celebrations at home glimmered briefly in the paintings of Antonio Canaletto and Francesco Guardi.

left
Deianira Abducted
by the Centaur
Nessus,
Guido Reni
After Deianira, the wife of Hercules, was abducted by the centaur Nessus, Hercules killed him with a poisoned arrow as he was about to carry her across a river. But the hero was himself fatally stricken when he tried on Nessus' bloodstained garment. Bursting with energy, this is the finest of several pictures Guido dedicated to the labors of Hercules.

below
The Labors of
Hercules,
Guido Reni
An assistant to the Carracci brothers and a member of their academy for life drawing, Guido Reni (1575-1642), known as Guido, preferred realistic effects in the manner of Caravaggio, while maintaining the tradition of classical antiquity – as in this series of vigorous pictures showing the labors of Hercules.

FLEMISH PAINTING
(14TH TO 15TH CENTURIES)

The brooding overcast skies, featureless horizons, and harsh winters of Flemish landscapes seem to favor a retreat into domestic privacy. The concept of beauty held here was not the same as the one held under the warm Italian skies. Here sensual pleasures had more appeal than those of the intellect; and a concern for material well-being held sway.

By the end of the 13th century, the Flemish feudal nobility was in decline. The knights of Flanders had been crushed by Philip the Fair of Burgundy in 1302, then were replaced by an elite of industrious but pleasure-loving merchants. By commissioning paintings and sculptures, they contributed to a flowering of the arts.

In the mid-14th century, the heiress of the count of Flanders married Philip the Bold, duke of Burgundy, who then annexed Flanders to his dukedom. His successors, Philip the Good and Charles the Bold, made Flanders the cul-

tural hub of their new principality. Bruges, a leading port and financial marketplace, drew traders from all over Europe. At the same time, Ghent, Tournai, and Liege vied with one another in promoting and protecting the arts.

This golden age of Flanders was marked by a convergence of extremes: of ponderous sensuality, elegant luxury, and materialism, and of mysticism. Yet these frenetic contradictions merely masked the turmoil of the waning Middle Ages, as well as the intellectual disquiet fed by the philosophical speculations of such great mystics as Jan van Ruysbroeck and Thomas à Kempis.

Like its Italian counterpart, Flemish art was initially religious, but in the 16th century, as the Church's power and influence diminished, artists deserted monasteries in favor of princely courts and cities. Under the protection of massive town halls and belfries, a new art emerged, expressing piety in forms

HIERONYMUS BOSCH

With Hieronymus Bosch (ca. 1450-1516), the solemn, peaceable style of traditional Flemish painting abruptly swung toward the grotesque and the disturbing. A mystical painter, haunted by sin and problems of salvation, Bosch filled his paintings – they are at once archaic and powerfully modern – with a proliferation of bizarre

creatures and forms, giving free rein to all sorts of erotic fantasies, as in this *Ship of Fools*: a boat without a captain, loaded with drunken, lustful nuns and monks. Bosch was independently wealthy: he had no need to rely on patrons and could therefore paint whatever his imagination dictated.

The Invention of
Oil Painting
It was a Florentine,
not a Flemish artist,
who brought the
revolutionary
invention of northern
European painters to
Italy. According to
Vasari, Jan van Eyck
perfected the oil-
painting process. On
wooden panels
prepared with a
ground of white paint,
he built up thin,
transparent layers of
paint made of natural
pigments dissolved in
linseed oil. With this
technique, Flemish
artists could achieve
an infinite range of
colors and suggest
three-dimensional
space. They were also
able to model the
planes of faces and
render the
transparency of skin.
"These paintings,"
said the French writer
Germain Bazin, "in
which atmosphere and
light seem to envelop
everything in ethereal
fluid, lend such
powerful truth to
reality that merely
seeing them gives an
almost hallucinatory
sense of actual
presence."

borrowed from every-day life, character-ized by an increasin-gly detailed realism. Painters strove to render inner truth through minute obser-vation of external detail. They gave thanks to God by cele-brating creation.

Were the 15th-cen-tury Flemish artists really "primitives," as they are sometimes called? The term orig-inated in the Re-naissance to designate artists who did not draw inspiration from classical antiquity. Yet it hardly describes the Flemish painters of the late Middle Ages, whose art is nothing if not mature and balanced.

It was during this time that the distinctive flavor of Flemish painting materialized – a love of realism, of color, of harmonious

forms. For a century, Flanders saw a suc-cession of brilliant artists – the van Eyck brothers, Rogier van der Weyden, Direk Bouts, Hans Memling, Hieronymus Bosch. They influenced paint-ing in other European countries as well, including Spain, Ger-many, and Italy.

By the early 16th century, Bruges, as an artistic center, was falling behind the busy cosmopolitan port of Antwerp, which was more open to new fashions, par-ticularly from Italy. The artist who brought the Italian Renaissance to Fle-mish soil, Quentin Metsys, founder of the School of Antwerp, blended Flemish realism with the poetry of Italian painting. A century later, Peter Paul Rubens followed in his footsteps.

left
Detail of Saint Mary Magdalene,
Rogier van der Weyden
This elegant Mary Magdalene is part of the Braque family triptych, named for the family that commissioned the

work. The center of the triptych (now lost) showed Christ giving His blessing, with the two saints occupying the right and left panels.

BRUEGHEL "THE PEASANT"

The geographer Abraham Ortelius paid tribute to Pieter Brueghel the Elder (ca. 1525-1569) at his funeral by praising his careful observation of nature, but adding that "in all his works, there is more to see than what is painted." Shortly before his death, Brueghel asked his wife to burn several of his engravings, whose scathing observations might cause problems with the authorities. He was at first influenced by the fantastic world of Hieronymus

Bosch, but eventually he returned to the Flemish tradition of landscape painting. In his famous illus-trations of *The Months*, Brueghel painted peasants far removed from idealized Italian depictions of agri-cultural workers. His own peasants sweated and toiled in a cosmic cycle of death and rebirth. Against the man-centered pretensions of the Renaissance, Brueghel affirmed a universe in which the divine – not man – was preeminent.

center
The Beggars,
Pieter Brueghel
Painted in 1668, this Brueghel depicted the reality of everyday life without moralist undertones.
We can also see influence of Hieronymus Bosch.

In 1648, the Treaty of The Hague ratified the split between the northern provinces of Flanders, which had converted to Protestantism, and the Catholic territories to the south. The former were granted independence as the Republic of the Lowlands, or Republic of Holland. The southern lands remained under the dominion of the Spanish Hapsburg rulers, the Infanta Isabel and her husband, the Archduke Albert of Austria. Eager to mark the restoration of Spanish power in Flanders and to make it a bastion of Catholicism, they attracted artists there into serving the propagation of the Catholic faith.

The war-torn southern provinces offered huge opportunities to artists. The capital, Antwerp, had suffered under the iconoclastic intolerance of the Protestants. But now the returning Spanish outlawed the reformed faith and called on architects, sculptors, and painters to embellish the city and its churches. Spurred by the Counter-Reformation, the Church commissioned a growing number of artworks. Large-scale canvases were soon prominently displayed in palaces and churches. Seventeenth-century Flanders became the northern counterpart of Baroque Italy.

Among the many artists, one name stands out: Peter Paul Rubens. Before entering the service of the Hapsburgs in 1609, Rubens had worked in Italy at the court of the Gonzagas, the great art patrons of Mantua. After returning to Antwerp in 1608, he became the undisputed leader of the Flemish School. Commissions poured in, from altar paintings for Antwerp churches to portraits of royalty in every European country. To keep up with demand, he surrounded himself with disciples like Anthony van Dyck, Paul de Vos, and Jan Snyders, who painted portions of his canvases, while Rubens unified the compositions and added the final exuberant touches. When Rubens died in 1640, he was mourned throughout Flanders. Even after his death

RUBENS

Peter Paul Rubens (1577-1640) dominated 17th-century Flemish art. Under his influence, the artistic barriers between northern and southern Europe, already weakened by Metsys and Dürer, finally collapsed. Rubens decided to become a painter in 1600, while in Italy. He eagerly studied antique sculptures, acquiring a faultless technique as well as a perfect knowledge of traditional Italian painting.

Returning to Flanders in 1608, he opened his studio in Antwerp, where he produced works for the city, its churches and private patrons. He was at the height of his fame during the 1620s, creating immense compositions for churches and palaces, including a gallery in the Luxembourg Palace in Paris, where Marie de Médicis commissioned a series of paintings glorifying King Henri IV. This colossal work was a monument of the Baroque style, which Rubens helped spread through Northern Europe.

his dominance continued for most other Flemish artists had either studied under him or been strongly influenced by his art.

His leading disciple, Anthony van Dyck (1599-1641), had an equally brilliant career. In contrast to Rubens's Baroque effervescence, van Dyck cultivated a refined art tinged with melancholy. After an artistic pilgrimage to Italy, where he developed his own style under the influence of Correggio and Titian, van Dyck returned briefly to Antwerp, then moved to England to become the favorite portraitist of Charles I and the English aristocracy.

Jacob Jordaens (1593-1678), whose prolific energy made him closer to Rubens, depicted traditional Flemish themes of village fairs and festivities, to which he brought a sensual Rubenesque element. After Jordaens, David Teniers (1610-1690) was the only artist to continue painting landscapes with everyday peasant life. The dazzling period of 17th-century Flemish painting ended with a plethora of lesser masters, including Cornelius van Haarlem, Paul de Vos, and Jan Snyders. With the decline of the Flemish economy in the 18th century, the Flemish School faded away.

FLEMISH PAINTING

DUTCH PAINTING

Until the end of the 17th century, Flanders and Holland were both part of the same country. Swept up by the Reformation in the 16th century, the northern provinces seceded from Spanish rule under the leadership of William of Orange. In 1648, Spain agreed to recognize the independent Dutch Republic, whose intense commercial activity now brought it unprecedented prosperity.

Dutch artists took pride in their independente, country and shared a common enthusiasm for the everyday working lives of their countrymen. With their newly acquired wealth and social status, Dutch merchants were eager to have artists paint their portraits. Perhaps because they did not always have the means to commission individual portraits, they often sat for group pictures, with each participant paying his share in monthly installments. Hence the large number of sizable canvases depicting the members of citizen militias, guild banquets, and governing boards of hospitals, hospices, and poorhouses.

Three artists – Hals, Rembrandt, and Vermeer – stand out from among the many who were active during the golden age of Dutch painting. The truculent Frans Hals (1581?- 1666) was reputed to be a kind of ruffian, a fre-

quenter of taverns, who beat his wife and exploited his pupils. His painting is spontaneous, high-spirited, full of passion. His brush was guided not by theory nor by preoccupation with details but by an unerring sense of color and texture. His portraits reflect a love of freedom and extemporaneous expression, free from the meticulous tradition of earlier Dutch painting.

Harmenszoon van Rijn Rembrandt, the austere son of a miller from Leyden, gave up university studies to become a painter. In 1625, he set up his own studio. But recognition as an artist was slow in coming; only after absorbing Caravaggio's influence did he begin to make a name for himself. He settled in Amsterdam, where he received many commissions for paintings, particularly from local guilds. After the death of his wife and a series of financial setbacks, Rembrandt pursued his artistic quest alone, making no concessions to the tastes of contemporary patrons, who soon turned to other artists. His lofty spirituality and ever more audacious style found little favor; like Hals, he died in dire poverty.

Some twenty years younger than Rembrandt, Jan Vermeer (1632-1675) remains an enigmatic figure. So little is known about his life and activity as an

above
Gypsy Girl, Frans Hals
This "gypsy girl" with the charming smile and flattering décolleté is actually a courtesan, immortalized by Hals in a snapshot of astounding truth and immediacy. You can almost hear her time-worn invitation: "Would you like to come with me, young sir?"

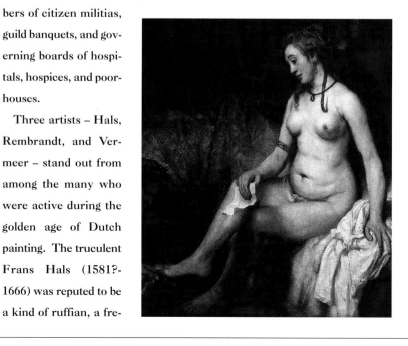

left
The Sacrifice of Abraham, Pieter Lastman
A historical painter and engraver, Lastman (1583-1633) was first influenced by Caravaggio, then by Rembrandt (who had been Caravaggio's pupil). These influences can be seen in the chiaroscuro bathing the scene, in which the angels stay Abraham's arm as he moves to strike Isaac.

bottom left
Bathsheba at Her Bath, Rembrandt
David, king of Israel, seduced Bathsheba, wife of Uriah. Then after having her husband killed in battle, he kidnapped and married her. Bathsheba gave David four sons, including Solomon. Rembrandt here represents Bathsheba bathing, which is how David first saw her. The king is absent from the painting; the only token of his presence is the letter in Bathsheba's hand, in which he confesses his desire to the guilt-stricken young woman.

Portrait of the Artist at His Easel, Rembrandt
Rembrandt's series of self-portraits records a life sacrificed to the pursuit of an artistic and spiritual ideal. In this canvas dated 1660, just two years before his death, Rembrandt painted his own image at the easel with astonishing sincerity and humility: the viewer is drawn beyond superficial appearance to the truth of the painter's soul.

The Lacemaker, Jan Vermeer
The model for this painting (executed around 1664) was probably Catherine Vermeer, the painter's wife. The small size of the canvas accentuates the intimate mood of this domestic cameo. Auguste Renoir said that, along with Watteau's Pilgrimage to the Island of Cythera, it was "the most beautiful work in the world."

artist that he is sometimes called the "Sphinx of Delft." His reputation rests on his genre scenes, although he also painted wonderful urban views. Indeed, Vermeer was a master at depicting ordinary men and women in domestic settings. No less than Hals and Rembrandt, he eschewed the anecdotal and went straight to essentials.

A master of tranquil, luminous effects, he was fond of using slanting indirect light to create a harmony between his figures and the objects surrounding them, and to enhance a very restricted

but subtle range of colors, chiefly blues, yellows, and reds, as well as shades of white and black. After Vermeer, the greatest age of Dutch painting came to an end. Crippled by an economic crisis, stemming partly from war with England and partly from foreign competition, Dutch life would never again foster such a favorable artistic climate.

The best Dutch painters of the 18th century merely repeated, less brilliantly, the lessons of the great masters of the previous century.

GERMAN PAINTING

right

*Saint Ursula
Announces Her
Pilgrimage to the
Court of Her Father,
Master of the
Legend of Saint
Ursula*
*The anonymous
painter of the nineteen
panels of this
enormous polyptich
altarpiece (ca. 1495-
1500) is known as the
Master of the Legend of
Saint Ursula. The
panels illustrate the life
and martyrdom of the
saint, murdered by the
Huns while traveling
on a pilgrimage to
Rome with an escort of
11,000 virgins. The
original polyptich was
dismantled, and
separate panels are
now in the museums of
Cologne, Bonn,
Nuremberg, London,
and Paris (the
Louvre).*

In the Middle Ages, Germany was not yet a separate nation. It was a part of the Holy Roman Empire and was divided into a number of small states. As a result, many schools and artistic centers sprang up across its territory. These were dominated by two currents: one from the north, which imported the Flemish style through shipping contacts on the Baltic Sea; the other from the south, via Burgundy. The latter influence brought German artists in touch with classical sculpture, Burgundian realism, and the new principles of perspective.

Despite these influences, German art from the Middle Ages onward had its own character. In the early 15th century, it was still dominated by the International Gothic style. Around 1440, more realistic representations – free of the preciosity of the late Gothic – began to appear in the work of Stefan Lochner, sometimes called the "German Fra Angelico," as well as that of Lukas Moser and the Swiss painter Konrad Witz, a master at orchestrating effects and playing on the viewer's emotions. In the second half of the 15th century, the meticulous realism of the Flemish School and the influence of Italian experiments in perspective left

their mark on German painting. So did the technique of engraving (which then commanded a much wider public than painting), with its sharp contours, rigid lines, and flat tints. In Alsace, northern and southern influences merged in the work of Martin Schongauer, prefiguring the three great masters of the German Renaissance – Grünewald, Dürer, and Holbein.

These 16th-century German artists discovered the humanistic values of the Italian Renaissance, traveling south of the Alps to gain firsthand inspiration from the revival of interest in Greek and Roman mythology. Under the impetus of Martin Luther, the monk who rebelled against the corruption and worldliness of the Roman Catholic Church, a new reading of Scripture gave birth to the Reformation, a phenomenon that in turn exerted a strong moralizing influence on art. The Reformed churches granted little space to art, least of all to painting, considered prone to blasphemy. The traditional commissions from monasteries declined, replaced by orders from private patrons. A number of painters, including Holbein, were forced to imigrate to other countries for financial reasons.

HANS HOLBEIN

In 1531 Hans Holbein settled permanently in England, where he became Court painter and decorator to Henry VIII. There he painted a series of portraits of famous figures, including Anne of Cleves, one of the king's wives; members of court, such as Sir Henry Wyatt; and various officials, including the astronomer Nicolas Kratzer and Erasmus – absorbed in thought as he writes his commentary on Saint Mark's Gospel. These portraits reflect an unusually keen faculty for observation, respect for truth, remarkable texture, and a sense of decorum that reveals the influence of the Italian Renaissance. The status of his sitters, their positions and functions within society, is invariably indicated by the outward signs of their rank, clothing, and jewelry.

left
*Four Portraits by
Hans Holbein*
*From left to right:
Nicolas Kratzer,
Erasmus, Anne of
Cleves, Sir Henry
Wyatt.*

Portrait of the Artist
Holding an
Erynganeum,
Albrecht Dürer

*The greatest German
painter of the
Renaissance, Dürer
painted this self-
portrait in 1493, when
he was twenty-two
years old. He was on
the point of becoming
engaged, which*

*explains the thistle
plant (symbol of desire
or fidelity) he holds in
his hand.*

Annunciation with
Two Saints,
Bartel Zeitblom

*Zeitblom (ca. 1450-
1517) belonged to the
Swabian School and
was influenced by the
great Alsatian painter
Martin Schongauer,
who was himself
influenced by the
Flemish artists Van der
Weyden and Dirck*

*Bouts. According to
Christian tradition,
Saint Anne was the
Virgin Mary's mother,
which accounts for her
many representations
in religious paintings.*

In the end, the Reformation's impact was twofold. It shattered European cultural unity, and it gave birth to modern Germany. Martin Grünewald (1455-1528), an artist steeped in religious feeling, blended the pessimism of the waning Middle Ages with the fresh ideals of the Renaissance, reflecting a blend of influences that also characterizes the work of Albrecht Dürer (1471-1528). A towering figure in 16th-century German art, Dürer never lost touch with the uncompromising realism and medieval mysticism of his early years. Through his travels, he was exposed to Flemish and Italian influences. He was the first German artist to employ perspective, and to base his art on a detailed observation of nature. After Hans Holbein (1497?-1543) – a master portraitist who shed the Gothic heritage as a result of his encounter with Italian art – the great period of German painting came to an end. After two centuries of relatively minor achievement, it enjoyed another renaissance with the 19th-century painter Caspar David Friedrich, the Nazarene Group, and Adolph Menzel.

GERMAN PAINTING

ENGLISH PAINTING

Lady Macbeth,
Henry Fuseli
*Shakespeare's world,
full of sound and fury,
fascinated the Swiss
artist Fuseli, domiciled
in England. This
nightmarish vision of a
moonstruck Lady
Macbeth, terrifying
those around her as she
wanders wildly
through the
passageways of a
castle, torch in hand, is
characteristic of the
gloomy, morbid
romanticism of this
painter.*

center right

Landscape with
Distant River and
Bay, Joseph Mallord
William Turner
*Not the eye of a
cyclone, but Turner's
vision – bordering on
abstraction – of a
landscape. Here line
gives way to pure
color, and reality
becomes illusion. In
the late 19th century,
the French
Impressionists
acknowledged their
debt to this English
precursor.*

Clearly, the fact that Britain is an island has marked the history of Great Britain and British painting for centuries. Isolated from the European continent, England was long shielded both from invasion and from foreign influences. John Bull has remained unshakable, and so has the English passion for green fields, rainswept skies, and silver seas, and its patriotic pride in the elegance of its gentlemen, the dreamy winsomeness of its ladies, and the fair complexion of its children – themes that English artists have always delighted in painting.

Yet it was a Flemish artist, Anthony van Dyck, who, during the reign of Charles I, captivated the English aristocracy. With his genius for blending portraiture and natural scenery, he founded the English portrait school. He was followed by Sir Joshua Reynolds, first president of the Royal Academy, who placed his models in bucolic settings and boldly depicted them as they appeared in real life. Squarely in the tradition of van Dyck, Thomas Gainsborough (1727-1788) began his career in a French studio and later settled in the fashionable city of Bath, where he painted the local gentry. Born toward the end of the 18th century, Thomas Lawrence (1769-1830), the son of an innkeeper, became the favorite portrait painter of kings, popes, and aristocratic figures.

Apart from portraiture, landscape painting is unquestionably British art's foremost contribution to the history of painting. John Constable (1776-1837), a revelation at the 1824 Paris Salon, wholly renovated the genre with his use of a broad range of fresh, lively colors. His contemporary Joseph Mallord William Turner (1775-1851) went even further. With his remarkable sensitivity for natural phenomena, Turner broke away from academic art and bathed his landscapes in hazy, luminous, atmospheric effects that heralded Claude Monet and perhaps even modern abstract painting.

Visionaries in their own field, William Blake (1757-1827) and the Swiss-born Englishman Henry Fuseli (1741-1825) were the pre-eminent artists of English romanticism. The poet, painter, and illustrator Blake was immersed in the poetry of the Bible, Dante, and Milton. He painted fanciful mystical scenes inspired by supernatural visions. Drawing on the works of Michelangelo and the writing of Shakespeare, Fuseli's paintings express a shadowy world of nightmares and demons, aglow with morbid eroticism.

below

Conversation in a
Park, Thomas
Gainsborough
*The importance of this
portrait of the
Andrews couple by
Gainsborough
transcends its balanced
composition and fresh
colors. It marks the
emergence of a new
class of landowners in
the 18th century and
the importance of rural
property ownership to
British prosperity.*

bottom left

View of the Lagoon
near Venice,
Richard Bonington
*Like Turner, the
landscape painter
Bonington traveled to
Italy and was
entranced by Venice.*

SPANISH PAINTING

Spanish artists dwell neither on angelic sweetness nor on serene beauty, but on mysticism, death, pride, and violence. Spain's history is a long chronicle of invasion and reconquest, of wars and crusades, from the arrival of the Visigoths in the 5th century to the Arab conquest in the 8th century and the *reconquista* by the Spanish king to the expanding Spanish empire and the discovery of America.

By the early Middle Ages, foreign influences – the art of French illuminated manuscripts, Moorish, Byzantine, Romanesque and Gothic art, not to mention the inspirational impact of the Franciscan Reformation – had combined and coalesced in Spain. Nevertheless, a genuinely native art also flourished in Catalonia in the 13th century, with painters like Ferrer Bassa and the Serra brothers .

After reconquering their territory from the Moors, Spain's Catholic monarchs gave Spanish culture a new direction, marked at once by the Inquisition and by hospitality to artists from abroad. From Jaime Huguet to Pedro Berreguete, Spanish painters interpreted the Flemish style in their own terms. The 16th century ushered in an age of grandeur under the reign of Charles V; he maintained the tradition of hospitality toward foreign artists, inviting Gerard David from Bruges and John of Flanders to his court. Later, Philip II turned to Italian painters. Doménikos Theotokópoulos, otherwise known as El Greco (1541-1614), reached Spain via Italy from his native Crete, bringing with him powerful Byzantine and Venetian influences. Settling in Toledo, El Greco made Spanish spirituality his own, painting visions of ecstasy and suffering in a unique idiom that aspired to the hereafter.

Toward the end of the century, the revolution of Caravaggio's dramatic chiaroscuros captivated the Spanish artist José de Ribera (1591-1652), who painted portraits of beggars as well as visions of martyrs. Also influenced by Caravaggio was Francisco de

Zurburán (1598-1664), who combined mystical ardor with a shrewd eye for detail.

Paradoxically, it was when Spain's political and economic power began to decline that its literature and painting rose to heights never attained before or since. Diego Vélazquez (1599-1660), a devotee of Titian, was the least mystical of Spanish painters. Nevertheless, he ushered in the golden age of Spanish painting, which included such artists as Zurburán, Ribera, and Murillo.

When the grandson of Louis XIV, Philip of Bourbon, became the ruler of Spain, he naturally called in French artists. Their worldly, even courtly, art was ill suited to the Spanish temperament. His successors, Ferdinand I and Charles II, also turned to French as well as Italian artists. Only one genuinely Spanish artist appeared in the 18th century: Luis Meléndez (1716-1780), a gifted painter of still lifes. Francisco Goya (1746-1828), much like the more illustrious of

Vélazquez ended his career as grand master of the Royal Palace, painting portraits of great psychological depth and technical virtuosity. After him, Bartolomé Estebán Murillo (1618-1682), a painter of monastic and picaresque scenes, blended religious devotion with sentimentalism in pictures whose subjects were alternately saints and the downtrodden.

his forerunners, was a passionate artist with a predilection for drama and wild excesses, cruelty, and satire. An unusually versatile painter, he excelled in a variety of genres, from frescoes to tapestry cartoons, portraits, and historical scenes. Haunted by hallucinatory visions, it was Goya who brought the unique Spanish genius back to life.

left
Christ on the Cross Worshipped by two Donors, El Greco
Painted around 1580, shortly after El Greco's arrival in Toledo, this work embodies the Greek, Roman, and Venetian influences that marked his painting. Born in Crete, El Greco studied in Titian's workshop in Venice and was influenced by the Mannerists in Rome. Their style clearly influenced this Christ on the Cross. *Indeed, its colors and the flowing, elongated form of the Christ figure, standing out against a stormy sky, prefigure the famous* Burial of Count Orgaz, *painted six years later. El Greco shows us the painting's two donors (who gave the work to a convent in Toledo) in prayer at the foot of the cross.*

bottom right
Brother Juniper and the Beggar, Bartolomé Estebán Murillo
On a trip to Spain in the 19th century, French poet Théophile Gautier wrote of Murillo: "The honor and the curse of Seville is Murillo. You will hear nothing but his name spoken." Indeed, Murillo was the most famous Spanish painter – not only in Spain but throughout Europe. He owed his success to the solidity of his technique and to the charm with which he interpreted piety in ordinary life.

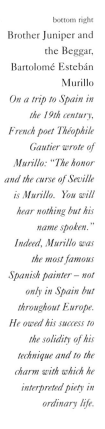

The Department of Sculpture

The Louvre's Department of Sculpture is the distant beneficiary of the former Royal Collections and of the Museum of French Monuments – which was opened by the painter Alexandre Lenoir to safeguard ancien régime works from pillage during the French Revolution. As early as 1824, the Galerie d'Angoulême, the core of the future Department of Sculpture, was exhibiting works dating from the Renaissance and the Enlightenment alongside sculptures from antiquity. Works from the Middle Ages did not enter the collection until later in the 19th century, when museum curators and collectors who had developed a taste for medieval works convinced the public of their importance. In 1871 the department, encompassing medieval, Renaissance, and modern sculpture, became an independent section of the Louvre, although it did not function continuously and independently until 1893. The lion's share of the collection is French sculpture – particularly open-air sculpture, exhibited in the Cour Puget and the Cour Marly. Italian Quattrocento and Renaissance sculpture is splendidly represented. The pieces from the Flemish and Northern Schools, although few in number, are of the finest quality.

THE DEPARTMENT OF SCULPTURE

THE DEPARTMENT
OF SCULPTURE

below
Galerie
d'Angoulême
*From 1824 to 1848,
the Louvre's first*

*sculpture collections
were exhibited in the
five rooms of the
Galerie d'Angoulême
(named in honor of the
duke of Angoulême's
victories in Spain
in 1823).*

center right
Museum of French
Monuments, Jean-
Lubin Vauzelle,
ca. 1796
*This painting depicts
the entrance hall of the
museum.*

preceding double page
The Cour Marly
*The Cour Marly
displays sculptures that
originally stood in the
grounds of the Château
de Marly, Louis XIV's
country residence. The
king paid close
attention to the
landscaping of the
gardens. He even
placed plaster models
of statues in the
grounds before deciding
whether to assign firm
commissions to the
artists.*

The Louvre, along with the Victoria and Albert Museum in London and Germany's Berlin-Dahlem, is one of the rare museums to devote a whole department to sculpture. The department, which offers a panoramic view of French statuary and a rich glimpse of non-French sculpture, was once the Museum of French Monuments, created by Alexandre Lenoir during the French Revolution.

The first of the Louvre's rooms dedicated to the history of sculpture, the Galerie d'Angoulême, was opened in 1824 during the Bourbon Restoration. It set out to display the various currents that have flowed through French sculpture. Works on display ranged from collections inherited from the royal residences, such as the open-air statues of the Cour Marly, to "acceptance pieces" (masterpieces presented by artists in support of their application for membership in the Royal Academy of Painting and Sculpture), to more recent works commissioned by the French state. In 1893 the Department of Sculpture became independent of the Decorative Arts Department. Donations helped swell the collections of Italian and French statues. In 1936 these were exhibited in a new display in the Pavillon des États, but due to lack of space, 18th- and 19th-century pieces were excluded from the exhibit. This exclusion (which involved a rich sampling of the most representative works) was partly resolved, however, by the new layout adopted in 1969 and 1971 at the Pavillon de Flore. In the new Louvre "economy," the Department of Sculpture now benefits from a major redistribution of space: the great outdoor statues are exhibited in the glass-roofed courtyards and terraces of the Cour Marly and the Cour Puget. For the first time sheltered spaces flooded with natural light and rich in architectural perspectives can compete with open-air settings in the display of monumental statuary.

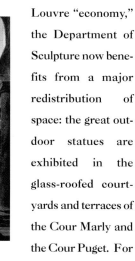

above left
Swabian Donor
*Having been in the
Louvre since 1520, the
Swabian Donor is
now surrounded by
newly installed
collections. Here it is
seen through the
staircase of the
Northern Schools
Department.*

below
Hunter at Rest, or
"Adonis," Cour
Marly, Nicholas
Coustou, 1710
*This statue by Coustou
reminded Louis XIV of
the pleasures of
hunting in which he
loved to indulge. But
this hunter would not
remain at rest for long:
as early as 1716, he
found a new home in*

*the Tuileries gardens.
He was later moved to
the Louvre to become
part of the museum's
collection.*

right
Museum of French
Monuments, Léon
Mathieu Cochereau,
1793-1817
*This painting depicts the
Salle du XVIIᵉ Siècle.*

MUSEUM OF FRENCH MONUMENTS

In 1793 Alexandre Lenoir was assigned the management of a depository of works that had been confiscated under revolutionary laws from émigrés, abolished guilds, and churches. Gradually Lenoir converted this depository into a museum of French monuments, setting up exhibition rooms in the former Convent of the Petits-Augustins. It was the first time that such works – they were mainly sculptures – had been presented in chronological order. Lenoir also created an "Elysian garden," in which funerary monuments (largely imitations of ancient works) were displayed in a manner that anticipated the Romantic spirit ; it was to have a lasting influence on 19th-century artistic imaginations. The museum opened to great public acclaim. Its popularity endured until Louis XVIII abolished it on December 18, 1816.

THE ROMANESQUE MIDDLE AGES

Medieval sculpture, by nature essentially religious, was originally integrated into an architectural whole that is virtually impossible for a museum to reproduce. Sculptures taken from church tympanum, and figures once ensconced in niches, are now displayed independently of the structures to which they formerly belonged, and the vibrant colors they once sported have long since faded. We see them in the Louvre today abstracted from their living context; they reflect the history of sculptural technique rather than the history of "monuments."

The revival of sculpture during the Middle Ages sprang from a historical context favorable to learning. The 11th to the 13th centuries saw a massive surge in monasticism, spearheaded by the great congregational reforms at Cluny and Cîteaux. Monastic institutions sprang up all over Europe, as the Church struggled to impose a basic universal moral code. Romanesque art flourished in these institutions: it sought not only to make a statement of faith but also to offer theological instruction and an explanation of the world's mysteries.

Romanesque sculpture is thus inseparable from the religious archi-

tecture of the day, which had developed a novel and more rational physical layout for church building. This new order incorporated various standard forms

of sculpted decor – tympana of portals, capitals, and vaults – which themselves became integrated fixtures. Thus bound to its existing architectural setting, Romanesque sculpture favored the bas-relief technique over sculpture in the round; isolated statues of wood or precious metals were rare in this period. The Romanesque portal, whose form was fully defined by around 1100, consisted of a large half-moon tympanum decorated with bas-reliefs and erected on a lintel above the door, which was framed by sculpted pillars. A Christ figure, as well as figures from the

accepted classical concepts: the Romanesque body was lengthened, shrunk, or twisted to fit into its setting. Romanesque sculpture was marked by high stylization, with profuse exploitation of geometric folds in drapery, concentric circles to indicate knees, and tragic, hollow-eyed faces. The Louvre houses a panorama of this sculpture in its multi-faceted regional forms: in Burgundy, for example, proportions are elongated and the relief rather low, while in the Auvergne region and Provence, the figures are more compact and the relief is much sharper.

REDISCOVERY OF THE MIDDLE AGES

In the 17th and 18th centuries lovers of medieval art were rare. The word *Gothic*, synonymous with an earlier era, had a pejorative connotation. The 19th century, however, was more attuned to this long-rejected art. Admirers of medieval art inspired a number of cultural "movements." Some were purely faddish, such as the "troubadour" cult, which yearned for the return of epic court poetry; others were historical or archaeological. All gave new prestige to these monuments of a vanished France. The campaigns they launched,

spearheaded by the writer Prosper Mérimée and elaborated by the architect and writer Eugène Viollet-le-Duc, were an authentic rescue operation, designed to make the Middle Ages better understood. Collectors of medieval art donated beautiful works to the Louvre. Once firmly rooted there, the arts of the Middle Ages regained their place and found a staunch supporter at the École du Louvre in Louis Courajod.

othic art, which took off
during the 13th century
and endured until the 15th

G othic art, which took off
during the 13th century
and endured until the 15th
century under the name of
Flamboyant Gothic, was an
inherently French art, and more
particularly the art of the
Capetian dynasty. Its testing
ground was the cathe-
drals themselves, par-
ticularly those of
the Île-de-France,
Picardy, and Cham-
pagne regions. The
primitive Gothic style
of the abbeys of Saint-
Denis and Sens,
which appeared dur-
ing the 12th century,
evolved into a more
classical style that is
best seen in three
cathedrals where it
reached its zenith:

the heavens: more an emo-
tional than a cerebral impulse,
it comes from the heart. Every
detail celebrates divine glory and
the miracle of the Creation.

The search for symbolism
and allegory, a Byzantine legacy
widely used in Romanesque,
now yielded to a
desire to replicate the
forms of nature. A
new kind of artistic
realism was born,
especially in sculp-
ture. Sculpture in the
round, neglected for
nearly eight cen-
turies, resurfaced to
vie with the bas-
reliefs integral to
Romanesque art.
Gothic sculptures
stood out from their
architectural sup-

Chartres, Reims, and Amiens.
Romanesque masses gave way to
structures three times higher in their
upward surge. The Gothic
cathedral was at once the
symbol and the expression
of faith ascending toward

ports in a more pronounced fashion than their predecessors. With their more faithful
reproduction of the human
body, they paved the way for
the portraiture that would
emerge in the late 14th and
early 15th centuries.

above
Saint George and
the Dragon, from
Gaillon, Michel
Colombe, 1508-1509
*Colombe was
influential in
preparing his
contemporaries for the
art of the Renaissance.
His Saint George
and the Dragon
exemplifies the grace
with which he achieved
the transition in his
own work.*

center right
Tombstone of Jean
Casse, Canon of
Noyon, Sainte-
Geneviève, Paris,
middle of 14th
century
*The tombstone of this
cleric, who is buried at
Sainte-Geneviève in
Paris, emphasizes the
splendor of his
vestments and of the
weeping funeral
procession of patron
saints and relatives.
Above his head is a
rendering of the Last
Judgment, a reminder
of Christian hopes and
fears.*

bottom left
Virgin with Headless
Child, Northern
France, third quarter
of the 13th century
*This statue reflects the
fervor surrounding the
cult of the Virgin. The
sumptuous folds of her
clothing, and the inlaid
glass, looking like
lavish jewelry,
accentuate the majestic
feel of the work.*

left center, below
Philippe de
Commynes and
Wife, Convent of
Grands-Augustins,
Paris, early 16th
century
*De Commynes (1447-
1511), a historian
during Louis XI's
reign, had a tombstone
made for himself and
his wife (they are
represented here at
prayer). The tomb
marked their funerary
chapel in the
Convent of the
Grands-Augustins in
Paris. Ransacked
during the French
Revolution, this
monument, along with
fragments of the chapel
decor, was one of the
first pieces to enter the
Museum of French
Monuments.*

bottom right
Virgin and Child,
Monastery of
Cîteaux, second
quarter of the 14th
century
*This statue comes from
the famous
Burgundian monastery
of Cîteaux, where the
cult of the Virgin
flourished under Saint
Bernard in the 12th
century. Nearly two
hundred years later, the
monks continued the
tradition of glorifying
the mother of Jesus,
who is supported here
on her jutting hip.*

Gothic realism was enhanced by an infusion of humanity that had been absent from Romanesque sculpture. Faces lost their stiffness or their air of blank command and instead were imbued with tenderness or pathos. This variety of expression and feature, coupled with the figures' postures and the drape of their garments, accentuated their individualization. Christian iconography began to draw upon new decorative motifs and themes, inspired by both the Old and the New Testaments.

Instead of the terrifying theme of the Last Judgment, commonly found in Romanesque sculpture, more serene motifs were employed. Renderings of Christ the Savior abounded, along with the prophets and the saints, on the tympana of cathedrals in Paris, Amiens, Rouen, Reims, and Bourges.

Worshippers in search of divine intercession often turned to the Virgin, whose origin, like theirs, was human. She became the object of an increasingly widespread cult, reflected in the growing number of cathedrals dedicated to Notre Dame (Our Lady). Typically, she sits radiantly upon the carved decor of the western tympanum, crowned and enthroned, her figure second only to Christ himself in prominence. In statuary in the round, she is represented as the Virgin with Child, breast-feeding or playing with her son. As the Middle Ages waned, she was increasingly depicted as a sorrowful mother, lamenting the death of her child.

In the late 15th century, the Gothic style flowered into more mannered, exuberant forms, which earned it the name "Flamboyant." Northern Europe continued to develop this late Gothic style, which was characterized by sumptuous decor, complexity of forms, sensuality, and the use of polychromy. Meanwhile, Italy – relatively resistant to Gothic art – was rediscovering antiquity, a first step toward the humanism of the Renaissance.

INTERNATIONALIZING GOTHIC

From its 12th-century origins in the Île-de-France region, Gothic art was rapidly disseminated by wandering artists, along trade routes, and through exchanges among the various courts. By the 14th century, a whole range of decorative Gothic styles were in wide circulation. "Prefabricated" solutions to decorative or architectural problems were continually exchanged. The distinguishing characteristic of this international Gothic style was a tendency toward fluid, curvilinear stylization, blending elegance and refinement with restrained vitality. Cathedrals, chapels, and palaces blossomed all over northern Europe, where the style was easily identifiable regardless of the country. Eventually artists and patrons grew weary of Gothic and sought out new forms that would lead to the Renaissance.

THE RENAISSANCE

before the newcomer eclipsed its predecessor. To the decorative elements typical of Gothic statuary were juxtaposed new themes and forms – foliated scrolls, grotesque ornaments, and volutes – borrowed from Italy at the urging of the various royal and princely courts, all inclined to humanism. As can be seen in the works of Michel Colombe, an *imagier*, or "image-maker," from Tours, and his acolyte Jean de Chartres, the Gothic legacy receded slowly. It was replaced by a new feeling for humanity and a resulting clarity of composition, to which sculpture gave full expression. On his return from his first Italian expedition, Charles VIII invited Italian artists to embellish the castles of the Loire valley. From his château at Amboise, the Italian influence spread to Blois and Chaumont, then to the château at Gaillon in Normandy.

Ponce Jacquiot (1515-1572) was influential in the diffusion of Italian motifs and represented the first generation of the French Renaissance, as did the sculptor Jean Goujon (1510-1563). Appointed sculptor to the king, he worked in the châteaux of Anet and Écouen and above all in Paris. His first

below
The Battle of Senlis, Michel Anguier, ca. 1663
This bronze gilt relief was sculpted for the funerary monument of Henry I, duke of Longueville. It is now in the Orléans chapel of the Church of the Célestins in Paris. The "Longueville monument" still extols

the memory of this once-illustrious family.

W as the Renaissance a radical break with the Middle Ages or merely a later manifestation of the medieval spirit? Did Italy really spearhead the movement, or did it begin in northern Europe? At which moment, and where, did people feel that they were witnessing the advent of a new direction for humanity, vastly different from the preceding one? Historians are still divided on the issue. One person who maintained that the Renaissance began with the northern European school was Louis Courajod, curator of the Louvre's Department of Sculpture in the late 19th century. Courajod believed that 14th- and 15th-century Franco-Flemish Gothic realism laid the foundations for the 16th-century Renaissance.

The debate is complex, but it is now accepted that the transition from late Gothic to Renaissance happened gradually, and that the two styles coexisted

above
Funerary Spirit, Tomb of Christophe de Thou, Church of Saint-André-des-Arts, Paris, Barthélemy Prieur, late 16th century
This funerary spirit comes from the tomb of the first president of the Paris Parlement. Prieur succeeded Germain Pilon as sculptor to the king in 1594 and is often considered Pilon's artistic successor as well. This funerary spirit is much freer than stiffer, more conventional figures by the same artist.

center left
Saint Luke the Evangelist, Jean Goujon, latter half of the 16th century
This bas-relief comes from the decoration of the rood screen of the Church of Saint-Germain-l'Auxerrois in Paris. It reflects Goujon's artistic pursuit of both the sacred and the profane.

JEAN GOUJON AND PIERRE LESCOT

Clearly Jean Goujon was one of the sculptors most prized by French kings. Closely associated with designing their palace, the Louvre, he also worked from 1544 to 1545 on Saint-Germain-l'Auxerrois, the chapel of the kings of France. But the most fascinating thing about Goujon is the perfect understanding he had with the architect Pierre Lescot, as manifested at the Louvre in the Henry II Wing in the Cour Carrée. The architectural elevation serves as a setting for a sculpted allegorical decor that essentially glorifies royal government; but the setting is enhanced rather than dominated by the decor. As with the *Fountain of the Innocents*, antiquity – tempered by Mannerist grace – sets the dominant tone.

right

Nymphs and Tritons,
Fountain of the
Innocents, Paris,
Jean Goujon,
1547-1549
*Fascinated by classical
Greek sculpture,
Goujon wedded his
historical inspiration
to the Mannerist style
of his contemporaries.
The nymphs and
tritons of the
Fountain of the
Innocents (where
19th-century copies
have replaced the
originals) glorify the
power of water and
pay homage to the king.*

below

Tomb of Valentine
Balbiani, Germain
Pilon, 1583-1585
*Balbiani reclines
languorously on her
tomb, peacefully
reading – in grim
contrast to the aged,
decrepit woman at the
tomb's base. Pilon has
pushed a medieval
custom – the depiction
of recumbent effigies of
corpses – to its limits
by using every resource
within the range of
Mannerism.*

work in the capital was the rood screen of Saint-Germain-l'Auxerrois. Soon afterward he began work on the *Fountain of the Innocents* (in Paris executed between 1547 and 1549), where graceful water nymphs embody the sensual pagan spirit of the Renaissance. At the Louvre Goujon provided statues and reliefs for the exterior decoration, while his caryatids in the Salle des Bals are a reminder that this artist – who translated the work of the Roman architect Vitruvius into French – contributed greatly to the rediscovery of antiquity. His works reveal an admiration for Greco-Roman statuary. They also betray the influence of Italian artists of the Fontainebleau School, such as Francesco Primaticcio, Benvenuto Cellini, and Il Rosso Fiorentino.

The second generation of French Renaissance sculptors were grouped around Germain Pilon (1528-1590), the most powerful French sculptor of the late 16th century. He too was influenced by Italians,

notably by Primaticcio and the Mannerist movement. He quickly developed his own manner, however, especially for tomb sculpture and portraiture – a field in which he proved himself a worthy heir of the Gothic sculptors.

In the late 16th and early 17th centuries, Mannerism flourished in France with the second Fontainebleau School. Barthélemy Prieur, Pierre Biard, and Pierre Franqueville, a disciple of Giambologna (sculptor of the *Chained Slaves* for the base of Henry IV's equestrian statue), gave the movement new momentum. Mathieu Jacquet, also a product of this school, struck out on his own to pursue a high degree of realism that was tempered by the delicacy of his style.

Until around 1640 a few French sculptors stood out over the others: Jacquet, Jacques Sarrazin, and Simon Guillain (a bronze worker) were clearly heirs of the school of Pilon, while the brothers François and Michel Anguier, influenced by Italy, found expression in dynamic theatrical forms.

center left

Flying Angel,
Ligier Richier,
ca. 1550-1560
*This flying angel,
executed either by
Richier or by someone
from his studio, was
inspired by the graceful
infant Jesus in the
Chapelle des Princes de
Sainte-Maxe in Bar-
le-Duc, Lorraine.*

following double page

Triton, Nereid, and
Eros, Gérard van
Opstal, late 17th
century
*Swimming among the
Tritons, these beautiful
young Nereids,
daughters of the sea
god Nereus, adorn the
splendid Cour
d'Amphitrite. Van
Opstal (1595-1668),
highly sought after for
the perfection of his
compositions, set this
submarine idyll on a
marble slab. The work
was acquired in 1669
for the Royal
Collections.*

In 1661, when the young Louis XIV shook off cardinal Mazarin's tutelage, the balance of artistic influence in France tilted toward antiquity. Between 1661 and 1685 French classicism (a blend of the Apollonian ideal with a more restrained Baroque) became the dominant style, largely due to the efforts of Jean-Baptiste Colbert and Charles Le Brun. It was at this time that the institution of "acceptance pieces" came into being. These were works on themes selected by the Royal Academy of Painting and Sculpture for execution by artists to whom membership had been granted. Royal commissions also imposed a degree of unity in the handling of monumental statuary, brilliantly represented in the Cour Marly by the works of Antoine Coysevox, Guillaume Coustou, and Antoine Le Pautre. Under the glass covering that protects the

Finance Ministry's former courtyard stand sculptures conceived for royal estates, particularly the gardens of the Château de Marly, after 1679. Here a bountiful water supply facilitated the construction of a series of embanked basins descending to an ornamental pond decorated with two of Coysevox's equestrian groups, *Mercury* and *Fame*, each astride Pegasus. In 1719 these groups were moved to the Tuileries entrance, then were replaced in 1745 by two new groups commissioned from Guillaume Coustou: *Escaped Horses Recaptured by a Groom.* During the French Revolution, these horses in their turn were moved to the entrance of the Champs-Élysées. Many other statues (some twenty in all, including *Hippomenes* and *Apollo*, are exhibited in the Louvre) decorated the basins and undergrowth of Marly, which was ransacked during the Revolution.

THE COUR MARLY

Conceived as an open-air space, this courtyard (once used as a parking lot by the Ministry of Finance) displays monumental statues from the former royal residence of Marly, which were originally intended to decorate gardens, in a "natural" setting. Daylight pours through the vast glass casing, and the natural look is enhanced by boxed shrubbery reminiscent of the orange trees prized by Louis XIV. The courtyard stands in the center of the Department of Sculpture, newly installed in the former quarters of the Finance Ministry. Instead of vast stretches of parked cars, where "nature is dominated by man," visitors now see a vast panorama of sculpture through the arcades of the peristyle.

right

Milo of Crotona
Devoured by a Lion,
Pierre Puget, Parc
de Versailles, 1682
*This statue by Puget
retells the story of the
aging athlete who
overestimated his own
strength and was
devoured by a wolf
(rendered as a lion by
Puget).*

left

Cato of Utica, Jean-
Baptiste Roman and
François Rude, 1840
*Begun by Roman in
1832, this statue was
not completed by Rude
until 1840. The
political context in
which it was sculpted
was oppressive, and
the work stands as a
heroic profession of
Republican faith.*

below

Saint James the
Lesser, Jacques
Clérion, 1669
*This "acceptance piece"
by Clérion, presented
in 1669, reflects the*

*predilection of the Sun
King's century for
strong religious
sentiment.*

Few provinces in France remained immune to the dominant style of Versailles. In sculpture the provincial schools produced a major spokesman in Pierre Puget (1620-1694). Originally from Provence, Puget received his training in Rome, alongside Pietro da Cortona, and in Genoa, where he was immersed in the Baroque. He first made a name for himself in 1657 with the *Atlantes* he created for the town hall in Toulon, which drew the attention of the Louis XIV's influential superintendent, Nicolas Fouquet. Puget carved a highly flattering allegorical figure for Fouquet: a *Gallic Hercules* bearing the arms of France. After the fall of Fouquet in 1661, his successor as intendant, Colbert, claimed the sculpture for himself.

In 1670 Colbert commissioned Puget to create three works for Versailles: *Milo of Crotona, The Meeting of Alexander and Diogenes,* and *Perseus and Andromeda.* Puget responded with a spectacular demonstration of the increasingly popular Italian Baroque style. But his artistic boldness and expressive power, as well as his fierce independence, kept him on the sidelines of court-sponsored activity.

Around 1700 Rococo art peaked in the park grounds at Marly. Today the Cour Marly also exhibits bronzes and bas-reliefs by Martin Desjardins, who decorated the Place des Victoires in Paris with a colossal statue of Louis XIV (destroyed during the Revolution), flanked by *Chained Captives* and by bronze reliefs.

below

Chained Captives,
Martin Van den
Bogaert, known as

Desjardins, 1686
Desjardins executed his
Chained Captives *to
complement the
triumphant equestrian
statue of Louis XIV in
the Place des Victoires.
The piece represents the
nations whose defeat
led to the 1678 Treaty
of Nijmegen: the Holy
Roman Empire,
Spain, Brandenburg,
and Holland.*

above center

Nymph with Shell,
Antoine Coysevox,
Parc de Versailles,
1683
*This graceful nymph by
Coysevox originally
stood in gardens at
Versailles.*

SCULPTURE TECHNIQUES

A three-dimensional art, sculpture is always in relief. The work's degree of projection from a plane or concave surface is described as low, medium, or high relief – low relief being only slightly raised and high relief being nearly detached from the surface. Work in full relief – cast in the round – is called statuary. The sculptor's range of working materials is very wide. Each demands a particular technique, sometimes requiring the artist to collaborate with a specialist, most often a craftsman skilled at giving the medium preliminary form, dressing it, and working it into shape. The technical difficulties involved in creating sculpture have always conferred prestige on sculptors and their work. Apart from architecture, no other art has played so great a civic role – not to mention its effectiveness as propaganda.

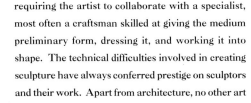

FROM THE 18TH CENTURY TO NEOCLASSICISM

With the death of Louis XIV in 1715 and the regency of Philip of Orléans, the solemn and ceremonial style of Versailles gave way to a manner marked by unrestrained love of life. The artists of the day – including architects and decorators such as Gilles Marie Oppenordt, interior decorators such as Jean Le Pautre and Toro, painters such as Pillement and Antoine Watteau, and gold- and silversmiths of the caliber of Jean Meissonnier – worked for the regent and a wealthy clientele of art lovers, assuring the supremacy of the new French style. It flourished from 1730 to 1760 and was to have as far-reaching an influence as the Gothic style had enjoyed. Sculpture, hitherto an official art, often monumental, intended to be admired by the masses, now moved out of the public eye and the royal gardens and into the privacy of homes. The first Rococo sculptors retained their attachment to mon-

umental or religious and funerary statuary. But their successors eagerly began to create a profane and worldly art, culminating in busts or effigies of private citizens. Henceforth portrait sculpture would reach an aristocratic and even middle-class clientele, eager to perpetuate their images in marble.

At the same time, sculptors were in demand for interior decoration. In this vein Claude Michel (better known as Clodion), the creator of statuettes and bas-reliefs representing voluptuous themes that blended Boucher's sensuality with influences from antiquity, won a well-deserved reputation. Sculpture that was arrested in the act of creation and left unfinished would arouse interest until the 18th century, when collectors who preferred the spontaneity of rough drafts to the perfection of completed work eagerly sought terra-cotta casts and small bronzes.

"ACCEPTANCE PIECES"

The Royal Academy of Painting and Sculpture, founded in 1648, monitored artistic production and set itself up as the guardian of Beauty. It also it offered a level of instruction that guaranteed artists recognition of their work, as well as numerous commissions – royal for the most part. Would-be members had first to be accepted by the Academy, then were required to execute an "acceptance piece" on a predetermined subject. Such pieces were most often presented mounted on slabs, a form that the Louvre has respected in its displays. These acceptance pieces give an idea of the artistic vitality of the period from Louis XIV's reign to the abolition of the Academy in 1792.

Neoclassicism

A round the middle of the 18th century, a backlash against the Rococo style emerged that sought to return to the sources of antiquity, inspired by the archaeological finds at Pompeii and Herculaneum. Marking the transition to Neoclassicism, Jean-Antoine Houdon (1741-1828) dominated late 18th-century sculpture. With the work of this artist, whose realistic style accentuated both the anatomical and the psychological truth of his sitters, Neoclassicism found its favorite niche in portraiture. The most illustrious of Houdon's contemporaries, from George Washington to Napoleon, sat for him. This passion for portraying illustrious men (encouraged by the count of Angivillers's order for twenty-eight statues of France's geniuses for the Grande Galerie) reached its peak during the Revolution and the Empire.

An ideal of austere, heroic beauty now prevailed, best illustrated by the work of Denis-Antoine Chaudet, who decorated Paris's Panthéon, and of Claude Ramey, who portrayed Napoleon. But this rigorous tendency coexisted alongside a softer, more gracious mood, represented by the work of sculptors Joseph Chinard and Antonio Canova. The reign of Neoclassicism ended with the Bourbon Restoration, when artists like François-Joseph Bosio and James Pradier were drawn to a more elegiac style inspired by a newly rediscovered Greece.

The ideal of absolute truth, of realism, risked bringing sculpture to an impasse. To avoid it, artists could return either to a pre-Classical style or to a more ostentatious Baroque. The Romantics chose the latter solution.

Pompeii and Herculaneum

The 18th-century rediscovery of Pompeii and Herculaneum, followed by a craze for archaeological digs, injected new vigor into the old aesthetic debate over antiquity.

For although the artistic production of Rome was well known (with some Roman works credibly attributable to Greek artists), the discovery of the ruins of once-beautiful cities set artists on fire. Painters rediscovered colors they had once merely dreamed of – such as "Pompeiian red" – which became the rage in contemporary decoration; while sculptors drew powerful new inspiration from this freshly uncovered testimony.

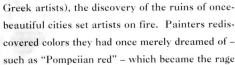

ROMANTICISM

Fevered and impassioned by temperament, Romantic sculptors found it irksome to have to submit to the constraints implicit in handling heavy materials – or to devote the time necessary to create "finished" works of art. In short, sculpture was not a major factor in the artistic upsurge that unseated the academic old guard during the first half of the 19th century. Even sculptors deeply committed to the new movement were reluctant to be drawn into Romanticism's excesses. *Orlando Furioso* by Jehan Duseigneur (an artist linked to the literary world of Petrus Borel, Théophile Gautier, and Gérard de Nerval) strove to reconcile features of antique statuary with the dramatic theatricality of the Romantics. The influential sculptor Pierre-Jean David d'Angers (1788-

1856) devoted his talent to honoring the illustrious figures of the day, from René de Chateaubriand to Victor Hugo, in a series of bas-reliefs completely devoid of militant revolutionary spirit. François Rude, an ardent Bonapartist, dominated Romantic sculpture, just as his masterpiece *La Marseillaise* dominated the Arc de Triomphe. The expressive force of that famous bas-relief is as powerful as that of Rude's free-standing statues, such as *Monge* and *Marshal Ney*. Rude's contemporary Antoine-Louis Barye (who was close to Delacroix) earned the well-deserved nickname "Michelangelo of the Ménagerie." He loved animals and spent a great deal of time studying the interplay of their muscles and flesh at the Jardin des Plantes. His bronze animal studies richly reflect his observations.

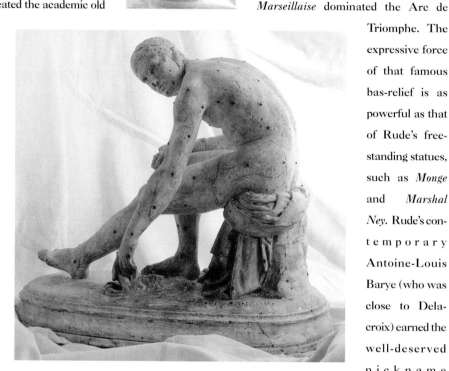

THE MATERIALS

Materials can be classified according to the techniques required to work them. Clay, wax, plaster, and stucco require modeling; the same materials, plus bronze and glass, call for casting; and stone, wood, ivory, and bone have to be carved. Stone was the most frequently used material in the early days of sculpture, particularly in its most prestigious form, marble. Wood (fibrous, compact, light, and requiring delicate handling) was the most commonly used material in regions where stone was scarce and was essentially reserved for interior design. Bronze, an alloy of copper, pewter, and zinc, was used chiefly for open-air statues, even though it served in the creation of small-scale statuary as well. Early in the 19th century, bronze was being used for the serial production of casts.

Italian Sculpture

In contrast to the Louvre's abundance of French statuary, sculpture from the foreign schools – displayed in the Denon Wing – is relatively scarce. The Italian Middle Ages (11th to 13th centuries) are illustrated with only a handful of Romanesque religious works from Umbria, Florence, and Pisa. Despite the tentative appearance of naturalism (which would be fully expressed in Gothic statuary), these works still show traces of Byzantine influence. But under the

chisel of Nicola Pisano and his acolytes, works of greater expressive power, such as the Baptistery pulpit in Pisa, were soon to emerge. The 14th century saw the triumph of nudes and profane beauty, of sculpture in the round over relief. Knowledge of nature and man grew

increasingly complex. Florence was the cradle of the early Renaissance – the late 14th and early 15th centuries. Lorenzo Ghiberti chiseled delicate, pathos-filled bas-reliefs of the life of Christ for the bronze doors of the Baptistery in Florence – starkly contrasting with the tormented style of Jacopo della Quercia and the inspired vitality of Donatello. Strongly influenced by the art of antiquity, Donatello transposed his heroic vision of man into marble and bronze: it was a vision in which the backward look at antiquity betrayed the angst characteristic of the transition period in which Donatello lived. For Donatello was the herald of the new art that was already conquering Italy and that would later prevail throughout Europe.

The New Sculpture Rooms

Shuttled from pillar to post ever since its creation, the Louvre's sculpture collection found a new setting in 1993-1994, one that offers a full display of the whole collection. It now complements much more vividly the spirit of the museum's Decorative Arts and Painting departments.

The French collections are displayed in the rooms once occupied by the Finance Ministry. Two covered courtyards house works originally intended for outdoor viewing: the Cour Marly (formerly occupied by the Finance Ministry), and the Cour Puget (formerly home to the Cour des Caisses). Schools of foreign sculpture – Italian, Spanish, and northern European – are laid out in new rooms located near the museum's Denon entrance, to the north and west of the Cour Visconti.

From the day in 1824 when the Galerie d'Angoulême opened its doors to exhibitions of Renaissance and modern sculpture, Michelangelo's *Slaves* has welcomed visitors. Michelangelo Buonarotti (1475-1564) was the emblematic figure of the Renaissance in all its splendor. Although he was brilliant in all artistic fields, his genius was most evident in sculpture. Pope Julius II summoned the artist to Rome to build for him a magnificent tomb, a colossal task that he worked on intermittently from 1505 to 1545. He never completed it, perhaps defeated by the challenge of fusing his personal turmoil and the turbulence of the times into an expression of universal suffering. But over the years, he imbued his *Slaves* with the full power of his fantasies, fears, and hopes.

Julius II's successor, Leo X, commissioned Michelangelo to sculpt the tomb for the Medici Chapel in Rome's Church of San Lorenzo. The sarcophagi of the Medici dukes Lorenzo and Giuliano are set above reclining larger-than-life figures symbolizing Day and Night (for *The Active Life*) and Dawn and Evening (for *The Contemplative Life*). The figures betray Michelangelo's hesitation between stoic resignation and Christian hope. Exhausted by years of struggle and uncertainty, Michelangelo turned increasingly to architecture and then to painting, abandoning sculpture until the very end of his life, when he created his *Pietà*. Mannerism, which his own art illustrates, was to influence many sculptors, from Benvenuto Cellini to Giambologna, and from Pierino da Vinci to Adrien de Bries. It would resurface later in the Baroque style, celebrated by another great Italian, Lorenzo Bernini.

THE NORTHERN SCHOOLS

German Gothic sculpture was expressionist in spirit from its beginnings in the 13th century. The 15th century saw the blossoming of the Beau Style, as exemplified in the Louvre's *Virgin and Child* from Salzburg. Each region had its particular style, a diversity accurately reflected in the museum's rooms devoted to the Northern Schools.

Gothic art was swiftly implanted in Flanders and the Netherlands. Sculpture there evolved into a more mannered Franco-Flemish style, which was balanced by a movement favoring realism, led by artists like Claus Sluter. In the early 16th century, a classical backlash occurred, making its appearance in the decorative sculpture of the day. Toward the late Renaissance, Mannerism became more popular, strongly marking artists like Adrien de Vries – who would later adopt the Baroque.

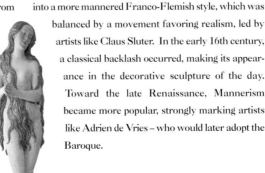

The Department of Decorative Arts

The Louvre's Department of Decorative Arts is a cornucopia of masterpieces. They range from crown jewels, medieval works of ivory and enamel, furniture from the royal residences, and tapestries, to cameos, scientific instruments, and works of gold, bronze, porcelain, ceramics, and majolica. Until very recently, the collection was housed in the Cour Carrée, where the display arrangements – overcrowded viewing cases with tapestries hung above them – had remained the same since the late 1930s. But with the reopening of the Richelieu Wing (former home of the Finance Ministry) and the annexation of the second floor of the Pavillon Sully, the department has found much-needed breathing space. The layout of the reorganized collection now allows for a much more rational and extended display. Presented in chronological order, the collection offers visitors a panorama of decorative objects produced between the end of antiquity and the early 19th century.

The Department of Decorative Arts dates back to the inauguration of the Louvre museum in 1793, when it was intended to house the vases and furnishings of the Garde-Meuble de la Couronne (the Crown Furniture Repository, the government department responsible for furnishing the royal palaces). The collection did not become an autonomous department of the museum until 1893. Before then pieces were moved from department to department, by whim and random decision. Today they have been arranged in a spacious area that gives full play to the beauty and singularity of each object.

The original collection included the *pietra dura* vases and Renaissance bronzes of the Garde-Meuble de la Couronne, which entered the Louvre in 1796, as well as the medieval treasure confiscated from the Abbey of Saint-Denis in 1791.

From its inception the collection was of exceptional quality. Over the years it has been enlarged and enriched by acquisitions, donations, and bequests. In the early 19th century the purchase of the Edme-Antoine Durand collection brought in thousands of antiques and a few hundred objets d'art (stained-glass windows, enamels, ceramics) from the Middle Ages and Renaissance. The purchase of painter Pierre Révoil's collection expanded the department to include furniture and tapestries. When Louis-Napoleon purchased the bulk of the Marquis Campana's collection,

the Louvre acquired one of the world's richest troves of Italian Renaissance faience. The Charles Sauvageot bequest resulted in the display of pottery by Bernard Palissy.

Not until the end of the Second Empire did the Louvre give pride of place to items from the 17th, 18th, and 19th centuries. In the early 20th century, thanks to the contributions of the Mobilier National (successor to the Garde-Meuble), furnishings and bronzes from the palaces of Saint-Cloud and the Tuileries entered the Louvre. Subsequent bequests by the Rothschilds and Camondos (and more recently from Niarchos, David-Weill, and Grog-Carven) have added furniture, tapestries, gold- and silversmiths' work, glass, and porcelain to the department's collections.

Despite its broad range of objects of such outstanding quality, the Department of Decorative Arts does not seek to replace more specialized museums. Rather, it offers a selection of quite exceptional works, the modern counterpart – on a much vaster scale – of the collections of such potentates as Rudolf of Habsburg and the Medici.

The collection is now housed on the second floor of the Richelieu Wing and in the area around the Cour Marly and the Cour Puget, while furniture is in the north and west wings of the Cour Carrée. The apartments of the duke of Morny are located in the southwest corner of the Cour Marly, on the second floor.

THE TREASURE AND ABBEY OF SAINT-DENIS

In the 5th century Saint Geneviève (patron saint of Paris) had a church built to house the holy remains of the martyred 3rd-century Roman bishop Denis and his companions, Rusticus and Eleutherius. King Dagobert enlarged the building and its treasure, and it later became his burial ground. Though it was famous from the outset, the abbey's days of true splendor began in the 11th century.

The tale of Denis's martyrdom is

rich in anecdotal detail. After he was decapitated, he is said to have carried his own head to his grave in the village where the abbey now stands. In 1052 the monks of Regensburg claimed to be in possession of the martyr's remains. The Saint-Denis tomb was opened: in it were found relics of the Passion. Early in the following century, the great Abbé Suger enlarged this treasure (intended as a testimony to divine splendor) with a gift of a gold-plated tomb.

Byzantine art had already come into being by the 4th century, but it did not attain perfection until the 6th-century reign of the emperor Justinian. It underwent periods of decline and rebirth until 1453, when Byzantium finally fell to the Turks.

Although the Byzantine decorative style developed out of late imperial Roman art, it had its own distinctive characteristics. The craftsmen of Constantinople adapted the traditions of the late Roman Empire to Christian ends. Shaped by this religion and by the role of the emperor, who represented God on earth, Byzantine art also drew on the art of the Middle East and Egypt. It was characterized by predilections for the human figure and for flat rather than sculpturesque forms; a love of jeweled luxury; extreme stylization of figu-

rative forms; floral or foliate motifs; and exquisite craftsmanship.

In the 8th century the Iconoclast Controversy ended with a rejection of the cult of holy images, ultimately bringing Byzantine art's first golden age to a virtual close. Religious orthodoxy and the cult of images were reinstated in 843, and a second golden age of Byzantine art began. Under the Comnenus dynasty (1081-1185), it was evolving toward mannerist elegance – a development cut short by the sack of Constantinople in the early 13th century by Western Crusaders. A final renaissance, fertile in icons, mosaics, and frescoes, blossomed under the rule of the Palaeologus dynasty (1261-1453).

Before the Turkish conquest, Byzantium had already transmitted its artistic traditions via Italy to the Middle Ages.

below
Enamel medallions, France, 13th century
On a small scale, these medallions presage the decorative genius that went into the exquisite rose windows of medieval cathedrals. They once adorned a pair of gloves believed to belong to the bishop of Le Mans.

left
Icon of the Crucifixion, School of Novgorod, 16th century
This Russian Crucifixion (an instance of the far-ranging influence of Byzantine art) is imprinted with the expressive power of a Christian empire ultimately doomed to fall to the Turks. Mary, Saint John, and two other figures, symbolizing the throngs of the faithful, bend toward the body of Christ and herald his triumph over death.

above left
Saint John the Theologian, gilt bronze, Russia, 16th century
This plaque was part of an iconostasis, a screen dividing the sanctuary from the main body of the church.

below
The Transfiguration, Constantinople, ca. 1200
This portable icon

treats the same themes and possesses the same decorative strengths as the interiors of monumental Byzantine churches.

left below
Icon of Saint George, portable mosaic, Constantinople, early 14th century
Legend has it that the 3rd-century Saint George, the young and handsome prince of Cappadocia, encountered and vanquished a dragon.

Easy to whiten, polish, and handle, ivory has been used as a medium for carving since prehistoric times. The ancient civilizations of the Middle East and Mediterranean used it to make religious objects, to decorate furniture, and to fashion heads and hands for monumental statuary.

Byzantine artists used ivory extensively to create religious, political, and decorative works. In the 5th and 6th centuries, ivory plaques sculpted in low relief were hinged together to form diptychs honoring Byzantium's successive consuls. The Louvre possesses the most beautiful of such plaques – the Barberini Ivory. Byzantine carvings provided inspiration for Charlemagne's Renaissance, as well as for Ottonian art in Germany, which fostered the development of German, English, and Flemish workshops.

During the Gothic period the French workshops were the most active in Europe: in the 14th century Paris rose to be the major center for the production of sculpted ivory. By the 15th century, however, the most exquisite pieces were coming from northern Italy, particularly from the workshops of the Embriachi and Visconti. The art of ivory was revived in the second half of the 16th century, when workshops turned out objects worked with a lathe. Throughout the 17th century demand for religious or mythological statuettes, portraits, snuff boxes, and marquetry furniture (in which André-Charles Boulle in particular excelled) remained constant. Thereafter porcelain supplanted ivory and continued to do so until the 19th century.

IVORY

Carolingian and medieval artists drew inspiration from the ivories of Rome and Byzantium. Ivory, which came to Europe predominantly from Africa, was a much sought-after trading item. After a period of relative scarcity in the 10th and 11th centuries, it became plentiful again following the opening of European trading posts on the Atlantic coast of Africa. European cities, particularly Paris, became great centers of ivory sculpture. Craftsmen of the Gothic period, attuned to court poetry of epic and courtly love, created a much wider variety of works and softened the forms handed down to them from Romanesque art. Despite their intimacy, the monumental élan of works reflects the grandeur of the cathedrals.

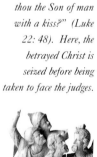

The royal treasure of the Abbey of Saint-Denis became part of the Louvre's collection during the French Revolution and was the nucleus from which the Department of Decorative Arts evolved. Founded in 630 by the Merovingian king Dagobert, who enriched the treasure with gifts of his own, the abbey has served as a royal burial place ever since. Its prestige was enhanced by the fact that it included the relics of Saint Denis, considered the patron saint of France. During the Carolingian period, the treasure was enlarged by Charlemagne's grandson, Charles the Bald, who was the secular abbé of Saint-Denis from 867 until his death in 877. During this period the treasure received the Cup of the Ptolemies, a famous 3rd-century Egyptian cameo vessel used as a chalice for the coronation of queens; its serpentine paten is inlaid with gold fishes, and it is mounted in cloisonné enamel.

The jewelry case of Charlemagne – a portico in gold and precious stones, surmounted with a large antique intaglio – as well as carved ivory book covers were also added to the treasure.

In the early 12th century, thanks to Abbé Suger (who served as minister to Louis VI and Louis VII and as regent of France while the king was away during the Second Crusade), the abbey became the fountainhead of the new Gothic art. Suger was also responsible for acquiring precious *pietra dura*, or rock-crystal vases, such as the famous liturgical urn known as the Eagle of Suger, of either Egyptian or Roman origin. The urn remained at the abbey until the French Revolution. Suger wrote that he had found an antique porphyry vase from the Roman Imperial period in a chest at the abbey and converted it into an

above
Arm Reliquary of
Saint Luke, rock
crystal, 1337-1338
*This reliquary, made
in Naples for Queen
Sancia of Majorca,
evokes Saint Luke's
authorship of one of
the four Gospels. It is
a monstrance (or
"viewable") reliquary,
in which the relic is
visible through the
rock-crystal section
of the arm.*

below right
Reliquary of the
True Cross, triptych,
repoussé gilt-silver
chased and engraved,
after 1254
*The remains of the
True Cross, discovered
in 326 by Saint
Helena, mother of the
emperor Constantine,
were disassembled.
The two largest pieces
were given to the
basilica built to mark
the site and to the
Church of the Holy
Cross in Jerusalem.*

left center
The Alpais Ciborium,
Limoges, before
1200
*This ciborium, or
receptacle for holding
the consecrated wafers
of the Eucharist, was
once a funerary chalice.
With its engraved and
chased gilt-copper,
enamel, appliqués,
and gems, it heralds
the birth of the Gothic
style.*

below
Scepter of Charles V,
gold, treasure
of Saint-Denis
*This scepter relates the
life of Charlemagne,
who sits enthroned at
its summit. The fleur-
de-lys below
Charlemagne's throne
was originally covered
with a layer of white
enamel.*

RELICS

A relic is a fragment of a saint's body or an object crucial to the history of Christianity. No matter how magnificent they were, gold, precious stones, and fine goldsmith work paled in value compared with relics: they were the only "real" treasure, the irreplaceable link between the human and the ineffable. Throughout the Middle Ages, relics were the foundation of a church's or a convent's prestige and the guarantors of its continuing prosperity. They (and the reliquaries in which they were kept) were also objects of theft. Dealers specialized in the trade of these priceless fragments – while prelates worried that the faithful were being deceived by forgeries. It was reported that false relics were so common in the 11th century that their authenticity was put to the test through ordeal by fire. If they passed through unscathed, they were judged authentic – and of course if they burned, they were considered fakes.

"eagle" with the help of a special mount he ordered for it.

His successors continued to embellish the treasure of Saint-Denis until it reached its zenith in the 14th century. In addition to the relics of Saint Denis himself and his martyred companions Rusticus and Eleutherius, the abbey also held relics of the Passion and of Saint Louis, who was canonized in 1297. These relics drew pilgrims who journeyed from all points of the compass. In the 14th century the abbey received some of its most remarkable pieces: the ring of Saint Denis, the ring of Saint Louis, and the reliquary statuette of the Virgin and Child, donated by Queen Jeanne d'Evreux. Charles V, a great

Abbé Suger (1081-1151) was raised at the Abbey of Saint-Denis along with the future king Louis VI. Appointed abbé in 1122, he was determined to add further luster to the abbey's renown. It kept closely in touch with contemporary innovations in architecture and drew on them to build a basilica that marked the beginning of Gothic architecture. There, in the true Benedictine spirit, he set out to transpose the "immaterial" aspect of God's kingdom into precious stones and decorative objects. At the abbey he built up a treasure composed of votive objects, such as crosses and candlesticks or ciboria, patens, and chalices. The treasure also boasted holy books, ostensories, and liturgical vestments. Certain priceless relics, such as the spear that pierced Christ's side, were also associated with the treasure, which was constantly enriched by donations.

lover of art, donated coronation regalia, royal objects that had invariably aroused awe and curiosity. Since the late Middle Ages, Saint-Denis had been collecting coronation paraphernalia from France's Merovingian and Carolingian kings.

According to a 17th-century inventory, the treasure of Saint-Denis was made up of 445 objects; illustrations of them were published in Dom Michel Félibien's book, *Histoire de l'abbaye royale de Saint-Denis en France* (1706). During the Revolution a few regalia objects were miraculously spared pillage and were later turned over to the Louvre in 1793. But the bulk of the treasure disappeared: only a hundred or so pieces in all found a home in the Louvre.

above right
The Eagle of Suger, liturgical ewer, treasure of Saint-Denis, 1147
From an Egyptian or Imperial Roman vase, Suger created this "eagle" in 1147. "This stone," he wrote, "deserved to be set among gold and precious stones. It was of marble, but now it is more precious than marble." The vessel testifies to the goldsmiths' skill in suggesting the bird's threatening posture by the addition of a few naturalistic flourishes.

below right
Chasuble, Bohemia, mid-14th century
The delicacy of the embroidery adorning this chasuble – the lavish vestment worn over the alb and stole during celebration of the Eucharist – breathes tenderness into scenes from Christ's childhood. The procession of the Magi, come to worship the infant, may reflect the splendor of the court of 14th-century Bohemia, where the chasuble was produced. Gothic forms like these had long since diffused from their birthplace, the Ile-de-France, to inspire creative efforts in other parts of Europe.

below
Reliquary Statuette: Virgin and Child of Jeanne d'Evreux, 14th century
This gilt-silver statuette was given to the Abbey of Saint-Denis in 1339 by Queen Jeanne d'Evreux, widow of Charles IV the Handsome. It is one

of the rare surviving examples of a large Gothic statuette made of precious metals. It illustrates the tender and idealized cult of the Madonna during the 14th century. The reliquary fleur-de-lys in her right hand was said to contain some of the Virgin's milk, part of her veil, and some of her hair.

Chased Enamelwork

Enamel, a vitreous paint that dries to a hard glossy surface, has been used for decoration since the first millennium B.C. in Asia. *Enamel* designates both the material and the art object itself. Medieval enamelists used several techniques. In the cloisonné technique the enamel was poured into compartments, or *cloisons*, whose shape was dictated by the design and which were formed by a network of raised metal strips. In champlevé, or chasing, enamels of different colors were poured into grooves engraved on the object's silver, gold, copper, or bronze surface; once hardened, they were polished down to the same level as the surrounding metal surface. In *ronde-bosse* enamel was applied to convex surfaces. And in painted enamels colored enamel was painted onto a metal surface. The champlevé technique was very much in vogue in Byzantium, spread throughout Europe, and reached the peak of its popularity in 12th- and 13th-century Romanesque art. It had three major schools: Mosan (especially at Liège and Huy), Cologne, and Limoges. Limoges was the most fertile of the three. Its enamelworkers adopted the Romanesque style in the 12th century: highly stylized figures in low relief against a blue background decorated with rosebuds, stars, foliage, or arabesques. Their champlevé enamels, generally on copper, decorated the usual range of church objects. In the 15th century the champlevé technique was supplanted by painted enamelwork.

below
Pair of Mirror Covers
Craftsmen offered covers made of two small decorated plaques to protect

mirrors. For decoration they drew upon courtly themes, whimsical motifs, or Christian iconography, such as these scenes depicting the baptism and the flagellation of Christ.

below right
Centaur, gilded copper, champlevé enamel, Meuse, ca.1170
This scene was once part of a group, since broken up, that probably illustrated the virtues and vices. The centaur is one of the few pagan motifs handled in this period.

THE DEPARTMENT OF DECORATIVE ARTS

above left
Warrior Fighting a Dragon, gilded copper, Meuse, ca. 1160-1170

left center
Concave Plaque, Limoges, second half of 12th century
King David announces – as indicated by the scroll he brandishes – that he will continue the work of Jacob. He did so, uniting the kingdom of Israel and making Jerusalem his capital.

below
Casket Shrine of Saint Martial, Limoges, ca. 1170
This casket shows episodes from the lives of Saint Martial, first bishop and patron saint of Limoges, and of Saint Valerius.

right
Self-portrait of Jean Fouquet, copper, enamel with gold paint, after 1451
This self-portrait served as the painter's signature on the diptych of Notre-Dame de Melun, commissioned by Charles VII's secretary, Étienne Chevalier.

Goldsmithing

During the Gothic period, goldsmithing held a place of honor among the arts. In testimony to the prowess of medieval goldsmiths, many of their works are still in existence. These craftsmen had for centuries belonged to a powerful guild. The naturalism of Gothic architecture and sculpture was echoed in gold jewelry, reliquaries, shrines, croziers, and other religious objects. The techniques were numerous: smelting (melting and fusing ores); stamping (imprinting a seal or design on the metal's surface); chasing (decorating the metal by engraving or embossing); gilding; repoussé work (decorating the gold with patterns in relief, formed by hammering or pressing on the metal's reverse side); and filigree (delicate and intricate ornamental work achieved with fine twisted gold wire). These techniques remained virtually unchanged for centuries.

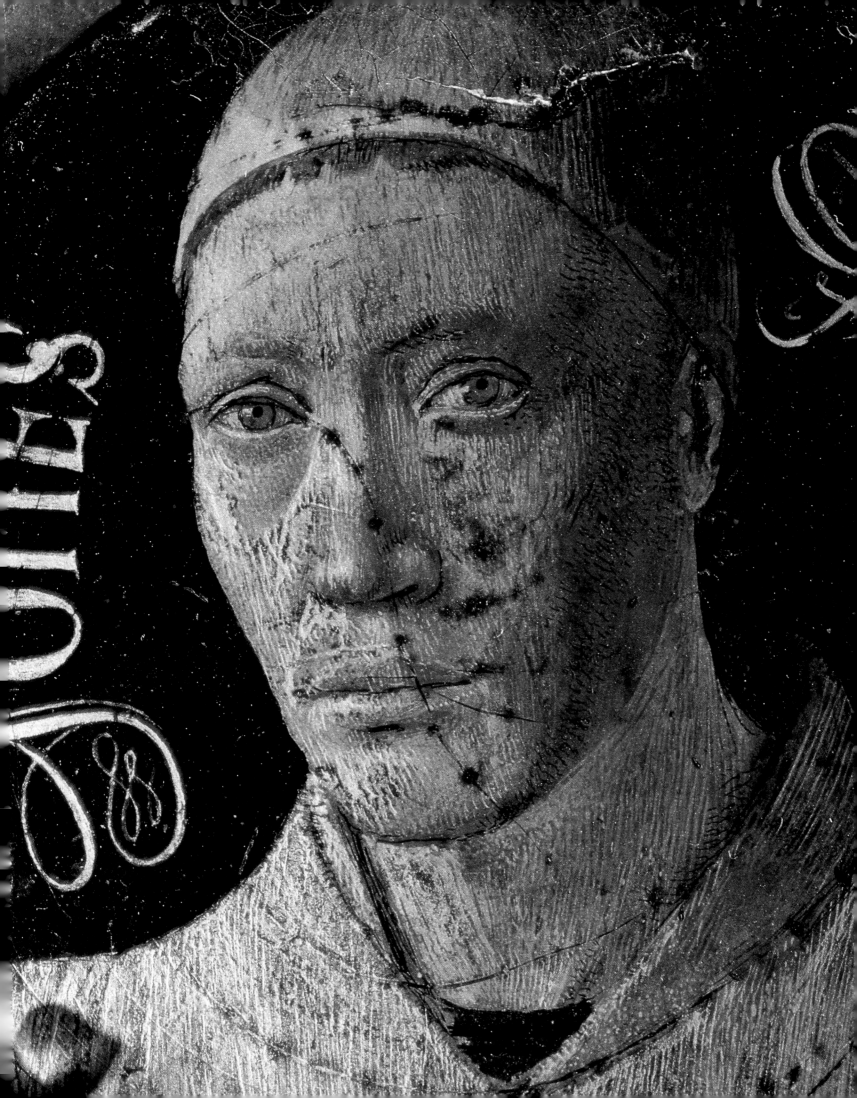

TAPESTRIES

At the turn of the 14th century, the well-established art of tapestry-making began a period of expansion. Paris – where the oldest and one of the largest word for tapestry is *arazzo*.

Making tapestries was time-consuming and demanding, and thus they were costly to obtain. But they were easily transported and served

below

below
Albarello, Spain, Manises, ca. 1430
The medieval pharmacopeia had evolved little since the antiquity. Physicians offered nostrums that had learned names but doubtful effects. Potters received princely orders for pharmacy jars and vases to store drugs and herbal medicine. An albarello was for dry preparations, and spouted vessels were used for liquids. The albarello, whose form originated in Persia, was a jar without handles, its neck and foot being slightly narrower than the body, which was often gently waisted.

above left, and right
The Story of Scipio: Battle of Zama and Reception of the Carthaginian Ambassadors, tapestry, Gobelins, 1688-1690
This tapestry, woven in the Gobelins factory, was copied from one created in Brussels some fifty years earlier for Francis I. A series of ten tapestries based on cartoons by the Italian painter Giulio Romano (1499-1549), they depict the feats of Scipio Africanus. Each of the tapestries illustrates an episode from the Punic War, culminating in Scipio's victory over Hannibal at Zama.

French tapestries was woven, the *Revelation of Saint John*, based on a cartoon, or preliminary sketch by Hennequin of Bruges – and Arras in Flanders were the leading centers. A tapestry is also known as an Arras (its old English name) or a Gobelins, from their places of manufacture. The Italian

to decorate and warm the walls of castles, churches, and even the tents of military leaders. In the 15th century commissions from the dukes of Burgundy and the kings of England helped Arras displace Paris, which was perpetually under siege in the Hundred Years' War. In addition to traditional narrative themes (religious sub-

center left and above
The Hunts of Maximilian, tapestry, Brussels, 1528-1533
This detail is from the scenes of March and April

MAJOLICA

Majolica, the old Italian term for all tin-glazed earthenware, was originally used in the 14th and 15th centuries for Hispano-Moresque lusterware (pottery having a metallic sheen) that was shipped to Italy from Spain and North Africa by way of Majorca in the Balearic islands. Since the 13th century, Islamic potters in Spain had so refined their ceramic techniques that their work was on a par with that of the gold-smiths, and their works were eagerly sought after.

Italy began by copying Islamic pottery ware, but by 1400 Italian workshops had created their own style. Florence, Caffagiolo, and Pisa developed a type of ceramics that soon reflected the first gleams of the Renaissance. So marked was Italian domination that an Italian pottery center, Faenza, gave its name to the French word for pottery: *faïence*.

below right
Ceremonial Basin, Italy, ca. 1425-1450
The lion, symbol of strength, bears the coat of arms of Florence.

jects, heraldic allegories, and *mille-fleur* motifs), new themes appeared – scenes from everyday life, hunting scenes, and love scenes – and were given richer colors than in the previous century. Flemish tapestry workshops began producing verdure tapestries, with leafy plants, richly scrolled foliage, or wooded landscapes. In the early 16th century, Brussels became the leading center of especially sumptuous tapestries woven with gold and silver thread. The weavers worked from cartoons by great Flemish painters such as Bernard

Van Orley (1488-1541), who inspired the famous *Hunts of Maximilian.* So great was the prestige of this work that Pope Leo X and all the princes of Europe commissioned tapestries based on cartoons by such Italian masters as Raphael. France, its workshops benefiting greatly from royal protection, struggled to compete with its Flemish rivals. Francis I created the royal workshop at Fontainebleau, and Henry II created the Paris factory. But on the European scale,

Brussels and Antwerp maintained their supremacy.

Only in the 17th century did French tapestry assume a major role. Henry IV lured two Flemish tapestry makers to Paris – Marc de Coomans and François de la Planche – setting them up in the Gobelins factory in 1607. Sixty years later the king's minister Jean-Baptiste Colbert officially founded the royal tapestry workshop there. Working on a vast scale, the Gobelins weavers reproduced old cartoons, such as those for the series known as the *Story of Scipio,* or created new series based on cartoons by Charles Le Brun. They were a source of inspiration for German, Italian, and Spanish factories. Elsewhere in France, factories at Aubusson and Beauvais produced both verdure and grotesque tapestries, the latter from drawings by the architect and ornamental designer Jean Bérain. In the 18th century, the art of tapestry-making evolved toward a graceful imitation of painting – and in consequence sacrificed its traditional character.

FROM MULBERRY TO SILK

Tapestries and carpets are well represented at the Louvre, but the art of fabric is displayed mainly in the form of furniture, hangings and curtains, and clothing. Examples range from Marshal Effiat's canopied bed to the cloaks of officers of the Order of the Holy Spirit, which are more than twelve feet long. Until the 16th century Italy, and particularly Florence and Venice, produced the finest European silks and velvets. But during the reign of

Francis I, the silk industry developed rapidly in Lyon, and France began to take the lead. Under Henry IV, the agronomist Olivier de Serres and Barthélemy de Laffemas developed mulberry tree cultivation and bred silkworms in the south of France in order to produce their own silk. In 1605 Claude Dangon of Lyon invented a loom for weaving large-scale patterns in varied hues, and fear of Italian competition came to at an end.

BRONZES

After a long eclipse, bronze was rediscovered during the Middle Ages, particularly in Italy, where Lorenzo Ghiberti and Andrea Pisano became famous for their high-relief medallions on the bronze doors of the baptistery in Florence. The art of bronze enjoyed less prestige in France during the same period, but it had gained in esteem by the 13th century, when

great recumbent statues of the bishops of Amiens were created. During the Renaissance, largely due to the passion for antiquity, bronze became more popular and its uses more diversified. No longer reserved for monumental statuary, it was used for statuettes and other small objects, such as candlesticks, small boxes, and hand bells. Venice

and Padua led in production. In Padua, Bartolomeo Bellano trained the greatest Italian bronze worker of the Renaissance, Andrea Briosco, known as Riccio (1470-1532). (The Louvre has devoted an entire room to displaying Riccio's work, including such masterpieces as *Arion*, *Shepherd with Pipes of Pan*, and bas-reliefs from the Della Torre tomb in Verona.) At the same time, another art form – the medal – was becoming more popular, largely under the influence of Antonio Pisanello (1395-1455). Another great bronze worker was Jean Boulogne, known as Giambologna (1529-1608), a sculptor born in Flanders and active primarily in Florence. He is also well represented at the Louvre, where a rotunda is named after him.

PEWTER

In the 16th century France competed with Germany and northern Europe for supremacy in pewter-making. The use of this alloy, although considered less noble than bronze and less precious than silver, was widespread. Highly malleable, it was used from the Middle Ages onward for civil and religious objects: jugs, pitchers, goblets, saltcellars, sacred vases, chalices, and baptismal fonts. A more elaborate, purely decorative variety, "display pewter," was developed in the 16th century, first in France, then in Germany. Pewter was cast in clay, brass, or stone molds; the decoration was then etched in or carved intaglio with a chisel. The Louvre houses a few masterpieces in pewter, notably the work of François Briot, a 17th-century French Mannerist metalworker. His crowning work is known as the Temperantia Dish.

RENAISSANCE EARTHENWARE

below, center
Display Plates, Italy
left: *One of Deruta's specialties was* belle donne, *which adorns this striking plate, intended for display on an opulent dresser.*

right: *Majolica from Casteldurante was reputed for its original decorative designs, notably those in the* cerquate *style – adorned with oak leaves – or a* trofei *(hung with trophies), as in this example.*

center: *Made in Urbino around 1530 after an engraving by Barthel Beham, this plate is typical of the so-called* istoriati *style.*

THE DEPARTMENT OF DECORATIVE ARTS

Man has known how to shape and fire clay since prehistoric times. When they are coated with impermeable enamel or an other kind of glaze, clay forms are known as ceramic. In the 16th century Italy led Europe in ceramic production. As early as the second half of the 15th century, the Tuscan city of Faenza – which gave its name to the French word for majolica, *faïence* – was thronged with potters' workshops, the most famous being the Casa Pirota. Ceramicists turned for inspiration to themes that were popular in painting, decorating their pieces with masks and fantastic or grotesque beasts. Other factories included those of Caffagiolo, where the Medici were active patrons of the arts; Urbino, which surpassed Faenza at the end of the century;

Casteldurante, where artists found inspiration in Raphael's paintings; and Deruta, in Umbria, famous for the quality of its blues, which imitated Chinese porcelain. Majolica soon spread to France, where glazed terracotta also reached its apogee. Bernard Palissy (ca. 1510-1590), most famous of French potters, drew inspiration from nature. In Nevers, however, the Italian influence remained powerful: there the dukes of the Gonzaga family (originally from Mantua) welcomed artists such as Domenico Conrade and Giulio Gambini. Italian influence was strong in Rouen as well, home of the great French potter Albaquesne (1526-1559). He specialized in floor tiles decorated with heraldic designs, allegorical figures, and grotesques.

above left
The Abduction of Helen, plate, Urbino, ca. 1530
Paris's abduction of Helen, wife of Menelaus, is one of the crucial episodes of the Iliad. Created after an engraving by Barthel Beham, this plate too is characteristic of istoriati *majolica.*

center left
Abimelech Spying on Isaac and Rebecca, plate, Urbino, ca. 1525
This plate from the service of Isabella d'Este, duchess of Urbino, was commissioned from the duchy's most talented painter, Nicola da Urbino.

above
Plate, Manises, ca. 1450
I(esu) H(omine) S(alvator), "Jesus Savior of Men," is inscribed on this majolica piece, used for liturgical purposes.

right
Erotic Scene, plate, Deruta, early 16th century

FRENCH MAJOLICA IN THE 17TH AND 18TH CENTURIES

Although glazed earthenware remained the rule in popular art until the 18th century, majolica had been more important in the design of tableware and refined objects since the 17th century. The most prolific centers of production were the workshops of Nevers, which kept the Renaissance style alive until the 17th century. At that time Nevers adopted the "Oriental" manner of Rouen, which reached its apogee in the following century, and of Moustiers, which borrowed themes from the decorator Jean Bérain. Toward the middle of the 18th century, Rococo came into its own. Marseilles launched into maritime designs, while Strasbourg strewed its artifacts with roses and peonies. In Paris the Pont-aux-Choux factory produced a delicate white china inspired by goldsmiths' work. But at the end of the century, French pottery was displaced by English and German production.

Toward the middle of the 15th century, painted enamels on copper came very much into vogue in France and later in Italy, where they supplanted champlevé enamels. Until the 16th century Limoges would remain the capital of painted enamels. The technique involves applying a coat of black enamel to a metal surface; this background is then covered with several opaque white layers. The craftsman draws an outline with a nib or point and applies colors in powder form, then uses a brush to spread more white layers onto the lighter areas. The piece is then glazed.

Decorative plaques often drew their themes from the Bible, as well as from illuminated books of hours and pagan themes from antiquity, restored to honor by the Renaissance. Rigorous draftsman-

ship, rich colors, and the use of both chiaroscuro and grisaille marked the work of the artists of Limoges.

By the first decades of the 16th century, these artists were signing their works. Most of them came from families that had long specialized in this art, such as the Pénicauds and the Limosins. The painter and enamelist Léonard Limosin, who worked for Francis I, created the famous *Portrait of Anne de Montmorency, Constable of France*, dated 1556, exhibited today at the Louvre. He also executed portraits of Francis I, Henry II, and Francis of Lorraine. Painted enamels declined in the 17th and 18th centuries, being used only for items such as snuff boxes, watch cases, frames, and miniature portraits.

THE ART OF LÉONARD LIMOSIN

Léonard Limosin (ca. 1505-1576) began as an enamelist for Jean de Langeac, bishop of Limoges. The best and most original of the Limoges enamel painters, he presented himself at the court of Francis I, who put him in charge of the royal enamel workshops at Limoges. He was influenced by the Fontainebleau School of painting, particularly by Primaticcio (his mentor), Il Rosso, and Nicolo dell'Abate.

He was a keen observer of Dürer's work, however, particularly the German master's engravings. A renowned portraitist, he was also a prolific creator of decorative panels, in which he focused on movement rather than volume. As head of a major enamel workshop, he collaborated with his two sons, as well as with Pierre Pénicaud and Jean Miette, an enamelist and painter.

STAINED GLASS

below and right center below
Medallion of Anne de Montmorency, Constable of France, stained glass, Château d'Ecouen, 16th century
Silver yellow and grisaille are applied lavishly to the laurel wreaths demarcating the Montmorency monogram. The proud display of arms and heraldry vaunts the power of this illustrious family.

bottom left
The Windfall, stained-glass fragment, early 16th century
The 16th century favored allegorical and edifying themes. Here a downpour of gold and precious stones streams from heaven into a bag held by a richly dressed man.

bottom center
Stained-glass fragment, early 16th century

Stained glass is inextricably associated with Romanesque and Gothic art, yet as technique it is older than both. It appeared in the Middle East as early as the 8th century and in the West during the Carolingian period (751-987). The 11th-century invention of the lead framework allowed for a greater variety of motifs, designs, and sizes than the old wooden frame. In the Romanesque period, colorless panes were often used to allow the maximum amount of light into the dark buildings. The designs, derived primarily from manuscript illuminations, were somewhat simple. During the Gothic period, however, church windows were taller and broader. They now illuminated not only the building but the faithful as well. Ornamental compositions gave way to representations of figures, not only religious but secular and pagan figures as well. Designs grew more complex and delicate; colors acquired density.

In the 15th century, when the Gothic style entered its Flamboyant phase, naturalism far overshadowed symbolism. At the same time, a new technique – the abrasion of sheets of flashed glass – permitted attractive gradations of color. In the 16th century transparent enamel pigments, which could be painted directly on to regularly shaped sheets of clear glass, freed the glass-stainer from the task of cutting colored glass pieces and fitting them into the lead frameworks. Stained glass had detached itself from its architectural support to become an art in its own right.

above left
Saint George, stained-glass fragment, 16th century
Conceived as a single piece, this fragment is painted with yellow and grisaille.

bottom right
Romulus, Numa Pompilius, stained-glass medaillon, *Romulus and Remus, according to the legend, were both raised by a she-wolf. Romulus, after killing his brother, went on to become the legendary first king of Rome. Numa Pompilius, Rome's second legendary king, was said to be the personification of its civil and religious legislation.*

right
Justice, stained glass, late 16th or early 17th centuries
This allegorical figure echoes themes innovated by the Fontainebleau School during the second half of the 16th century. The purity of the glass and the high quality of the enamels reveal an art at its apogee. Its most magnificent creations adorned royal and aristocratic chapels everywhere.

FROM GLASS TO STAINED GLASS

On the banks of the river Belus, it is said, Phoenician traders lit a huge fire, wedging it between boulders of saltpeter, to ward off the night cold. As the fire burned, the saltpeter fused with the silica of the sand and the ashes, and glass was born. But according to another legand, it was Tubalcain, the famous metallurgist, who was responsible for the invention of glass. Whatever its origins, glass was in use in antiquity, and there are very early traces of it in Gaul. By the 5th century, according to the historian Fortunatus, windows were fitted with glass panels that intensified light. By the 7th century, France led other European countries in applying the technique to its shrines. Once glass was mounted in window frames, the way lay open to an architectural art par excellence – stained glass.

FURNITURE AND ART DECO

above right
View of the Salle
Lebaudy

preceding double page
Martial Scene,
stained-glass
fragment,
early 16th century
Martial scenes, unless
based on biblical lore,
reflect the sovereign
order that regulated a
society still strongly
rooted in medieval
practices.

below
Shield of Charles
IX, chased iron
inlaid with gold and
enamel, 16th
century

In the center of the
shield, Marius brings
off a brilliant victory
over Jugurtha. A
gorgon's mask
dominates the scene,
while four chained
warriors attest to the
victory. Around the
rim, the letter K for
Karolus alternates
with oval medallions
to form a chain.
Battlefield trophies
and symbols of power
all celebrate the valor
of a king who
nevertheless was
unable to assume
power.

"Furniture" originally designated not only wooden furnishings, such as chests, tables, armoires, and chairs, but also the fabrics and embroidery that decorated them – carpets, hangings, and tapestries. In the early centuries of the French court, these items were stored in the Garde-Meuble de la Couronne and were constantly shuttled from royal castle to royal castle. Later, a distinction was made between furniture, primarily wooden, that was made by joiners and cabinetmakers; and furniture that was upholstered and decorated with fabric, which fell into the domain of the upholsterer. French furniture (the lion's share of the Louvre's furniture collection) can be broken down into specific stylistic periods, for which there is not always an equivalent in other European countries.

In the Middle Ages (during the Romanesque and Gothic periods) there was little variety in furniture. The chest was a standard piece, serving both as storage space and as a seat. Equally familiar were tables – usually large boards supported by trestles. Beds were high and hung with canopies. At the end of the Gothic period, the dresser and cabinet made their appearance in noble and royal reception rooms; their decoration drew on architectural designs. By the 15th century techniques and tools had evolved to such an extent that furniture boasted sculpted decoration and marquetry.

The Renaissance saw new types of furniture appear with decorative motifs drawn from antiquity: for example, large tables and chairs were inspired by the heavy curule seats used by Roman magistrates. Later the Louis XIII style borrowed geometrical forms and motifs from Italy and Holland. The Louis XIV style was characterized by great opulence, tempered by classical restraint. Forms were heavy, colors tended to be somber, and the Baroque influence was discreet and muted. Some of the furniture from Versailles

right
Aspasia, appliqué
bronze decoration,
armoire attributed to
André-Charles
Boulle, 1710
Aspasia, the friend
of Socrates, Pericles,
and Alcibiades, was
also a lover of all
thinngs beautiful.
Here she is shown
discussing architecture
with Socrates, who
occupies the other leaf
of the armoire door.

center left
Detail,
Bird Cabinet,
Germany, painted
ebony and ivory,
17th century,

below
The Abduction of
Helen, detail on
ceremonial buckler,
painted canvas on
wood, northern Italy,
16th century, circle
of Jules Romain

ARMOR AND WEAPONRY

For many centuries, weapons and armor were also works of art: artists like Dürer, Holbein, Jules Romain, and the painters of the Fontainebleau School were eager to leave their mark on the field. Since the Middle Ages certain cities had specialized in this type of production. In Italy, Milan was reputed to turn out armor and weapons of a quality surpassed only by the highly stylized armor produced in Germany. But with the spread of firearms in the 15th century and the increasing sophistication of gun-lock design, Italy and Germany yielded their place to the gunsmiths of France. There, in Paris and Saint-Étienne, the armorers' art attained its highest levels in the 18th century and during the Napoleonic era. The armor and weapons displayed in the Louvre are mostly ceremonial articles of royal origin, fully deserving their place in the pantheon of the decorative arts.

French furniture design now reveled in an

below

Armchair, château of Effiat, wood, velvet, and embroidered silk, mid-17th century

below

Armchair, Turkish cabinet of the Count of Artois au Temple, Georges Jacob, Paris, ca. 1777

above

Armchair, Saint-Cloud

This armchair was created for Marie-Antoinette for her château at Saint-Cloud.

THE DEPARTMENT OF DECORATIVE ARTS

meet growing military expenditures, it was melted down and was replaced by furniture – particularly two new forms, armchairs and console tables – of carved and gilded wood. The cabinetmaker André-Charles Boulle specialized in exotic woods and in metal-inlaid tortoiseshell. Louis XIV decoration was rigidly symmetrical, including wreaths, shells, and radiant suns. A transitional style, known as Régence, marked the passage to the new style that emerged under Louis XV. Inspired by such decorators as Antoine Le Pautre and Gilles Marie Oppenordt, the nimble and kinetic volumes of the Rococo style displaced the symmetry favored under Louis XIV. This trend was consolidated during Louis XV's reign, a time when France became the arbiter of fashion, design, and cabinetmaking techniques. In addition to inlay work in precious woods, cabinetmakers adopted varnished decors that imitated Chinese lacquer; they used brass or bronze for door handles and keyholes, as well as decorative patterns and designs.

unparalleled variety of forms, their elegance based on balance and harmony; the whole of Europe hastened to emulate it. A growing taste for comfort and social intimacy encouraged cabinetmakers and carpenters to experiment with newer models, on a smaller scale than previously, while the expanding maritime trade made possible a wider range of woods. These new designs, conceived in the first half of the 18th century, included the wing chair, the *marquise*, the *duchesse*, the *ponteuse*, and the ottoman.

Long after it was supplanted in Paris by the Neoclassical manner, the Louis XIV style remained firmly in vogue in the French provinces. Between 1760 and 1775, a transitional style emerged, reconciling elements of the Louis XV style with the straight lines brought into fashion by

above center

The Bird Cabinet

At the end of the 17th century, German artisans created sumptuous cabinets embossed with ivory on the exterior and very luxurious interiors.

below

Table de Toilette, after the drawings of the painter Nicolas Henri Jacob

This toilette,

entirely made of crystal, glass and bronze, belonged to the duchess of Berry.

below center

Cabinet with Clock, attributed to André-Charles Boulle, ca. 1710

THE "BOULLE" STYLE

In early 17th-century France, inlay work was used mainly in ebony cabinets. Concealed behind their dark exteriors were inner spaces that featured rare woods and precious materials in dazzling display. Ironically, the tribulations of the royal exchequer (which dictated the melting-down of solid silver furniture) gave inlaid furniture its finest hour. André-Charles Boulle (1642-1732) created an inimitable style inspired by the

sketches of ornamentalists – craftsmen who specialized in painting stucco and plaster work. Inlay work made it possible to produce magnificent furniture at low cost. The grace of line and the somewhat ostentatious wealth of contrasts between the precious woods and the metal inlays (pewter, brass, and gilt-bronze reliefs) masked the relatively low cost of materials resorted to for the sake of royal belt-tightening!

Neoclassicism. In the fourth quarter of the century, Neoclassicism consolidated its position, which endured until the fall of Napoleon's Empire in 1815. The Louis XVI, Directoire, and Empire styles were all expressions of Neoclassicism. More lavishly decorated, favoring the use of painted or gilded wood, wreaths, rosettes, and medallions, the Louis XVI style was eventually dethroned by the austerity (borrowed from ancient Rome) of the Directoire style and its successor, Empire. The latter was marked by the systematic use of mahogany (already in wide use by English cabinetmakers), set off by bronze. Its decorative arsenal included sphinxes, lions' mouths and paws, eagles, bees, acanthus leaves, and the Napoleonic monogram.

Created by Gabriel Lemonnier, these jeweled artifacts revealed the splendor of the French Empire to a dazzled world when they were put on display at Paris's Universal Exposition of 1855. Every component contributes to their magnificence: diamonds, emeralds, the eagles supporting the cross-surmounted globe, and above all the virtuosity of an art that raised high the reputation of France's jewelers.

below right
Settee, from the Count of Artois's Turkish Cabinet, second quarter of 19th century
Designed for the future King Charles X, this piece of furniture (its lines then resolutely modern) had no other purpose than to induce dreams of an imagined "Orient."

L'ORFÈVRERIE ET LES JOYAUX DU LOUVRE

Every king has accumulated treasures, with the jewel-studded work of goldsmiths constituting the pride of his collections. Whether emblems of power or items of ceremonial dress, the oldest of them are on display throughout the Department of Decorative Arts. But the Galerie d'Apollon, its magnificent decorative motifs conceived by Le Vau and Le Brun and given added luster by Delacroix's *Triumph of Apollo*, provides the most fascinating setting for such treasures. On display there are the objects most highly treasured by France's sovereigns – such as the Crown Diamonds, including the Sancy and the Régent. Acquired in 1717, the Régent diamond is considered the world's most beautiful by reason both of its purity and its perfect symmetry. Also displayed in the Galerie d'Apollon are Louis XV's crown and the diadem of Empress Eugénie, last sovereign of France.

After the fall of the empire came the Charles X style, marked less by the Neoclassical forms it inherited than by its use of light-colored citrus woods and dark-hued inlay work. The Louis-Philippe style, also inherited from Empire, dispensed with heroic allusions and rigid lines, preferring instead curved forms and middle-class comfort. With the accession of Napoleon III, French furniture design fell into a decline: craftsmanship retreated before the advance of machine-worked products, and creative invention gave way to pastiche and the juxtaposition of past styles, from Gothic through Renaissance all the way to Louis XV.

below
Separable *Duchesse*, Delannois, gilded beechwood, around 1760 to 1765
Divinely comfortable, this duchesse chaise

longue is made for a tête-à-tête.

above
Wing Chair "A la Reine," stamp of Jean Nicolas Blanchard, after 1771
A triumph of the Louis XV spirit, this bergère wing chair glorifies the pleasures of salon life.

The Department of Graphic Arts

*Whereas painting is a deliberate art,
the fruit of patience and of painfully
mastered technique, drawing is
a fugitive form, a mere roughing-out of
the work to come. It thus conveys
a sense of immediacy and can reveal
an artist's personality better than
the finished work. But drawings,
hastily committed to paper, are fragile.
This is why the Cabinet
of Drawings (it has retained its
pre-Revolutionary name) is one of the
Louvre's least known departments.
With some 120,000 works representing
all schools and nearly every period of
art history, the Department of Graphic
Arts, split between the second floor
of the Richelieu Wing and the Cour
Carrée and the first floor of the Denon
Wing, exhibits its treasures only on a
temporary basis. Prior authorization
is required for admittance
to the Consultation Room,
located in the former guest apartments
of Napoleon III. But the
Chalcography Rooms, where
the engraved plates are kept, are open
to the general public.*

previous double page

The Apotheosis
of Hercules, Charles
Le Brun, ca. 1650
*On his return from
Rome, Le Brun was
commissioned to
decorate President
Lambert de Thorigny's
town house on the Ile
Saint-Louis. In this
drawing, Hercules is
borne aloft from the
Elysian Fields on a
chariot pulled by four
fiery horses. This
preliminary study was
executed in black stone,
ink, brown wash, and
red chalk, with white
highlights.*

center

Crossing the
Rubicon, Jean
Fouquet, ca. 1480
*This illumination is
from a lost
manuscript entitled*
Histoire ancienne
jusqu'à César et
faits des Romains
*(Ancient History
Until Caesar and
Deeds of the
Romans), of which
four illuminated pages
belong to the Cabinet
of Drawings.
Considered one of the
leading illuminators
of his time, Fouquet
distanced himself from
the International
Gothic tradition to
express an uncon-
ventional vision of
nature and man,
foreshadowing the
classicism of the
Renaissance.*

BUILDING THE DEPARTMENT
OF GRAPHIC ARTS

When Louis XIV acquired the collection of the influential German banker Everard Jabach in 1671, he brought six thousand drawings into the Louvre and created a special section, the Cabinet of Drawings, to preserve them. At the death a short while later of Charles Le Brun, first painter to the king, the collection was enhanced with drawings from the artist's studio. The same thing happened with the death of two other court painters, Pierre Mignard and Antoine Coypel. Although the 18th-century cabinet failed to obtain the fabled collection of Pierre Crozat, powerful financier and treasurer of France, it did acquire the connoisseur Pierre-Jean Mariette's collection, adding a further thirteen hundred prints "of the finest quality."

Such were the beginnings of the Louvre's Department of Graphic Arts, successor to Louis XIV's Cabinet of Drawings. Because of their fragility, these works are not on permanent display, although temporary exhibits give some idea of the extraordinary wealth of the department's inventory.

Both Jabach and Mariette are archetypes of the kind of passionate collector whose acquisitions were the starting point for most of the Louvre's departments. Born into a wealthy Cologne family and raised among works of art, Everard Jabach (1618-1695) came to Paris to become director of the French East India Company. He was wealthy enough to acquire "masterpieces by the lot" from royal collections (those of Charles I of England and the duke of Mantua), and he owned examples from every school.

top left

Narbonne Altar
Frontal, Parisian
Workshop,
ca. 1375
*A major work in the
development of French
drawing, this grisaille
in black ink on white
silk, found in
Narbonne at the
beginning of the 19th
century, once adorned
a chapel altar during
Lent. It depicts the
Crucifixion and scenes
from the Passion of
Christ. King Charles V
and Queen Jeanne of
Bourbon are shown at
prayer. The elegance
and clarity of the
composition suggest
that the artist might
well have worked on
the illumination of the
Très Belles Heures
de Notre-Dame,
commissioned by the
duke of Berry.*

A SHORT HISTORY OF PAPER

A Chinese invention imported to Europe by the Arabs, paper is made from cellulose fibers found in plants. In Europe, with the expansion of linseed and hemp cultivation, cloth rags were used to make paper. Shredded, they were mixed with water, forming a liquid pulp that was then dried and pressed into a form. By the end of the Middle Ages paper had replaced parchment. In time, wood fibers replaced rags, machines replaced vats, and continuous rolls replaced single-sheet forms. The first papers were smoothed with a mixture of bone powder and glue spread on with a brush. From 1400, the treatment of the paper pulp made this undercoat unnecessary, and papermakers learned to dye the pulp, especially in blue. Such paper, known as "Venetian," was in demand for drawings with white highlights. At the end of the 18th century, artists selected paper according to the demands of their drawing technique: vellum for watercolor, slightly rough paper for pastel. In the 19th century, Ingres created a paper for line drawing and pastel: "Ingres paper" is still used today.

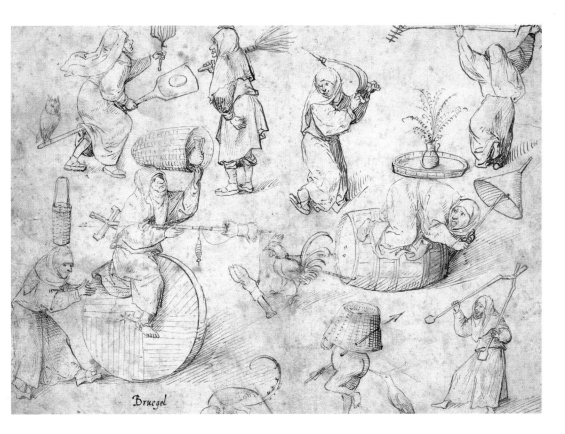

Pierre-Jean Mariette (1694~1774) was less flamboyant. Born into a family of booksellers and printers in Paris, in 1717 he went to Vienna to catalog Prince Eugene of Savoy's collections of drawings and prints. He continued his training in Italy, moving among scholars and collectors. Back in Paris, he was a regular visitor to the home of Pierre Crozat, where he mingled with lovers of art and with painters like Watteau. He soon became a full-fledged collector himself: giving up his job as a dealer, he devoted himself wholeheartedly to maintaining and enlarging his own collection. The first pieces he acquired were drawings from the Crozat collection, which contained sketches collected by the art historian Giorgio Vasari, Queen Christina of Sweden, and Jabach. One thousand of these drawings are now in the Louvre. They represent all the great masters, in particular Italian artists of the 16th and 17th centuries.

The other major 18th-cen-

tury collector was the powerful financier Pierre Crozat (1661~1740). His purchasing agents scoured Europe for works of art. In Urbino, for example, Crozat acquired many of Raphael's drawings. The paintings from the Crozat collection were sold to Catherine the Great of Russia via the writer Denis Diderot, and they form the core of the Hermitage's holdings.

Of the three men, Mariette is perhaps the most memorable: drawings were his chief love, and he collected nothing else. A true scholar, he stands apart from figures like Jabach and Crozat, who were above all men of wealth and power.

After these important acquisitions, the original Cabinet of Drawings was gradually enhanced with prints from the French and Northern schools. During the Revolution, the cabinet was integrated into the Central Museum of Arts. The collection doubled in size following the confiscation of émigré

fenedier klawsen

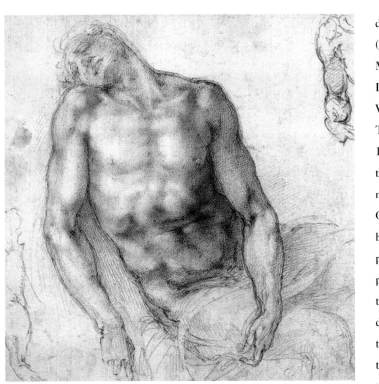

Dead Figure of Christ, Michelangelo
Michelangelo executed this study of a man's torso, along with two right arms, while he was working on the ceiling of the Sistine Chapel. Done in black stone, it reflects the artist's mastery of human anatomy and his sureness of touch.

facing page
View of the Val d'Arco, Albrecht Dürer, 1495
Executed on Dürer's return to Germany, after his first visit to Venice in 1495, this watercolor with additional touches in brush and India ink represents the Tyrolean village of Arco. The bold light effects reflect the influence upon Dürer of Italian masters.

property and Church holdings. When the Napoleonic Empire brought the Revolution to an end, the Central Museum was renamed the Musée Napoleon and given a flying start by its new director, Baron Vivant Denon. The most spectacular acquisition of this period came in 1806 with the collection of the historian Filippo Baldinucci, which contains Florentine school drawings from the 14th to the end of the 17th century. The museum also acquired some forty drawings by Jean-Baptiste Isabey and 838 drawings by the sculptor Edme Bouchardon.

Under the Second Empire (1852-1870), the acquisition of the Vallardi portfolio in 1856 brought some of Pisanello's most beautiful drawings to the Louvre. Leonardo's drawing of Isabella d'Este reached the museum in 1860. Donations and bequests from artists and their families, as well as state acquisitions, continued to swell the collection until the end of the century. The most important donors over the years have included Horace His de La Salle (1851 and 1878), Jacques Édouard Gatteaux (1881), Étienne Moreau Nélaton (1907 and 1927), Gustave Caillebotte, Count Isaac de Camondo, Baron Edmond

bottom right
Portrait of a Young Woman, Hans Holbein, 1522
Executed with a metal point and enhanced with red chalk and with white, this drawing belonged to the collection of the banker Everard Jabach before it was acquired by Louis XIV's Cabinet of Drawings. Renowned for his portraits, Holbein also painted many religious works. This portrait is a preliminary study for a head of the Virgin in the Retable at Gerst, Germany.

de Rothschild (1936), and Mr. and Mrs. David David-Weill (1947). Today, with 120,000 works, the Department of Graphic Arts boasts a comprehensive panorama of the art of drawing from the 15th to the 19th centuries.

Drawing reached its golden age during the 16th century in Italy. Patrons like the Gonzagas, the Viscontis, the Estes, and the Montefeltris found themselves vying for fame with artists, who were at last shedding their craftsman status to step forth as independent creators. It was the intellectual stature of painters such as Leonardo, Raphael, and Michelangelo that changed the artist's image and convinced contemporaries that a painting's conception, being an operation of the mind, was more important than its execution. This idea was upheld and disseminated by a student and friend of Michelangelo, the Florentine Giorgio Vasari (1512-1574). Director for fine arts of the Grand Duchy of Tuscany, Vasari was an architect, painter, writer, and collector and a pioneer. He left us the world's first history of art, his famed *Lives of the Artists*, published in Rome in 1550. Vasari is also behind the founding of one of the first collections of drawings,

above
Drapery for a Seated Figure, Leonardo
Leonardo was a student of the sculptor Andrea del Verrocchio when he did this gray wash drawing with white highlights, executed on canvas with a brush. The study would later serve as inspiration for his Virgin of the Annunciation, now in the Uffizi Gallery in Florence.

le 2 avril Biaz a envoyé nous demander une
feuille de papier pour donner la réponse de
l'empereur.

5 avril.
vers une heure.

Portes de Méquinez. la ville travaillé beaucoup.
grandes arcades contre le mur à gauche entr'ouvertes
portes.

La même porte en se
retournant sur la grande
place

porte garni de tôle.

top left
The Last
Sacrament,
Nicolas Poussin
*Poussin's name is tied
to the 17th-century
debate that pitted
advocates of the
primacy of line
(Poussin's camp)
against the champions
of the superiority of
color, led by Rubens.
Perfectly balanced,
theatrically staged,
this drawing in pen
and brown wash
unites all the virtues
of classicism, of which
Poussin was a leading
exponent.*

previous double page
Moroccan
Sketchbook
EugèneDelacroix,
*Delacroix, first of the
Orientalist painters,
reached Morocco in
1832 as part of King
Louis-Philippe's
diplomatic mission to
the sultan. Over the
course of six months he
filled several
sketchbooks and
notebooks, of which
three are now in the
Louvre. These sketches,
in lead point and
brown ink, often
enhanced with
watercolor, vibrate
with the painter's avid
curiosity about the
landscapes and
Muslim customs of
North Africa.*

Florence's Uffizi Gallery (where he was the first to classify paintings by period), and the creation of a drawing academy. He saw drawing as the "central principle" of art, a notion that went unchallenged in the education of artists of the time. Many theories on drawing cropped up in Renaissance Italy. They pitted advocates of "line" against those of "color," a debate that would consume generations of artists. In the 17th century, followers of Poussin argued that drawing was the "masculine principle" of art, while those of Rubens claimed that color was primordial. In the 19th century came the line-color duel between Ingres and Delacroix.

As a clue to the artist's personality, drawing gradually gained recognition as art in its own right, to such a degree that sketches were sometimes preferred to the painting itself. Because many drawings are unsigned, a whole body of expert scholarship emerged that focused closely on problems of attributing a work to one artist or another. "Scientific attribution" involves conducting a veritable police-style investigation of significant details that are likely to identify a drawing's creator. "Instinctive attribution," on the other hand, relies on intimate knowledge of an artist and his work.

Another clue to attribution lies in the fact that drawings from large collections are identified by a mark stamped on the reverse side. Drawings can also be displayed in a distinctive montage, like those of Everard Jabach; glued to a "heavy white paper with a gilt border," like Vasari's; or surrounded by a pen or wash-drawn frame, adorned with a scroll and bearing an attribution. Mariette presented his

center left
Man in Turban,
Rembrandt
*From his youth,
Rembrandt was
attracted to portraits.
Among his numerous
studies of heads, this
one stands out for its
subject's exotic
nature – although the
model's turban might
merely have been a
prop – and the
spontaneity and
precision of the
drawing.*

bottom right
Naiads and Triton,
François Boucher.
*At the peak of his
career, around 1753,
Boucher executed this
study (red chalk, black
stone, and white
highlights on brown
paper) for the Gobelins
manufactory.
A brilliant example of
his talent for drawing
naked figures –
in unimpeachably
Rococo vein.*

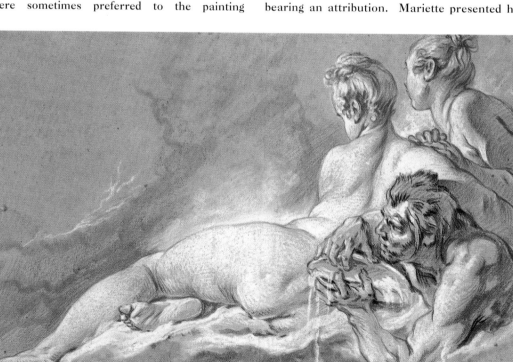

To Every Medium, A Pencil or Brush

The type of pencil or brush used in drawing produces a variety of textures and effects, allowing us to classify them by genre.

Pencils come in different grades, running from hard (lead, silver, graphite) to soft (charcoal, black stone, red chalk). Lead points were the most common, because of the ease of erasing. The graphite point appeared later, in 1660, and was the forerunner of the drawing pencil. It was easy to use but fragile: not until the 16th century did artists learn to seal it with a fixative. Black stone leaves a matte trace, in contrast to the shinier effects of pencil. It was used especially for drawings of nudes and portraits. Since the Renaissance, artists have favored red chalk for portraits and landscapes.

The brush, used since prehistoric times, led to the use of watercolors, which enjoyed their peak in the 19th century.

Often the most telling clue in identifying a work's creator is the technique employed.

Here the study of materials used in drawing (paper, brushes, pens, inks, different grades of pencils) is most instructive. Each century had its favorite technique: metal points in the 15th century, black stone in the 16th, brown wash in the 17th, red chalk in the 18th, watercolor in the 19th. This diversity is reflected in the Graphic Arts Department's superb catalog: from Mantegna to Millet, Rubens to Corot, Dürer to Fuseli, Poussin to Delacroix, and Leonardo to Ingres, it musters all the great names in the history of art.

drawings on blue paper with a gilded border and thin white line, with his initial in a circle. All the major museums stamp their drawings. Following the original initials of the court painters Antoine Coypel and Robert de Cotte, the Louvre has attributed the following stamps since 1789: "MN" (Musée National), "RF" (République Française, for the First, Second, and Third Republics), "N," in an oval surmounted by a crown (Napoleon I, used again for Napoleon III), and for the contemporary period, "ML" (Musée du Louvre) in an oval.

The Department of Egyptian Antiquities

On May 15, 1826, Charles X signed the decree creating a department of Egyptian monuments in the Louvre and appointing the pioneering Egyptologist Jean-François Champollion as its curator. Champollion had to start from scratch: The museum had no Egyptian collection worth mentioning, merely a few objects acquired under the ancien régime, plus some twenty-five hundred pieces from the Durand collection, acquired in 1824. Champollion also had to create a suitable exhibition space. Four rooms on the upper floor of the south wing of the Cour Carrée had been selected, but Champollion felt the proposed decor was ridiculous. He wanted "neither marbles nor embellishments in the Roman or Greek style," preferring instead a style that echoed Egyptian art. His wishes were only partially respected: Egyptian references were restricted to details in the painted decor. Although three of the ceilings had Egyptian themes, the Egypt they portrayed was a civilization seen through European eyes. Their titles spoke for themselves: Egypt Saved by Moses; The Egyptian Expedition Under the Orders of Napoleon; The Study and Spirit of the Arts Revealing Egypt to Greece.

THE DEPARTMENT OF EGYPTIAN ANTIQUITIES

Champollion was responsible for purchasing the Egyptian department's first two major collections: those of consuls Henry Salt and Bernardino Drovetti. But in the absence of a consistent acquisitions policy, the department grew without excessive concern for ethics or methodology. Questionable pratices ended in 1858 when Auguste Mariette was appointed director of antiquities projects in Egypt. Mariette instituted a "division of finds" procedure, whereby the fruits of an excavation were

shared by Egypt and the country sponsoring the dig. This policy continued until Tutankhamen's tomb was discovered in 1922.

Since then (with the exception of occasional gifts, such as the colossal statue of Amenhotep IV that was given to the Louvre by the Egyptian state in thanks for French help in rescuing the Temple of Abu Simbel), the Egyptian government has kept strict control over treasures unearthed from its soil. Yet the Louvre's Egyptian department has continued to grow, especially from the recent transfer of the Egyptian collection from the Bibliothèque Nationale, followed by that of the Musée Guimet and donations from private individuals. As a result of the remodeling undertaken during the Grand Louvre project, visitors can now view four thousand Egyptian objects, arranged in an area of some four thousand square yards that covers both floors of the Pavillon Sully. The Coptic collection will be exhibited in new rooms created around the Cour Visconti.

THE MASTABA OF AKHETHOTEP

This mastaba, or tomb, has been one of the treasures of the collection since 1902. Like many Egyptian works now in European museums, it was acquired, with Egyptian permission, in a desperate attempt to preserve it from the unchecked looting in that country. The chapel-like tomb arrived in pieces packed in fifty crates and was for years shrouded in mystery: the museum archives had no information even on the mastaba's original location in Saqqara. In 1991 an archaeological mission from the Louvre set out to search for the site. After six years of work, the results have exceeded all hopes – most of the complex has now been freed from the sand, along with important ruins. As a result, archaeologists have been able to reconstruct the original shape of the mastaba, which was much more complex than the small section now in the Louvre.

THE EGYPTIAN CAMPAIGN

From a military standpoint Napoleon's Egyptian campaign was a failure, but it generated enormous enthusiasm throughout Europe for the civilization of the pharaohs. It was also the

first step toward the creation (some fifty years later) of the Louvre's Egyptian collection.

The expedition, prepared in great secrecy, charged Napoleon with several missions. Officially he was to establish a semblance of order in a country teetering on anarchy – but his real purpose was to shift the war with England away from Europe and into the Mediterranean. Moreover, France's ruling Directory was relieved to be sending away a general considered "excessively ambitious."

Napoleon landed unchallenged at Alexandria, and on July 20, 1798, his army met and defeated the Mamluks, the military elite then ruling Egypt, in the Battle of the Pyramids. The French victory opened the way to Cairo – and to a brief respite from Bedouin harassment of French troops in the Egyptian countryside.

But Napoleon's tranquillity ended in August when the British destroyed the French fleet at the Battle of the Nile. In an uprising in Cairo in October, three hundred French soldiers were killed in the name of holy war. Napoleon then moved his theater of operations to Syria – where combat casualties and an outbreak of plague decimated his army. On August 23, 1799, to the outraged astonishment of his soldiers, Napoleon returned to France. The Egyptian dream, which for many had turned into nightmare, ended on August 31, 1801, with the expedition's surrender to the British.

THE EGYPTIAN ENIGMA

During the Greek and Roman occupation of Egypt, the hieroglyphic inscriptions engraved in the temples (the most recent of them dating to A.D. 394) were understood only by a handful of Egyptian priests. During the Greek era, many texts were written about the ancient Egyptian language, while its religion spread throughout the Mediterranean region. Later, under Roman rule, many Egyptian monuments were taken to Rome to further the glory of its emperors. Once the native Egyptian priesthood disappeared, the key to the ancient Egyptian language was lost, and the civilization of the pharaohs locked its secrets away. But if the language was forgotten, the ancient civilization itself was not: during the Middle Ages, Egypt lay on a major route to the holy land, and later it became a source of wealth for traders. An exotic land, it remains eternally alluring to travelers seeking to pierce its secrets.

THE DESCRIPTION OF EGYPT

right
Scholars of the Egyptian Commission, preliminary drawing for *Description of Egypt*
Often the butt of soldiers' humor, the scholars compensated for their lack of material resources with their enormous enthusiasm for the country they were discovering.

left
Allegorical Composition with Vivant Denon, drawing, Benjamin Zix, 1811
In 1802 Denon was appointed director general of museums. He reorganized the Louvre (renamed the Musée Napoléon) and accompanied the imperial armies throughout Europe to personally select artworks from defeated enemies. This painting shows Denon at the height of his glory, sitting in his office, which is packed with Egyptian, Greek, and Roman antiquities, some of them imaginary.

Work on a monumental compendium called *Description of Egypt* began in 1809, while Napoleon's empire was still intact, and was completed in 1822, under the reign of Louis XVIII; the topographical map was finished under Charles X in 1828. These seventeen volumes (eight volumes of text, nine of illustrated plates) were the final fruit of the scientific studies undertaken during Napoleon's Egyptian campaign. The book represented a decisive first step in the development of Egyptology. Fifty-one scholars were recruited by the mathematician Gaspard Monge and the chemist Claude-Louis Berthollet to form the Commission of the Sciences and the Arts and accompany the expedition. Their task was to study all aspects of the country their army was preparing to conquer, with special emphasis on ancient ruins, physical environment, customs, and institutions.

On August 22, 1798, the Institute of Egypt was born in Cairo with Monge as president and Napoleon himself as vice-president. Scholars and intellectuals scoured the countryside, visiting half-buried temples and nego-

tiating furiously with soldiers to gain more time to explore the ruins. All too soon, however, came the forced departure of the French. Although they abandoned to the English the bulk of the treasures they had amassed, including the Rosetta Stone (only the naturalists managed to preserve their collections), they nonetheless brought back precious documentation – books and drawings of monuments surveyed, essays read at meetings of the institute, and personal journals written during their travels and explorations. All these went into the laborious compilation of the *Description of Egypt*.

below
Profile of the Sphinx, Vivant Denon
Denon had only two hours to visit the pyramids – which explains this very inaccurate image of the sphinx. The headdress and angle of the neck do not correspond to those of the actual sphinx, which has the body of a lion and the head of King Chephren.

center left
Engraving with watercolor highlights, Pierre-Joseph Redouté
Nicolas-Jacques Conté was entrusted with supervising the engravings for the Description of Egypt. *He developed a device to reproduce the original shades of the watercolors executed in situ by the expedition's painters.*

VIVANT DENON

Dominique-Vivant Denon, elevated to the rank of baron during the empire, is a perfect example of the enlightened 18th-century man. He was eclectic and ambitious; although he lived in troubled times and sometimes came dangerously close to compromising himself, he carved out an exemplary career. He began as a diplomat, first in Russia and then in Naples, where he was already an enthusiastic "hunter of antiquities." He owed his participation in the Egyptian expedition to the empress Josephine, who interceded with her husband after he judged Denon (who was fifty-one) "too old" to take part. He was among the handful of men whom Napoleon picked to return to France with him, and in 1802 he published his *Voyage to Lower and Upper Egypt*. This impressionistic travel journal, illustrated with engravings made from drawings "executed for the most part with a pad on the knees or even on horseback," was immensely successful.

THE TIME OF THE CONSULS

below

Bernardino Drovetti
A former officer from the Piedmont region of Italy, Drovetti earned distinction in the French army during its Italian campaign. Like the British consul Henry Salt, he gained the trust of Mohammed Ali, who issued them with firmans *(decrees) allowing them access to excavation sites.*

During the first few decades of the 19th century, Egypt was a magnet for "Oriental" enthusiasts, thanks to the success of Denon's *Voyage to Upper and Lower Egypt* and the subsequent *Description of Egypt*. Torn as it was by civil war between the Mamluks and its new pasha, Mohammed Ali, however, Egypt was not a particularly safe travel destination. Nevertheless, it drew a large number of treasure hunters, like Giovanni Battista Belzoni, who had worked for Henry Salt, British consul in Egypt since 1815, and then for Bernardino Drovetti, French consul after 1802. Belzoni was locked in a relentless struggle with Jean-Jacques Riffaud, an explorer from Marseilles, over the richest finds and the first rights to promising sites. Accounts of these wars are legendary: Belzoni once stole a small obelisk that Drovetti had unearthed at Philae, fanning an already inflamed situation. Belzoni even claimed that he had been fired at. Nevertheless, Egyptian archaeology owes a great debt to Belzoni and Riffaud. Belzoni was the first European to enter the Temple of Abu Simbel. He also discovered the entrance to Chephren's pyramid at Giza (known as "the second pyramid"). His name is forever linked to the Valley of the Kings, where he discovered three unknown pharaonic tombs, including that of Seti I. Riffaud's exploits may have been less spectacular, yet he can be credited for many of the works in the Egyptian departments of both the Louvre and the Turin museum, including some of the most famous in their collections.

right center

Facade, Great Temple at Abu Simbel, David Roberts
When Belzoni first reached Abu Simbel on September 9, 1816, three quarters of the entrance to Ramses II's great temple was buried in the sand. Lack of time forced him to abandon excavation before he reached the gate. He was unable to enter the monument until his second trip in 1817.

left

Mohammed Ali, August Couder, 19th century
In an effort to repulse Napoleon's forces, the Ottoman sultan, overlord of Egypt, appointed Mohammed Ali first pasha and then viceroy of Egypt. Of Albanian origin, Mohammed Ali used harsh measures to achieve a gradual consolidation of his powers: he executed English prisoners, displaying their heads on pikes in the streets of Cairo. In 1811 he invited the last Mamluk leaders to a reconciliation ceremony – where he had them slaughtered at point-blank range.

THE DROVETTI COLLECTION

European consuls active in Egypt amassed archaeological finds, then auctioned them off to the museum that offered the highest bid. Louis XVIII refused Bernardino Drovetti's first offering of 1,273 items, whereupon they entered the Turin museum in 1824. In 1825, when the king named Drovetti an officer of the Legion of Honor, the consul decided that all new acquisitions should go to France, his adopted country. With the support of Champollion, who was impressed by the Turin collection, Drovetti sent a giraffe to Charles X; it was received in triumph in Paris in July 1827. On December 15 of that year, the Charles X Museum was inaugurated with the collection acquired from the British consul Salt and some forty pieces of jewelry donated by Mohammed Ali. The second Drovetti collection, of 1,970 pieces held in storage at Marseilles, was then purchased for 200,000 francs and sent to Paris in February 1829.

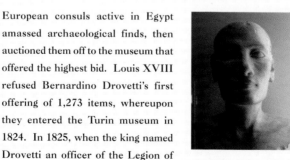

right

Great Hypostyle Hall, Amon-Ra Temple, Karnak, David Roberts
In 1817 the temple at Karnak looked like a mound of ruins buried in the sand. When Jean-Jacques Riffaud excavated outside the great hypostyle hall, seen here, he unearthed two previously unsuspected sanctuaries.

On August 18, 1828, Jean-François Champollion finally set foot on Egyptian territory. Along with Ippolito Rosellini, a professor of Middle Eastern languages from Pisa, he was joint director of the first scientific expedition sent to the Nile valley, a project jointly financed by France and the grand duchy of Tuscany. The era of archaeologist-consuls and wildcat digs was over: Mohammed Ali, influenced by Champollion's brother Jacques-Joseph, had placed "antique hunting" under official supervision.

In 1826 Champollion had been appointed curator of the Egyptian Gallery in the Charles X Museum. He had studied Europe's major Egyptian collections, including the first Drovetti collection in Turin and the Salt collection, also in Italy.

Champollion had been planning this trip for many years, and despite his poor health and the intense heat, he spared no effort to make it a success. Dressed Turkish style, he insisted on seeing everything personally. Less interested in excavations, he concentrated on making drawings and epigraphic surveys of monuments. He prided himself on being more meticulous than his archrival Jomard (director of the *Description of Egypt* publishing project), whom he accused of "neglecting to study the originals."

Champollion returned to France with a collection of two hundred objects for the Louvre, along with "four hundred and fifteen drawings, many of them colored on site," and Mohammed Ali's promise to give one of the two Luxor obelisks to France.

DECIPHERING THE HIEROGLYPHS

Champollion's (1790-1832) passion for ancient Egypt began in very early childhood, first at Figeac, then at Grenoble, where François Fourier, prefect of the Isère *département*, regaled him with stories of Napoleon's Egyptian campaign. Champollion spent his adolescence studying Eastern languages, perfecting his knowledge in Paris. He learned Coptic, the last incarnation (in a Greek alphabet) of the ancient Egyptian language. Using the wealth of documentation at his disposal, he learned to read the hieroglyphs of the names of Greek and Roman sovereigns who ruled over Egypt. On September 14, 1822, he deciphered the names of Ramses and Thutmose, thereby proving that the system he had evolved was not limited to Greco-Roman names. Barely had he announced the news of this deciphering than he collapsed from exhaustion. He then wrote his *Lettre à Monsieur Dacier* (the permanent secretary of the Académie des Inscriptions et Belles-Lettres), requesting him to transmit his discovery to the Collège de France.

CREATION OF THE DEPARTMENT OF EGYPTIAN ANTIQUITIES

Before he left for Egypt in 1828, Champollion wrote a long letter to Mohammed Ali, in which he warned about damage to Egypt's monuments and the need to "protect them against the assaults of ignorance and blind greed." But it was not until 1858 that significant controls were established, thanks to Auguste Mariette, appointed director of antiquities projects in Egypt. The task facing this former professor from the Collège de Boulogne-sur-Mer – who had become famous in 1851 for his discovery of the Serapeum at Memphis – was immense. He had enormous energy: he set up the first Department of Egyptian Antiquities, excavated sites as far south as the Sudan, and was merciless in his treatment of pillagers.

At Thebes he recovered some jewels belonging to a queen of the 17th Dynasty, which the regional governor had distributed to the women of his harem. He then placed them in the museum he had just created at Bulaq. He used every means at his disposal to serve the cause of Egyptian antiquities; he even wrote the outline for the libretto for Giuseppe Verdi's *Aïda* and actually helped direct the opera.

By 1952, the Department of Egyptian Antiquities was run by the Egyptian government, and in 1980 it was renamed the Organization of Egyptian Antiquities. As for Mariette, he was buried in the garden of the Egyptian Museum in Cairo, in an Egyptian-style marble tomb.

THE HIDING PLACE OF DEIR EL-BAHARI

In 1875 the sale by Theban dealers of fragments of funerary papyruses to tourists came to the attention of Gaston Maspero, newly appointed director of the Antiquities Department, who suspected that the residents were selling off the contents of a tomb. On July 5, 1881, after a three-month investigation, the culprits revealed the source of their pilfering: a hiding place dug into the side of a cliff at Deir el-Bahari.

Here 21st Dynasty priests had hidden sarcophagi containing the mummies of New Kingdom kings and queens to protect them from pillaging – practice already widespread in pharaonic times. It took three hundred workers six days to carry away the treasure. In Cairo the customs department scribe could not find the appropriate heading to enter the mummies on his books: he therefore applied the tax imposed on dried fish!

A Way of Life

Archaeologists who reached Egypt after the era of the consuls and the major expeditions were responsible for creating Egyptian collections in major museums. Without these museums, knowledge of the civilization of the pharaohs would have remained limited to a handful of connoisseurs. The visitor strolling through the Egyptian rooms in the Louvre is inevitably struck by the abundance of mortuary remains, our main source of information for understanding the customs and lifestyles of the ancient inhabitants of the Nile valley.

Egyptians took great care in preparing their tombs, and their obsession with conserving the body and earthly goods expressed a deep anxiety toward death and a passionate love of life. The scenes decorating the chapels of tombs therefore depict worldly pleasures and offer the deceased "all the amenities to be found throughout the country." Peasants and craftsmen worked to provide the owner of a tomb with an eternal source of food and material comforts. Not even the land was forgotten: tomb walls show scenes of hunters and dogs tracking game; on a river and in marshes, the deceased stands on his bark with his wife and children, waiting for birds to take flight from a papyrus thicket. Even more than a reminder of earthly distractions, these paintings glorified the deceased dignitary's importance by portraying him as eternally victorious over nature's wild forces.

above
Scribe's Writing Materials
This writing set includes a roll of papyrus, a papyrus cutter, a hollow palette with two recesses for red and black ink, and a wooden tablet. Wood was also used as a medium for writing.

right center
Illustration from the Book of the Dead, detail, painting on papyrus from Hornejiteph and Pui, late Ptolemaic – early Roman period
Called The Book of the Dead *by Egyptologists, such illustrated papyrus strips were either placed in a sarcophagus or rolled in strips around the mummy. Through the magic of image and word, they allowed the deceased to leave his tomb and enjoy earthly activities.*

below center
Model Boat, Middle Kingdom, ca. 2033-1786 B.C.

left
Ointment Spoon, painted wood, 18th Dynasty
Such spoons, probably used more for religious than for aesthetic or cosmetic purposes, extolled the charms of the naked female figure and reflected the symbolic values associated with aquatic flora and fauna.

right
The Agricultural Cycle, painting on dried mud, New Kingdom, Salt Collection
Wensu, a clerk-accountant in the state granaries, had the cycle of the seasons depicted in his tomb: tilling and seeding; the harvest; and bulls threshing the garnered grain.

The Nile

A "gift of the river" is how Herodotus described Egypt, which owes its entire civilization to the Nile. The river provided abundant water and was an unrivaled transportation channel; even gods and the deceased were said to travel by river craft. The Nile's annual flooding – personified in images as a spirit named Hapi, with blue flesh, a round belly, and drooping breasts – ensured the country's continued prosperity. Yet the river could be capricious: the flooding was sometimes too violent, destroying their efforts; or else drought could reduce the flow to a trickle, resulting (as in the pharaoh's dream) in years of famine. Unpredictable periods of famine were accompanied by a host of related disasters. Yet when Hapi returned, the Nile once again "filled the granaries, enlarged the warehouses, and gave goods to the unfortunate."

left

*Book of the Dead
Belonging to
Khonsumes,
papyrus, detail,
New Kingdom
During the New
Kingdom a collection
of formulae known as
the "Book of the
Dead" was placed in
the sarcophagus of the
deceased. It was
believed that with the
help of this "passport"
he would not long
remain in the
underground world
where he was buried.*

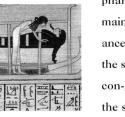

Before Champollion, knowledge of the ancient Egyptian religion was based on the often erroneous accounts of Greek historians. Once the hieroglyphs were deciphered, scholars could finally understand the meaning of the myths and reconstruct the sequence and meaning of ancient Egypt's elaborate rituals.

Egyptian mythology was based on a cyclical notion of time: the daily cycle of the sun, the annual cycle of the floods, and the cycle of generations in death and rebirth. It told of the geological formation of the Nile delta and how land was formed as the flood waters receded. This knowledge had inspired Egyptian creation myths: from the midst of primordial chaos, ruled by shadows and water, had emerged a hillock on which the god who created the universe first set foot. This order was constantly threatened by negative forces. The gods and their representative on earth, the pharaoh, waged a ceaseless battle to maintain the original harmony and balance, a battle reflected in many myths: the struggle of Horus, the dynastic falcon-god, against Seth, incarnation of the savage violence of the desert; and the wars waged by the pharaohs against the enemies of Egypt. In the chapels of dignitaries' tombs, scenes extolling the pleasures of life were not chance decorative sequences: the hereafter was populated by evil beings who had to be vanquished before the deceased could enjoy the abundance of eternal life.

*above
Anonymous Priest,
shea wood, Late
Period
In the name of the
pharaoh, priests were
responsible for
providing material
offerings to the divine
statues in the temples
to maintain their
sacred energies.*

*above left
Nebqed Papyrus,
New Kingdom
Egyptian funerals were
complex ceremonies
lasting seventy days.
First, in the
embalmers' quarters,
the body was
eviscerated, covered
with salt, and packed
with various
preservative materials.
It was then wrapped
in strips of linen. Just
before the sarcophagus
was closed, the ritual
known as the Opening
of the Mouth was
performed to revitalize
the senses.*

*center left
Head of the God
Amon, diorite,
New Kingdom*

*below
Coffins of
Tamutnefret, Singer
of Amon, painted
wood, New Kingdom*

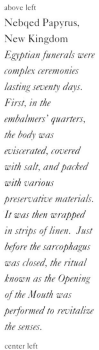

THE MYTH OF OSIRIS

Egyptian sources offer no coherent account of Osiris's adventures; the god is known to us today through a text by Plutarch, written in the 2nd century A.D. Killed by his brother (and enemy) Seth, Osiris was resurrected by the goddesses Isis and Nephtys, who were transformed into sparrows and beat their wings to give him the breath of returning life. Horus, born from the posthumous union of Osiris and Isis, succeeded his father – but only after a violent struggle with Seth, who contested his sovereignty. This myth served a dual function: it underscored the value of mortuary rituals (since everyone could hope to share Osiris's resurrection), and it legitimized the transmission of royal power from father to son.

The Egyptian rooms in the Louvre contain artworks from a civilization that appeared more than five thousand years ago. With the exception of the final period – the Coptic era – all the objects share a figurative language that followed immutable rules. The consistency was necessary: if the artwork failed to follow the rules, it lost its power to re-create life. This deeply conservative outlook was inherent in ancient Egyptian thinking. The art of the Nile val-

FROM THE PREDYNASTIC ERA TO THE MIDDLE KINGDOM

primarily from the cemeteries they left behind. Before 3500 B.C. artistic and religious objects were largely made of stone, including vases, cosmetics palettes, and weapons (maces and knives); terra-cotta pottery was also fashioned by hand. By the second half of the third millennium B.C., the first signs of a social hierarchy appear, with statuettes of bearded men – undoubtedly portraits of leaders of competing communities. The development of relief

above, and center left, below
Female Figures,
Naqada III,
crocodile bone
*Most early human
statuettes made by the
Egyptians were small
and of clay. Some,
however, were of ivory
or – as with these
figurines – of bone.
They are crudely
sculpted: the arms and
legs are barely roughed
out, and the sexual
characteristics are
exaggerated. In one
case the breasts are not
well defined, while in
both figures the hips
are wide. Still
unresolved is whether
the inscriptions on the
bodies represent
tattoos.*

center left
Head of King
Djedefre, quartzite,
Old Kingdom
*This head of Djedefre
is covered by the linen
nemes headdress and
bears a uraeus, or
cobra – a protective
goddess – on the
forehead. The king's
expression is one of
absolute sovereignty.
Discovered at the
mortuary complex of
Abu Roash, this head
probably belonged to a
sphinx, a hybrid
creature with the body
of a lion and head of a
man, meant to
symbolize the
pharaoh's
overwhelming power.*

ley was by no means static: the lessons of history, as well as contacts with the outside world, triggered changes of style and permanently enriched Egyptian culture's religious-artistic repertory.

The periods preceding the unification of Egypt under the sole authority of the pharaoh – the beginning of Egypt's dynastic history – are known

sculpture on stone and ivory, as well as painted ceramics, helps us understand the world of these predynastic Egyptians and retrace the steps that led to the institution of the monarchy.

The Thinite period was the great era of unbaked brick architecture, while the first great stone monuments,

below left
Knife from Gebel
el-Arak, Naqada II,
hippopotamus tusk
and flint
*The task of chipping
away the narrow
parallel flakes on a
knife blade was
extremely time
consuming,
but it is
character-
istic of
objects from
the predynastic
era. The relief
sculpted on both sides of
the ivory handle testifies
to the violence that
reigned among the
communities then living
along the Nile valley.*

essentially tombs, date to the Old Kingdom. During the 3rd Dynasty (ca. 2700-2620 B.C.) the architect Imhotep designed an enormous complex extending over thirty-eight acres for the pharaoh Djoser. It included the king's tomb, above which rose a step pyramid and several related buildings. With a few rare exceptions, the smooth-sided pyramid remained the characteristic form of royal tombs through to the end of the Middle Kingdom, around 1603 B.C.

Dignitaries of the Old Kingdom, such as Akhethotep, constructed mastabas as funerary monuments. Other striking examples of stone architecture may be found both on the Giza plateau and in regional burial places. The men who commissioned these tombs – all elite members of the pharaoh's entourage – adorned the walls of their chapels with a wide variety of figurative scenes. These scenes provided a catalog of earthly activities that – through the magic power of the image – they could contemplate forever. Royal and private statues were intended to last for eternity,

freezing the image of the sovereign and his servants in perpetual youth. In this way, all the conditions necessary for an ideal afterlife were achieved.

After the troubled times of the First Intermediate Period, which ended around 1938 B.C., a new culture evolved, adopting and modifying earlier models. Middle Kingdom pharaohs, who restored the monarchy, claimed to descend from their illustrious predecessors. They even went so far as to imitate the layouts of earlier mortuary complexes. Learning from past mistakes, these kings erected statues of themselves throughout the land to demonstrate their authority. The iconographic types by which they represented themselves reflected their administrative policy, as in the many images of Sesostris III. Since almost all the workshops (apart from a handful in the Old Kingdom) were established in the vicinity of the capital, production sites multiplied, resulting in a much wider variety of styles and themes.

After the expulsion of the Hyksos – minor Asian kings who held the Egyptian throne from 1650 to 1550 B.C. – the Theban prince Ahmose founded the New Kingdom, an era of stability and prosperity. The pharaohs of the 18th and 19th Dynasties carried out an aggressive foreign policy, and their victories brought a flood of booty and tributes that enriched the court and the temples, particularly that of Amon-Ra at Karnak. The monumental proportions of these edifices, and the wealth of their decor, reflect a society sure of its own values.

With the exception of Amenhotep IV and his successor, the rulers of the New Kingdom abandoned pyramidal forms for their tombs. Instead, they dug immense hypogea (subterranean burial places) in the Valley of the Kings. The pharaoh's remains were placed in these enclosed spaces, which were decorated with countless images depicting hybrid creatures and a fantastic universe. From here they were meant to travel through the darkness of the night, then be reborn like the sun. Only the scenes that show the king being welcomed by the deities of the pantheon offer a peaceful vision of the afterlife. But in the chapels of the tombs of dignitaries, the artists deployed all their imaginative powers to re-create sumptuous earthly pleasures and the beauty of nature.

Until the reign of Amenhotep III (ca. 1403-1365), sovereigns and their subjects were often portrayed in a mannered, sophisticated style. Amenhotep IV (who became Akhenaton and reigned from 1379-1362 B.C.) broke with what he considered excessively conventional standards of beauty and fostered a new aesthetic, based on a concern for authenticity. Later works dating from the Amarna era were more harmonious in form. But this episode was short-lived: Akhenaton was unable to impose his drastic religious reforms outside the capital, and after his death the old order was restored by Tutankhamen. Although some of the artistic works in following years still retained a vestige of concern for naturalism, most statuary of the era of Ramses consists of stereotypical, immutably serene portraits of notables, clothed in transparent, pleated garb.

below
Cosmetics Spoon, wood, 18th Dynasty
The figure of a non-Egyptian bent under a heavy burden is a common theme on cosmetics spoons.

center right below
Statuette of Queen Tiy, enameled schist, 18th Dynasty
Tiy (whose statue was originally accompanied by that of her husband, Amenhotep III) wears a tight-fitting dress decorated with vulture feathers. The bird's skin covers the heavy wig, from which rise two tall plumes, an emblem of New Kingdom queens.

THE DEPARTMENT OF EGYPTIAN ANTIQUITIES

left above
Kneeling Statue of Nakhthoreb, quartz, 26th Dynasty
The torso is naked, Old Kingdom style. an archaic manner to affirm his links to the past.

below
Funerary Mask of Khaemwaset, gold, 19th Dynasty
The son of Ramses II, Khaemwaset loved archaeology and undertook major restoration work in the Memphis region, particularly in the Serapeum, where he decided to have himself buried. Auguste Mariette discovered this mask on his mummy, in the chamber of a sacred bull.

right
Man's Head, Known as the "Salt Head," painted limestone, New Kingdom
This is one of 4,014 objects sold in 1824 by British consul Henry Salt to Charles X for the sum of 250,000 francs.

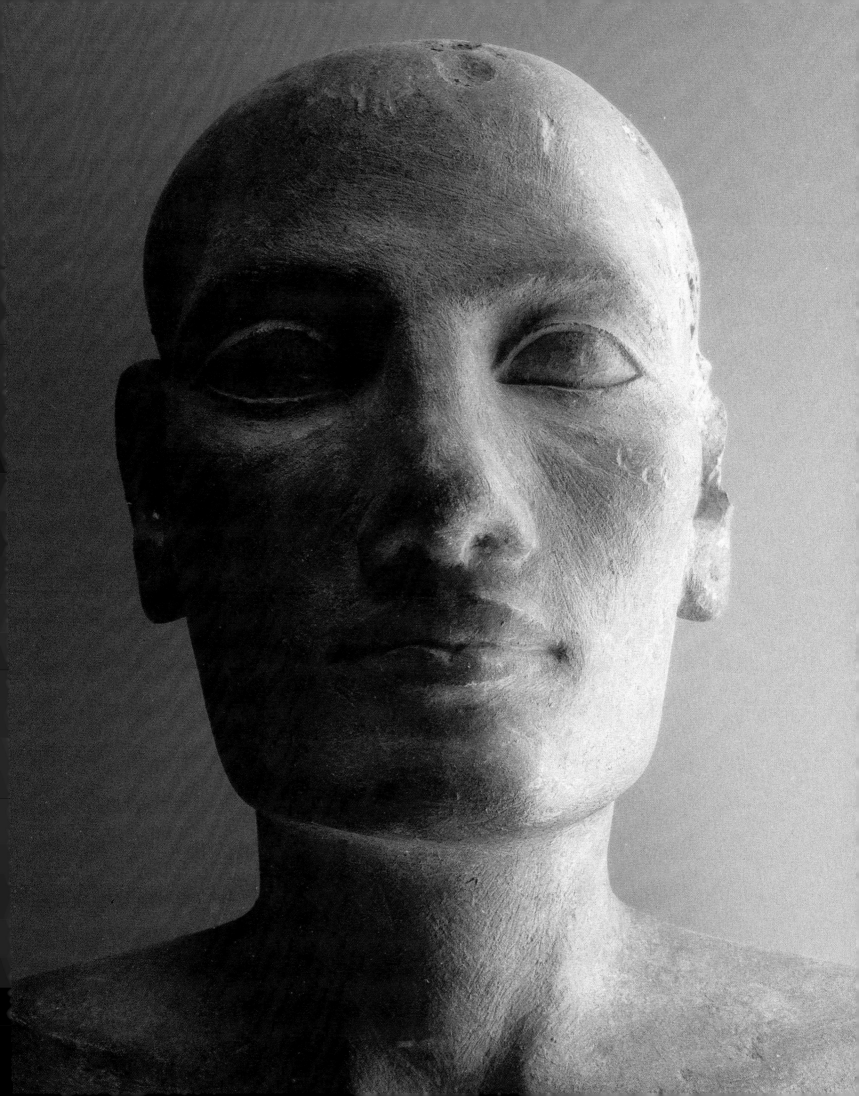

The best record we possess of the turmoil racking Egypt at the end of the New Kingdom is the microcosm of Deir el-Medina, a village of craftsmen employed on the construction site of the royal necropolis. These employees of the pharaoh, angered by the treasury's perpetual delays in paying them, went on a series of strikes. The less scrupulous among them participated in pillaging pharaonic tombs. On several occasions groups of villagers could escape attack by Libyans from the west only by taking refuge in nearby temples. In 950 B.C. Deir el-Medina seems to have vanished from the face of the earth. This incident occurred at a time of conflicting and competing powers. Egypt's legitimate 21st-Dynasty ruler resided at Tanis, in the delta, but his authority was contested by the great priests of Amon, who also claimed the title of pharaoh – whence the name of Third Intermediate Period (ca. 1080-664 B.C.) to describe the early years of the third millennium. Although weakened institutions and social misery are inimical to the arts, some workshops continued to produce high-quality objects, particularly in metal, including the treasures found in the untouched tombs of Tanis and the statue of Karomama in the Louvre, made of electrum, silver, and bronze inlaid with rose gold.

Starting with the 22nd Dynasty (945-889 B.C.), the rulers had foreign names, first Libyan, then (much later) Nubian. In the Late Period, which began with the 25th Dynasty (747-702 B.C.), Egypt enjoyed only fleeting moments of independent rule as the country was conquered and occupied by a succession of invaders: twice by Persia, then in 332 B.C. by Alexander the Great. Artifacts from these troubled centuries possess the sobriety of the earliest dynasties, in total opposition to the sophistication and luxury of the Middle Kingdom. Was this sobriety a reflection of the austerity of the times, or was it a determination to assert the ancient heritage of the pharaonic culture against the assaults of alien civilizations? The upheaval in Egyptian national consciousness is reflected in the appearance of a new kind of realism – one that carefully reproduced bone structure and skin texture and

created free-standing heads that exude a peculiar lassitude.

This tendency toward individualization continued during the Ptolemaic period (332-30 B.C.), when the country was ruled by descendants of Alexander's general Ptolemy (who had acquired Egypt when Alexander's empire was carved up). Two artistic styles coexisted in the Nile valley at this time: one (produced by the occupiers) was inspired by Greece; the other was wholly in the Egyptian tradition, producing works that filled the great numbers of native Egyptian temples built during those years. The priests, fully aware that they were the last guardians of the ancient religion, turned these temples into sanctuaries for knowledge that seemed doomed to disappear. A glut of pictures appeared on the temple walls, painted in a turgid style, with learned cap-

tions that disclosed the keys to rituals and beliefs that the Egyptian priesthood had hitherto hugged jealously to itself.

In 31 B.C., after Octavian defeated the fleet of Cleopatra VII and Anthony and became emperor under the name of Augustus, Egypt fell under Roman control. A few offspring of this cultural overlap emerged, such as the portraits at Faiyum. But the most important event at the beginning of this era was the spread of Christianity throughout the country by desert monks, particularly Saint Anthony of Egypt, Pachomius, and Macarius. The art of the Copts (a name given to Egyptian Christians by the Arabs who later invaded the country) drew more freely on Greco-Roman influences than on Egyptian ones. But it gradually modified the pagan theme by attaching Christian meanings to it.

**THE DEPARTMENT
OF EGYPTIAN
ANTIQUITIES**

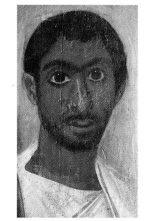

Department of Greek, Etruscan, and Roman Antiquities

It was in Greece that the Mouseion, the ritual site dedicated to the muses, originated. Richly decorated shrines arose in homage to the daughters of Mnemosyne and Zeus, as did establishments for worship and higher learning, such as the Mouseion of Alexandria.

Today the Louvre displays Greek, Etruscan, and Roman works from classical antiquity. These collections tell as much about the history of the three civilizations as about the discoveries by adventurers and scholars that led to their resurrection. Greek antiquities take us back through twenty-five centuries of remarkable discoveries to the sources of Western art. Next came the art forms of the Etruscans, a people whose origins are still partly veiled in mystery. And from the early Republic to the last days of the Empire – from paganism to Christianity – Rome contributed its diversity, wealth, and portraiture.

LANDMARKS IN ANTIQUITY

(ALL DATES B.C.)

EVENTS	CULTURAL DEVELOPMENTS
Bronze Age, 2900-1050	3000-2000 Cycladic art
2000-1400 Minoan civilization (Crete)	
2000-1600 Greeks reach mainland	
1900-1600 First Minoan palaces	
1650 Beginning of Mycenaean civilization	1650-1500 Mycenaean grave-circles
1600 Eruption of Thera (Santorin)	1600-1500 Large Minoan mural painting
1500-1450 Second Minoan palaces	
1400-1150 Mycenaean palaces	
1300-1260 Trojan War?	
1200-1050 End of Mycenaean civilization	
	1125 First use of iron
Dark Age, 1050-800	
	1050 Protogeometric ceramics
1000 Greeks in Asia Minor	
Archaic Period, 800-500	900 Geometric ceramics
800 The first cities	
776 First Olympic Games	
From 770 Greek colonization in Mediterranean, Black Sea	750 Homer, Hesiod
	650-600 First coins minted
	620 Black-figure ceramics
600 Founding of Marseilles	600 First *kouroi*
561-510 Tyranny in Athens	
	530 Red-figure ceramics
508 Cleisthenes in Athens, beginning of democracy	
Classical Period, 499-323	
499-480 Ionian Revolt: Greek-Persian Wars (Marathon, Thermopylae, Salamis)	472 *The Persians* by Aeschylus
477-432 Athenian supremacy, expansion	470-435 Phidias' creative period
	465 Temple of Zeus in Olympia
	447-438 Parthenon
451 Pericles supreme in Athens; dies of the plague in 429	442 Sophocles' *Antigone*
	431 Euripides' *Medea*
431-404 Peloponnesian War between Athens and Sparta	423 Aristophanes' *The Clouds*
406-367 Dionysius the Elder tyrant of Syracuse	
404-354 Sparta, Athens, and Thebes struggle for supremacy	399 Trial and death of Socrates
	370-340 Scopas and Praxiteles at their creative peak
	340-300 Creative period of Lysippus
359-336 Reign of Philip of Macedon	
338 Philip of Macedon subdues the Greek cities	
336-323 Alexander the Great reigns: conquest of Persian Empire	335 Aristotle founds the Lyceum
Hellenistic Period 323-330	310 Zeno founds the Stoic school in Athens
323-281 Alexander's successors: the Diadochi kingdoms	300 Epicurus founds his school in Athens
	300-290 Colossus of Rhodes
280-230 Supremacy of Ptolemies in Egypt	250-150 City of Pergamum
263-133 Kingdom of Pergamum	
230-188 Roman intervention in the East	200-197 *Nike of Samothrace*
212 Romans capture Syracuse	188-170 The Great Altar, Pergamum: *War of the Gods and Giants*
168 Battle of Pydna: the Romans in Greece	
146 Romans sack Corinth	
129 Creation of Roman province of Asia	
	88 *Venus de Milo*
64-63 Rome reorganizes the East	
31-30 Actium: Egypt becomes a Roman province	

THE MEDIEVAL REDISCOVERY OF GREECE

Few people in medieval Western Europe were interested in pagan antiquity. Not until the early 14th century, when universities began to teach the Greek language, and a flourishing trade in old manuscripts, medals, and small artifacts began, did Italians develop an interest in ancient Greece.

In the 15th century this interest intensified. Classical scholars exhumed ancient texts. Patrician families gained prestige by displaying collections of ancient works of art. Cyriacus of Ancona, one of the first antiquarian travelers to Greece, claimed that its "monuments and inscriptions were more faithful witnesses of Antiquity than texts by ancient authors." It was the birth of a brand-new movement – the rediscovery of the

past through the study of its material remains.

Over the next three centuries, every country, every royal court took part, with the English and French in the lead. Through their ambassadors, and the efforts of roving architects, painters, and scholars, they began to accumulate collections. Jacob Spon (1647-1685), who coined the term *archaeology*, returned from a journey to Greece with a report that would guide his successors until the 19th century.

The discovery of Herculaneum in 1709, followed by that of Pompeii, fueled enthusiasm for anything linked to antiquity. Then came the German scholar Johann Winckelmann, the founder of art history. By the end of the 18th century, Europe was living in antiquity.

ENGLISH ARCHITECTS

The English played a key role in promoting "the Greek manner." Early in the 17th century, Thomas Howard, earl of Arundel (1585-1646), amassed a superb collection of antiquities. In the following century, with the backing of the Society of Dilettanti (founded in 1732), the painter James Stuart and the architect Nicholas Revett studied the ruins of Athens. From 1751 to 1753 they established a detailed layout of the Acropolis and studied the ancient city's major buildings, including the Theseum, a temple dedicated to Hephaestus. (Its name is derived from its decorative friezes, which illustrate the adventures of Theseus, founder of Athens.) Back in England, they built a Doric temple resembling the Theseum. In 1769 the potter and artist Josiah Wedgwood founded workshops that produced imitations of the Greek vases discovered in Italy (and attributed at the time to the Etruscans).

I
n a torchlit ceremony on November 9, 1800, First Consul Napoleon Bonaparte and his wife, Josephine, inaugurated the new Museum of Antiques in the Louvre's Petite Galerie . In addition to works from the Royal Collections, the collections of émigrés, which had been nationalized during the Revolution, the museum displayed fabulous treasures that had recently been looted in Italy by soldiers of the victorious general-turned-first-consul. They included such extraordinary pieces as the *Laocoön* group and the *Apollo Belvedere*, taken from the Vatican; the *Dying Gaul* and the statues of the two sacred sister rivers, the Nile and the Tiber, removed from Rome's Capitol Museum; and four horses from St. Mark's in Venice. There

were also innumerable lesser works of art taken from the renowned collections of the Albani, the Braschi, and other prominent Italian families. The flag fluttering at the head of Bonaparte's procession carried a bold maxim: *"Greece let them go, Rome lost them at last, / Their fate changed twice and now will hold fast."* The prodigious spoils borne by the French victors would now be administered by the former curator of the Capitol Museum. The scholar Vivant Denon, a true Renaissance man, was appointed museum director, and in 1803 – before the French Empire was even proclaimed – the museum was rechristened the Napoleon Museum. Seat of the most prestigious museum in the world, Paris had become the new Athens.

THE ROYAL COLLECTIONS

The Caryatid and Lower Empire Rooms have housed Greek antiquities since the 16th-century reigns of Francis I and Henry IV. Most of the pieces, whether by donation or purchase, came from Italy. In addition to the Royal Collections, the Louvre has three large 17th-century private collections – those of Cardinals Richelieu and Mazarin and of the marquis de Nointel. The first two, assembled by two art lovers and high-placed civil servants, are relatively eclectic in nature. The third is something else again. De Nointel, Louis XIV's ambassador to Constantinople from 1670 to 1679, roamed the Aegean Sea and Greece gathering steles, bas-reliefs, and inscriptions. In 1722 his collection was turned over to the Académie des Inscriptions et Belles-Lettres, but during the post-Napoleonic Restoration it was returned to the Louvre.

---

below
Bronze nymph, 1st or 2nd century A.D. *Discovered in Belgian Gaul, this bronze statuette may be one of Niobe's children, fleeing the arrows of Artemis.*

center right
Salle des Antiques (Antiques Room) *High pedestals and alternating columns and statues create the sweeping perspective of the Antiques Room. At the far end is the* Laocoön *group. Formerly the Petite Galerie, one of Anne of Austria's summer apartments, the room was converted between 1798 and 1800 to house the former Royal Collections and the war booty brought back from Italy by General Bonaparte.*

GREEK, ETRUSCAN, AND ROMAN ANTIQUITIES

---

above left
Emperors' Room, drawing, 19th century *The Emperors' Room in the Museum of Antiques was depicted in an anonymous 19th-century drawing of the French school.*

right
Laocoön and His Sons, engraving, Marco Dente, 1527 *Discovered in Rome in 1506 and seized by French troops in 1797, the* Laocoön *group was the crown jewel of the museum in 1800. The marble statue, from which this engraving was made, is now once again back in the Vatican Museum. Dating from early in the 1st century, it depicts the punishment of a Trojan priest of Apollo who had profaned the god's temple.*

below left
Diana with Fawn, Roman copy of Leochares *The original of this statue, a bronze attributed to the 4th-century-B.C. Attic sculptor Leochares, was said to represent the goddess Diana and her brother Artemis. This 2nd-century Roman replica in marble is the centerpiece of the Antiques Room in the Louvre.*

With the fall of the Napoleonic empire, the museum lost part of its collections, despite the skillful resistance of its director, Vivant Denon. Yet the new rooms added to the Museum of Antiques died not go empty: they proved more than necessary, given the intense interest in antiquity and the museum's policy of regular acquisitions. Between 1808 and 1863, it purchased the Borghese collection, the finest pieces from the Albani collection, the Tochon collection, the collection of Chevalier Edme-Antoine Durand, and the Campana collection. Toward the end of the 19th century, the Rothschild family gave the Louvre marbles from Miletus and Didyma and the silver pieces from the Boscoreale treasure. Meantime, scholars and art historians like Visconti, Quatrèmer de Quincy, Haller von Hallerstein, Cockerell, Foster, Creuzer, and Müller were broadening the historical approach to ancient Greek art.

As far back as ancient times, Greek and Roman statues, paintings, sarcophagi, and vases had been migrating around all the civilized areas of the world. By the late 18th and early 19th centuries, this traffic had taken on alarming proportions, largely as a result of increased rivalry among European nations and the inauguration of new museums (like the British Museum, founded in 1759, and the Glyptothek in Bavaria, in 1830). Lord Elgin stripped the Parthenon of fifteen metopes, plaques from its frieze, and sculptures that had adorned its pediments. The frieze from the Temple of Bassae in Arcadia, discovered in 1811, traveled to Britain, while the statues from the Temple of Aegina ended up in Bavaria. The least concern of Greece's Ottoman rulers was to preserve a past that nourished rising national sentiment and the dreams of young Western Europeans.

LA VENUS DE MILO EST TRANSBORDÉE DU NAVIRE LE GALAXIDI A BORD DE LA GOËLETTE L'ESTAFETTE

vessel. The French quickly intervened, cut short the loading operation, bought the Venus, *and transferred her to the French schooner* Estafette.

left
Nasir ed-Din, engraving, 1873
Nasir ed-Din, shah of Persia from 1848 to 1896, began his reign determined to modernize his country. On his first voyage to Europe in 1873, he came to France and visited the Louvre. Here he views the Venus de Milo, *lit up by torches and portable lamps as she rises above a sea of helmets and cocked hats.*

far left
Apollo Sauroctonos, attributed to Praxiteles
The Athenian sculptor Praxiteles (active between 370 and 330), portrayed Apollo in powerful middle age. Apollo was usually presented as less muscular, more graceful and supple.

left
Aphrodite of Cnidos, Roman copy of Praxiteles
Exhibited around 340 B.C. in an open-air setting, the statue offered spectators a glimpse of the first great female nude in the history of Greek art.

above
House of Consul Fauvel, Louis Dupré
The painter Louis Fauvel, who settled in Athens in 1784, was named consul of France in 1803. A connoisseur of Greek antiquities, Dupré painted him among his treasures at his home in the center of the Agora. It would later become a museum.

VENUS DE MILO

Discovered in 1820 on the island of Melos (Milo), the figure was first misidentified as Aphrodite. It arrived in the Louvre in 1821 after a series of coincidences: it was found by a peasant and at the same moment by a young French navy recruit. In turn a naval sublieutenant informed the French ambassador in Istanbul of the find. The ambassador purchased it and gave it as a gift to King Louis XVIII, who donated it to the Louvre. The face and posture are typical of the Greek classical tradition, yet the realistic sense of movement is more characteristic of the period around 100 B.C. She was assembled from a number of fragments, and her missing arms have inspired a thousand speculations. The Bavarians discovered one of her feet; it is said to have been used as a model for a sculpture of dancer Lola Montez's foot!

On March 25, 1821, the orthodox archbishop of the Greek city of Patras raised his flag in revolt against Sultan Mahmud II. Greece burst into flames, and the islands rose in rebellion. A fleet was raised, Greek foot soldiers seized control of the Morea peninsula, and in January 1822 independence was proclaimed at Epidaurus. But the Turks went on the offensive and slaughtered the population of the island of Chios.

Aroused by philhellenist groups, public opinion all over Europe spurred governments to intervene. In 1830 the sultan was forced to recognize first Greece's autonomy, then its independence. But disturbances and then civil war followed. The solution devised by the Great Powers was to impose a king on the newly independent country – Otto of Bavaria, who ruled until 1862. During his reign archaeology developed into an organized activity. Laws were passed, a national museum was opened, and a Greek archaeological society was formed. Athens was the focal point of the king's concerns: he placed the Acropolis under the aegis of the Greek archaeological services, which partially restored its monuments. When it opened to the public in 1835, tourists as well as scholars gained access to it.

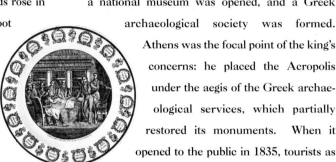

Once Greece was independent, rivalry arose among the Great Powers over the exploitation of its artistic treasures. In concert with the Greek government, they ratified the first convention on government – sponsored digs in 1875, dividing up the various excavation sites among them. As the scholars toiled, museums, including the Louvre, flourished.

left
Philhellenic
Committee
This porcelain dish depicts the French committee presided over by the poet Chateaubriand.

center left
King Otto Enters
Athens
The son of King Ludwig I of Bavaria, "lover of Greece and Lola Montez," had been designated king of the new state. He organized a governmental archaeological department and began restoration work on the Parthenon.

right
Crowned Male Head
This head, of unknown origin, dates back to the middle of the 1st century B.C. In the background is a statue of Melpomene, and behind her, Apollo Sauroctonos.

HEINRICH SCHLIEMANN

Heinrich Schliemann (1822-1890), the son of a German pastor, a self-taught polyglot, indigo merchant, gun-runner for Russian forces, banker for California gold prospectors, inveterate traveler, and student at the Sorbonne, decided in 1868 to devote his life to archaeology. Convinced that Homer's Troy was located at Hissarlik, in Turkey, he began an archaeological dig there in 1871. Over the course of twenty years, digging almost uninterruptedly, he unearthed a number of successive occupation levels, later known as Schliemann's Seven Cities of Troy, which spanned four millennia, as well as the famous treasure of King Priam. At the same time, he exhumed "Agamemnon's mask" from the tombs at Mycenae, started digs at Tiryns and Ithaca, and opened the world's eyes to the Mycenaean universe.

The first traces of Greek art appeared in the Cyclades, where a prehellenic civilization (3200-2000 B.C.), largely ignored by Pericles and his contemporaries, produced refined marble figurines. As for the Cretan and Mycenaean worlds of the second millennium B.C. Greeks of the archaic and classical eras could conjure up only a few hazy memories of them. Until the middle of the 8th century, art found expression chiefly in ceramics. However, during the geometric period (900-700 B.C.) the first shrines, wood-columned temples, and alphabetic inscriptions appeared. Silhouettes of warriors, charioteers, and flautists were incorporated into decorative geometrical patterns. They steadily grew more limber and lithe, breaking free of triangular configurations, infusing shape with movement, and opening the way to the archaic period (700-480).

City-states, philosophy, poetry, stone temples, and coins all arose in the years spanning 800 to 600 B.C. In the middle of the 7th century, great standing statues of naked men (*kouroi*) and artistically draped women (*kore*) were carved from stone – limestone at first, then marble from Naxos. These statues were no longer funerary figures or relatively standardized offerings to the gods. They took on new life and character; they were freer and more expressive, doffing their stone corsets as the forms and canons of the East grew less influential.

It was a passage from immobility to movement, from geometry to life.

THE TWELVE LABORS OF HERAKLES

The son of Zeus and of the mortal Alcmene, Herakles (Hercules to the Latins) was the most popular hero of classical mythology. Half of the Twelve Labors he was forced to undertake took place in the Peloponnese, where he was born. There he strangled the Nemean lion, decapitated the many-headed Lernean hydra, captured the Erymanthean boar, destroyed the Stymphalian birds, and cleaned out the Augean stables. Then he captured the Cretan bull, tamed the man-eating Mares of Diomedes, procured the girdle of Hippolyta, queen of the Amazons, set out to capture the oxen of Geryon, removed Cerberus from Hades, and fetched the golden apples of the Hesperides. He fought with a club and protected himself with armor made from the remains of the Nemean lion.

CLASSICAL GREEK ART

Although the period from 490 to 323 spanned less than two centuries, it was filled with wars, struggles for supremacy, and diplomatic maneuvering. But for Greek art, as for literature and philosophy, it was a period of harmony and perfection in every field: painting, ceramics, sculpture, architecture, and funerary art. The rules its artists developed would set the standards for centuries to come. Far from imposing a uniform code, however, the canons that emerged during this period allowed for multiple approaches to excellence, never overshadowing the artist's personality. Thus in architecture the Doric order, which reached its zenith in the first half of the 5th century, and the Ionic order, which enjoyed a rebirth during the sec-

ond half, coexisted and even overlapped. In sculpture a severe style developed, as seen in the fragment of a funerary stele from Thessaly, known as *Exaltation of the Flower*. Classicism had two forms, one serene and naturalistic, as illustrated in the Panathenaic frieze; the other more sensual and dynamic, and expressing greater pathos. The *Apollo Sauroctonos*, for example, reflects a discernible move toward interiorization, even portraiture. Local customs and regional schools from Xanthus to Syracuse, from Bassae to Macedonia, and from Epidaurus to Halicarnassus also influenced artistic production. Original masterpieces from this period, particularly sculptures, are very rare. In later years the bronze pieces were often melted down and

GREEK MYTHOLOGY

While the definition of mythology among the Greek's varies according to the expert, one point of agreement is that religion and mythology were two separate entities. Religion concerned itself with rites, sites, city-states, and calendars. Mythology organized the collective imagination, empowering the Greeks to conceive, organize, and substantiate reality. Its forms were multiple, and its themes were in constant flux and sometimes even contradictory. A vast stockpile for each and every need and desire, it could be enriched, expanded, and reinterpreted at will. There were three kinds of myth: tales of the origin of the universe, the creation of man, and the invention of sacrifice; tales of the exploits of the gods and their progeny, their wars and their loves; and chronicles of heroes, which were sometimes arranged in cycles, such as the stories about Herakles.

---

above

Veiled Head of Woman, bronze
This replica of a bronze original from the middle of the 5th century could be a portrait of Aspasia, renowned for her beauty and her intelligence. But it might also be simply a common iconographical form – the veiled woman – in keeping with contemporary style, as the draped body next to it suggests.

left

Helmeted Athena
The goddess of war and wisdom, patroness of literature and the arts, Athena kept protective watch over Athens from the Acropolis. The Athenian Alcamenes, a student of Phidias, may have sculpted the original that served as a model for this Roman replica. With his classic, almost academic style, Alcamenes launched a new tendency imbued with humanity and softness.

above

Bronze Ex-Voto Plaque
This cut-out bronze ex-voto depicts an old man taking a young man by the arm. This scene has been interpreted as a depiction of the ritual homosexuality that was part of Greek and Cretan culture. Dating from the second quarter of the 7th century B.C., this plaque is believed to be one of the oldest remnants of a richly illustrated series.

left

The Battle in the Hall
The Louvre acquired this bell-shaped krater (a vessel for mixing water and wine for banquets) in 1985. It is from Campania (330-320 B.C.), and is attributed to Ixion. It depicts the famous "Battle in the Hall" from the Odyssey, *when Ulysses returned home to kill Penelope's suitors. He is assisted in the fight by his son Telemachos.*

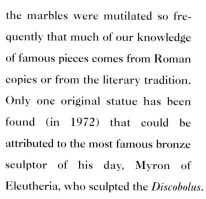

the marbles were mutilated so frequently that much of our knowledge of famous pieces comes from Roman copies or from the literary tradition. Only one original statue has been found (in 1972) that could be attributed to the most famous bronze sculptor of his day, Myron of Eleutheria, who sculpted the *Discobolus*.

Athens, under the protection of Athena, dominated the artistic movement of the 5th century B.C. There were powerful links between its political system – democracy – and its art. For the first time, works of art commemorated collective historical and political experiences. These works were for the most part commissioned by the civic community, which from 450 onward was led by Pericles (490-429). The impulse in rebuilding the Acropolis, the holy citadel whose buildings the Persians had destroyed in 480 and 479, was to bear witness to the power and glory of Athens. Public financing of the reconstruction project was established by decree: it came from the output of the silver mines of Mount Laurium and

from tribute-money from allied states. The artists involved included the sculptors Polyclitus, Phidias, and Alcamenes, and the architects Callicrates and Ictinos.

Between 447 and 406, an extraordinary complex of buildings arose on the Acropolis: the Parthenon, with its two friezes – one Doric, alternating metopes and tryglyphs, and the other Ionic, a long continuous strip – the Propylaea, the Erechtheum, and the Odeon. Each monument and bas-relief celebrated the history and exploits of Athena and Athens. Everything emphasized this inextricable harmony of Doric and Ionic styles – a harmony as firm as the harmony that had reunited the city to celebrate its goddess. Her colossal statue – 36 feet tall, sculpted by Phidias in ivory and gold and mounted on wood – was housed in the Parthenon. Soon after it ended, the ancients already invoked the "century of Pericles" to immortalize this fleeting moment when Athens was the crucible of a new art – Greek classicism.

HELLENISTIC ART

The word *Hellenistic* was coined at the height of the Romantic movement by the German historian J. G. Droysen to designate the fusion of Eastern and Western traditions between 323 B.C. (the death of Alexander the Great) and 30 B.C. (the Roman occupation of Egypt). Ever since Droysen, these two dates have demarcated the Hellenistic era, although certain crucial artistic developments preceded this period.

Hellenistic art was created over an immense geographical region that extended from the Adriatic to the Indus and embraced an endless variety of inhabitants, religions, civilizations, and art forms. Greek and Macedonian conquerors settled everywhere: in Egypt, in Bactria, and along the shores of the Persian Gulf. In theory the political regimes of the region were united under the domination of a king, yet these cities, kingdoms, and tribal federations were constantly at war. New metropolises like Alexandria, Pergamum, and Antioch emerged as centers of intellectual curiosity, philosophical speculation, science, and religion. Throughout the region a comman language – Greek – was spoken.

No single characteristic marks the Hellenistic style. Instead, there were interwoven currents, tendencies, experiments, and revivals. Some were rooted in local traditions; others reflected the taste of sovereigns or collectors or were derived from earlier styles. Culture burgeoned, blending baroque, realist, mannerist, and archaic features, veering from the small to the colossal, associating the traditional with the exotic – and perfecting the art of the mosaic.

above
Bronze Face
Dating from the late 4th or early 3rd century B.C., this bronze face illustrates how certain statues were made. Cast separately and undercut from forehead to ear, it once wore a helmet.

above
Nike (Winged Victory) of Samothrace
The Winged Victory *exudes a grace as powerful as that of the* Venus de Milo, *the* Mona Lisa, *and the caryatids.*

left center
Centaur Ridden by Eros
This copy of a 3rd-century B.C. original from Asia Minor was found in Rome during the 17th century; the centaur was a mythological predator of women.

below
The Three Graces
This Roman replica, given its low-relief treatment, might have been inspired more by a two-dimensional prototype (2nd century B.C.?). Originally

clothed, these daughters of Zeus, said to have been sculpted by Socrates, were nature deities who brought joy to the hearts of men.

THE NIKE OF SAMOTHRACE

Suffused with light, she seems to tremble in anticipation of flight from her lofty perch. This winged maiden comes from a shrine on the island of Samothrace. Discovered by Charles Champoiseau in 1863, the colossal statue was immediately sent to Paris. Over eight feet tall, she seems to skim the surface of her dark gray marble base, representing a ship's prow. The figure is positioned along a diagonal axis, its right side in three-quarter view, its wings outspread. The right hand, found in 1960, was raised and open, and the face was turned toward the spectator as if the winged woman were the harbinger of good news. She may have been announcing the Rhodian naval victory over Antiochos III of Syria in the early 2nd century B.C. The statue blends tradition and innovation, and its inscription may date from around 190 B.C. or 250 B.C.

facing page
Sleeping Hermaphodite
A certain Polyclees is said to have made the first plastic representation of a hermaphrodite. In this replica, the sexual ambivalence is partially masked by the sleeping position of the hermaphrodite.

ETRUSCAN ANTIQUITIES REDISCOVERED

Until the end of the 13th century, the Etruscans had disappeared from historical memory. Scholars knew only that the name Tuscany was derived from Tusci, the early inhabitants of the area, and that caches of treasure had been buried there. But virtually no one knew of the existence of the highly original and innovative Etruscan civilization. Its rediscovery came about as a result of the Italian Renaissance, when erudition, sheer luck, and politics converged.

The element of erudition was provided by Annio of Viterbo (1432-1502), a Dominican friar and theologian who published inscriptions from Etruscan monuments. He maintained that the Etruscan language was derived from Hebrew, and that the Etruscans were the descendants of Noah, and were therefore present from the beginning of mankind. It matters little that Annio's theories were highly imaginative, or that the inscriptions on which

he based his arguments were often forgeries, for as a result of his research the Etruscans finally reentered history.

The element of sheer luck was the outstanding quality of the artifacts unearthed during early excavations. In the first part of the 13th century, red-figure vases were found in Arezzo, followed by tombs whose paintings inspired Michelangelo and Leonardo da Vinci.

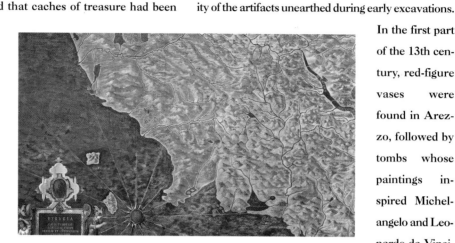

Urns and bronze pieces, including the exceptional *Chimera* and *Orator*, were also unearthed. These masterpieces joined the collection of Cosimo de' Medici, who claimed to be descended from the Etruscan kings. Here entered element of politics. The Medici and the city of Florence boasted of their great Etruscan ancestors, the first people to rule Italy. Parallels were drawn between the name Medici and the word *meddix*, believed to be Etruscan in origin and meaning "chief magistrate." Invokingan affiliation with the Etruscans was a con-

ETRUSCAN LANDMARKS (ALL DATES B.C.)

EVENTS	CULTURAL DEVELOPMENTS
2nd millennium: Arrival of the Indo-Europeans in Italy	
13th century: Arrival of the Lydians in Etruria	
8th century: Etruscans in central Italy; Greek colonization of Sicily and southern Italy	9th to 8th centuries: Villanovan art
	Ca. 7th century: First Etruscan inscriptions
616-509 Etruscan kings in Roma	
6th century: Expansion and height of Etruscan power	7th century: Era of Eastern influence
	540-510: Wall painting flourishes in Tarquinia
5th century: Decline of the Etruscan empire	
4th century: Etruscans retreat throughout the peninsula as Gauls arrive from the north; Roman expansion to the south	
2nd century: Roman Etruria	Ca. 10 A.D.: Last Etruscan inscriptions

venient way of opposing Rome's claim to be the ancestral and natural leader of Italy. In 1541 a Florentine Academy was founded: its aim was to prove scientifically that Etruscan civilization had predated that of all other peoples of Italy. The Florentine school was the center of European intellectual activity, and its arguments inspired further scholarly research. In the mid-16th century the French scholar Guillaume Postel began to study ancient Etruria. Thomas Dempster, an eccentric Scottish scholar, was commissioned by the grand duke of Tuscany to write a history of the Etruscans. In *De Etruria Regali Libri Septem*, he established continuity from the Etruscans to the Medici, supporting his theory with a systematic account of knowledge of ancient Tuscany. For unexplained reasons, Dempster's work, written around 1610, went unpublished for over a

century. The manuscript was finally discovered by Sir Thomas Coke, and Dempster's book – seven volumes on the Etruscans, with explanations, commentaries, and illustrations by eminent Italian scholars – was published in 1723. It brought the Etruscans into the European limelight. In 1726 the Etruscan Academy was founded in Cortona to encourage study of Etruscan civilization, and a new discipline – Etruscology – was born.

From the start Etruscology was a theater of contention, dominated by arguments over the origins and language of the Etruscans. It was not until the research of the Jesuit Luigi Lanzi (1732-1810) that serious progress was made. Lanzi offered the first credible readings and interpretations of inscriptions and art works, organized the Etruscan collections of Florence, and attributed the famous "Etruscan vases" to Greek craftsmen. This implied that the Etruscans – made fashionable by the paintings of Giambattista Piranesi and imitated by European ceramicists and furniture designers –

Etruscan Tombs
Etruscan tombs were a favorite sight for 19th-century travelers. This engraving depicts different tomb styles. They include the tomb of Porsenna (below at left), king of Clusium – modern Chiusi – described by Pliny the Elder in the 1st century A.D.

were not the direct heirs of the Egyptians but pupils of the Greeks.

During the first decades of the 19th century, at Vulci, Tarquinia, and Cerveteri (the ancient Caere), the discovery of the entire tomb-cities rich in vases, paintings, and golden artifacts brought wealth to antiquities

dealers. It inspired writers and artists and stirred the passions of discerning collectors such as Lucien Bonaparte, the Campanari brothers, and the Marquis Gian Pietro Campana. All over Europe exhibitions were held and museums opened (beginning with the Vatican's Museo Etrusco Gregoriano, named for Pope Gregory XVI, who inaugurated it in 1837). Learned societies arose, such as the Hyperborean Circle, founded in 1823 by German scholars and transformed six years later into the Institute for Archaeological Correspondence. The love affair with

Etruria was now a matter for science: collecting, classification, and the publication of learned reviews and books became the order of the day. Digs proliferated, particularly around the intact tombs when they boasted wall paintings, the quality and freshness of their colors were astonishing. Thus the Etruscans first became popularly known through the world of their dead. As a result, they were initially associated with images of demons, somber hues, and a morbid preoccupation with the infernal regions.

THE TOMBS

Thousands of Etruscan burial places have been discovered in Tuscany, of all shapes, sizes, and colors. Sometimes they were isolated tombs, sometimes cities of tombs with main avenues and side streets. They ranged from simple pits to grandiose sepulchral mounds decorated with urns or sarcophagi, from humble funerary monuments to elaborate stagings – so elaborate that they could even be laid out like a dwelling, with atrium, rooms, columns and capitals, beds and chairs; or else carved out of a rock, enclosing several generations of the same family or one individual alone. For a long time, tombs were the chief source for Etruscan researchers. They provided endless information on funeral rites and how they evolved; they cast light on the Etruscan belief in an afterlife and the strong bonds between the living and the dead. But the paintings, sculptures, inscriptions, and artifacts also proved to be an invaluable source of information on other aspects of Etruscan life.

THE ART OF LIVING

below

Pendant of Achelous
The horned head and bearded face of Achilles' rival, the

river god Achelous, is just over one and a half inches in height. Three different techniques were used in creating it: the head is worked in repoussé, most of the hair is stylized in filigree spirals, and the beard was shaped with extremely fine gold beadwork. This famous piece is from the Louvre's Campana collection and dates from the early 5th century. It betrays the influence of Greek mythology in Etruria.

left

Woman's Head
(ca. 350 B.C.)
A replica of Aphrodite's head, copied from Praxiteles' original.

Etruscology began with the study of necropolises, but in the second half of the 20th century it expanded to include the study of Etruscan houses. This shift followed archaeological digs in urban centers (Aquarossa, Marzabotto); shrines and temples (Pyrgi); ports (Gravisca); aristocratic dwellings (Rome); and palaces (Murlo). Etruscology is now recognized as an independent historical discipline in its own right: 1968 marked the "Year of the Etruscans," which included a traveling European exhibition (in which the Louvre participated) entitled "The Etruscans and Europe."

As a result, the Etruscans may have lost something of their mysterious aura, but they remain as fascinating as ever. They themselves predicted that their civilization would endure for ten *saecule*, or centuries. A very active civilization, the Etruscans smelted iron to build one of the largest industrial com-

plexes of antiquity, in Populania, opposite the island of Elba. They were fearless soldiers who erected, in Italy, the first known empire, stretching from the Po River valley to the Roman Campania. They were accomplished town planners and the first to build cities on the peninsula. They devised foundation rituals from which the Romans would later draw inspiration. Skilled farmers, they were unmatched in the art of drainage and drying out land areas. They loved games and festivals, banquets and sports, and appeared to be the most religious of people, recording their beliefs in sacred books and entrusting priests or *haruspices* – diviners who interpreted animal entrails – with keeping those beliefs intact. Even in the 5th century A.D., when the Etruscan language had disappeared for four hundred years, specialists could still recite certain passages.

left

Antefix with African Head
This antefix from Caere (Cerveteri) features the head of an African. Potters frequently used molds: after the clay was fired, the antefix was painted by hand.

center left

Funerary Relief
This plaque from a cippus, or grave-marker, from Chiusi depicts the laying-out of a corpse in an Etruscan ritual. This piece dates from the early 5th century B.C.

above

Antefix with Female Head
This antefix dates from the early 5th century B.C. and is part of the Campana collection. Found at Cerveteri, it was acquired in 1863. The face, with its arched brows and smiling mouth, reflects Greek inspiration.

MASTER MARINERS

The Etruscans were exceptional sailors. In fact, the Tyrrhenian Sea, whose waters lap their coast, bears the name the Greeks gave them: *Tyrrhenoi*. According to Homer, the Etruscans seized Dionysos when he arrived on the island of Naxos. To punish them, the god changed them into dolphins and covered their boat with vines. The legend is depicted on this black-figure cup by Exekias, which dates from

the last third of the 5th century B.C. But the Etruscans were more involved in trade than piracy; free ports where foreign traders settled were scattered along the Tyrrhenian coast. The Etruscans sought to control the maritime lanes of the two seas that bordered their empire, giving rise to conflicts with Greek merchants. The two powers continued to clash over mastery of the seas until the early 4th cenury.

ETRUSCAN ART IN THE LOUVRE

Recognized relatively recently as belonging to a distinct civilization that once dominated the Italian peninsula, Etruscan art narrowly missed being left out of the Louvre entirely. The Etruscan collection, created in the second half of the 19th century, is of fairly recent origin, but in artistic quality and historical appeal, it is one of the most brilliant collections outside Italy.

In the pre-Revolutionary Royal Collections, items from the workshops of Etruria were rare. In 1825, under Charles X, the Louvre acquired the collection of the Chevalier Edme-Antoine Durand, an eclectic collection with a great number of vases. Durand was a lover of antiquity, and in addition to the items he purchased in Italy, his collection also contained beautiful archaeological objects collected by the Empress Josephine and sold at auction by her son, Prince Eugène. These included a bronze oinochoe, shaped like the head of a man, that had once decorated the Great Gallery at Malmaison, the residence of the empress. Two years later, after the curator of the Egyptian Antiquities Department, Jean-François Champollion, asserted that the Louvre "had no beautiful objects in this sector," the museum purchased five urns from Volterra and a painting of a journey to the underworld for a ridiculously low sum. There was thus an element of chance in the beginnings of the Louvre's Etruscan collection.

The collection itself was not created until 1861, and one name – Gian Pietro Campana – became synonymous with it. Starting in 1831, the Italian marquis had amassed Europe's largest collection of Etruscan art in just twenty-five years, with approximately fifteen thousand pieces from Cerveteri, either excavated by his staff or purchased from dealers. In 1835 Pope Gregory XVI visited this extraordinary collection, which was scattered among several Roman villas. The visit made the collection world famous. But Campana overstepped himself: as director of Rome's pawnshop administration, he embezzled funds in order to enrich his collection. In 1857 the marquis was tried and sentenced to prison, and his belongings were confiscated and sold

left
Elongated Female Statuette
This bronze statuette, perhaps representing Aphrodite, was found in a sanctuary of Diana south of Rome. The solemn expression of the well-proportioned face contrasts with the marked lengthening of the body.

center
Oinochoe in the Shape of the Head of a Young Man
Found in Gabies and derived from attic ceramic models, this vase has been copied ever since antiquity.

left
Hunting Scene bronze plaque, with silver and copper inlays, 4th century A.D.

below
Filiform Statuette
This bronze filiform, cast by an Etruscan artist in the 3rd century B.C., could be the ancestor of a Giacometti. It comes from the area surrounding Ancona. The arms with open hands are positioned for a ritual offering, common in figurines like this one from central Italy that depict soothsayers.

by the papal authorities. Collectors and museums in England, Belgium, Russia, and France leaped at this opportunity to purchase Etruscan antiquities. The Emperor Napoleon III, who loved archaeology with a passion and was friends with the Campana family, was eager to elbow England and Russia out of the competition and anxious to donate such beautiful artifacts to the art world; he was also driven by a genuine educational mission. He dispatched his most trusted men to negotiate the purchase. The price was high: 4.8 million francs. Some considered it excessive. Napoleon III did not acquire everything he wished, but nearly everything – twelve thousand objects in all, incuding the *Husband and Wife Sarcophagus,* which the papal commission had earmarked for itself. The rest of the collection was dispersed between St. Petersburg (787 objects), Brussels, and Florence.

On May 1, 1862, the Campana Collection (now enlarged by additional purchases) inaugurated the Napoleon III Museum. The opening was a triumph, with more than six thousand visitors to the museum every Sunday throughout the month of July. Study guides were issued to

THE BRONZE ROOM

Etruria lacked a good supply of tin. So like the Greeks, the Etruscans plied "tin roads" that cut across the Alps or up the rivers to the land of the Gauls, where they could procure the mineral, essential for producing bronze. Hence a great number of Etruscan artifacts have found on French soil. The Etruscans, heirs to the great craftsmen of Villanova, became masters in the art of bronze, working both for domestic needs and for export. Thus, for example, a bronze vessel used for serving wine, originally from the Vulci workshops, found its way into the Celtic world. The scale of production was large, with forms varying according to period and tastes. There are basins, vases, fibulae, mirrors, cisterns, candelabra, statuettes, and statues, some of them, such as the *Chimera* of Arezzo, or the *Mars* of Todi, of extraordinary beauty.

scholars, workers, and artists. However, the Louvre and the Napoleon III Museum soon found themselves competing, sometimes acrimoniously, for acquisitions, and in October 1862 the Napoleon III Museum was shut down. The Campana collection was transferred to the Louvre. So that it could store and display only the essential items of this immense collection, the Louvre made three series of loans (in 1862, 1874, and 1893-1895) to other museums in France. No precise inventory of these loan items and their destinations was ever made. As a result, "Campana lots" are still hidden away in provincial museums today.

Since those early days, the Louvre's Etruscan collection has been enriched regularly, if at a less dizzying pace, by gifts and acquisitions. Furthermore, deposits made by Italian museums have enabled the Louvre to display articles from the Villanova era, a period from which the Louvre previously had not owned anything. Today the Louvre's Etruscan collection has earned equal standing alongside its Greek and Roman collections.

following double page
Vase with Silenus
Satyrs were rustic creatures, with a man's body and the legs of a goat. Sileni are distinguished from satyrs by their horses' ears and tails. The painter Micali, who created this amphora, was one of the most notable craftsmen in the Etruscan city of Vulci.

above
Young Man
This young male nude, in bronze, 4th century B.C., is reminiscent of Greek work, yet the face is characteristically Etruscan.

below left
Canopic Jar
This terra-cotta piece, 19.5 inches tall, dates from the second half of the 6th century B.C. One theory is that these funerary urns were intended to humanize the deceased.

ROME: FROM ROMULUS TO THE FALL

ROME:
FROM ROMULUS
TO THE FALL

In 754-753 B.C., it is said, Romulus founded Rome on the Palatine Hill. In the many legends surrounding the origin of the city, several key ideas about Romulus would remain alive in Roman minds right up until the fall of the Empire. Romulus was the son of the god Mars and of a mortal woman, a descendant of the Trojan hero Aeneas. He was a legislator, priest, and warrior – the ideal *imperator* – the kind of figure whom later Romans sought to emulate when they aspired to found, or re-found, a new Rome. The gods had chosen Romulus, and the new city was consecrated in their honor according to a specific ritual. Rome therefore became a holy city.

But Remus, Romulus' twin brother, met a violent death, and in consequence of this original sin, Rome was to be haunted by the specter of conflict and civil war. It would expand and grow stronger only by incorporating into its own populace the peoples it conquered.

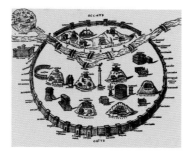

In 509 B.C. the Republic was established. A century under Etruscan kings had transformed the village on the Tiber into a city with solid walls, luxurious dwellings, and imposing temples. Its political and military institutions and its social organization had greatly changed. Yet Rome, which five centuries later would dominate the ancient world, was still scarcely different from the other city-states of Latium. Its conquest of the surrounding areas was enormously drawn out. At first, during the 5th century B.C., Rome was very much on the military defensive. Coveted by mountain tribes from outlying areas, weakened by an internal struggle between patrician nobility and urban plebs, it managed to survive only

POLITICAL ORGANIZATION

SPQR, Senatus Populusque Romanus – the Roman Senate and people – vaunted a unique double-headed sovereignty, that of the people and that of the Senate. Following the expulsion of Rome's kings, institutions soon arose that were based on three constituent components: the Roman people, the magistracy, and the Senate. The people, whom the courts defended, met in assemblies (*comices*) to elect the magistrates and to vote on legislation. The magistracies were collective and hierarchically structured. The Senate deliberated on foreign affairs, advised the magistrates, and guaranteed the maintenance of Roman traditions. There was a theoretical balance between monarchy, aristocracy, and democracy – a balance greatly admired in the second century B.C. by the Greek historian Polybius.

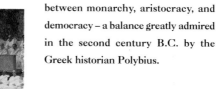

NADAGRA

EARLY ROMAN LANDMARKS

EVENTS

754-753 B.C.: Romulus founds Rome
753-617: Latin and Sabine kings

616-509: Etruscan kings
509: Republic established

405-395: Conquest of Veii
390: Gauls capture Rome
343-291: Conquest of central Italy

280-272: War against Taranto and Pyrrhus

264: First gladiatorial combats in Rome
264-241: First Punic War

218-202: Second Punic War (Hannibal)
215-205: First war in Macedonia

198: Rome in Greece
191-188: War against Syria

149-146: Third Punic War
134-121: The Gracchae

91-88: "Social war" in Italy
82-79: Sulla's dictatorship
73-71: Revolt of Spartacus
63: Catiline's conspiracy, Cicero's intervention
60: First Triumvirate: Pompey, Crassus, Caesar

49-46: Civil war
46-44: Caesar's dictatorship, assassinated in March 44
43: Second Triumvirate: Octavian, Mark Antony, Lepidus
31: Victory of Octavian at Actium

27 B.C.: Octavian receives title *Augustus*.
    (Rules until 14 A.D.)

14-68 A.D.: Julio-Claudian dynasty

69-96: Flavian dynasty

96-192: Antonine dynasty

167-175: First barbarian incursions
194-235: Severan dynasty. Empire reaches maximum growth

235-284: 3rd-century "crises": military emperor

284-305: Diocletian creates the tetrarchy
306-324: Constantine becomes sole emperor

324-337: Reign of Constantine

337-363: The Constantines
364-395: Valentinians and Theodosus

395: The Empire divided between Arcadius (East) and
    Honorius (West)
406: The barbarians cross the Rhine
410: Alaric sacks Rome

476: End of the Roman Empire of the West

CULTURAL DEVELOPMENTS

Ca. 770 B.C.: Thatched huts on the Palatine Hill
Late 8th-early 7th centuries: huts on site of Forum; first
    temples on Forum. Dedication of temple to Jupiter on
    Capitoline Hill

450: The Law of Twelve Tables

312: *Via* Appia (Rome-Capua)

272: Direct contact with Greek civilization
264: First gladiatorial combats in Rome

240: First tragedy written in Latin
219: First Greek surgeon in Rome

212: Syracuse sacked; artworks taken as spoils

188: Beginnings of "luxury" in Rome
185: First basilica on the Forum

133-129: Pergamum becomes a province of Roman Asia
    Minor

55: Pompey's theater
51: Caesar's *Gallic Wars*. Caesar's Forum

28: Pantheon in Rome

9: Dedication of the Ara Pacis
2 B.C.: Dedication of Forum of Augustus

Ca. 30 A.D.: Death of Christ

79: Vesuvius erupts
80: Colosseum; Forum of Trajan (Trajan's column); new
    Pantheon

212: All free inhabitants of the Empire become Roman citi-
    zens

250-251: First generalized persecution of Christians

313: Freedom of worship for Christians

330: Dedication of Constantinople

392: Pagan worship outlawed

413-426: Augustine's *City of God*
429-438: Theodosian legal code

through sheer tenacity. It took Rome ten years to capture Veii, an Etruscan city only twelve miles away. And when the Gauls invaded Rome at the beginning of the 4th century B.C., the city was unable to resist them.

Thereafter it sharpened its formidable military weapon – the legion – and secured the territories it conquered by settling colonies in them or incorporating them into the city. Praying faithfully to its gods for victory, Rome shook off its defeats and grew rich on war booty. Soon, manipulating a widespread network of alliances, it brought central Italy to its knees, and in the 3rd century B.C. it took advantage of the decline of the Etruscans to make hostile contact with the

Greeks in southern Italy. The latter appealed for help to Pyrrhus, the Hellenic king and military leader. But Rome shattered Pyrrhus' dreams of conquest. In 272 B.C. he was forced to withdraw, leaving Rome in control of all but the north of Italy. From then on, despite its century-long war with Carthage, the challenges to its institutions, its ambitious generals, local resistance, slave revolts, and debilitating civil wars, Rome was victorious time and time again. Within a century and a half, the whole Mediterranean basin would fall under its rule.

Octavian entered Rome in May of the year 44 B.C. to avenge the murder of his

THE PUNIC WARS

Founded by the Phoenicians in the late 9th century B.C., Carthage monopolized commerce in the western Mediterranean from its harbor on the North African coast, causing conflict first with Greece, then with Rome. War broke out, lasting from 264 to 241 B.C. Rome finally won, annexing its first provinces. In 219 war broke out again when a young Carthaginian

general named Hannibal crossed the Alps into Italy. He crushed several Roman armies, but Rome, buttressed by a loyal central Italy, managed to reconquer its lost territories. In 201 peace was signed, but fighting broke out again in 150. In 146 B.C., following a terrible siege, Carthage fell. Its citizens were enslaved, the city burned, and its soil cursed.

below

Trajan's Column
Trajan's column was flanked by the Greek and Latin libraries in the Forum built by Trajan. The hollow hundred-foot column contains a staircase leading to the lantern on top. The sculpted narrative celebrates the emperor's victory over Dacia (modern Romania) during Rome's two wars against the Dacians.

adoptive father, Julius Caesar. With a keen sense of propaganda, a flair for politics, and the help his father's friends and wealth, within fifteen years, Octavian had eliminated his rivals. In 27 B.C. the Senate ratified the extraordinary powers he had acquired and gave him the title *Augustus*. An entirely new political regime – the "Principate" – emerged. Founded on peace through victory, it was a monarchy in the guise of a republic. It was the Empire.

On August 19, 14 A.D., Augustus died at the age of seventy-six. The world he left behind him was radically different from the one he had entered. The conquered provinces were greater in number and were governed and defended more efficiently. Rome and Italy had been reorganized, society had been reformed and strengthened, and traditional religion had been renewed and immersed in a new religion – the imperial cult. A new model of civilization was offered to the provincial elite, who incorporated it and diffused it.

There were no rules of succession to guide Rome after the death of Augustus, but his heirs consolidated his legacy. The Empire ultimately stretched from the moors of Scotland to the cataracts of the Nile, from the dunes of Morocco to the banks of the Euphrates. It presided over countless languages, a multitude of cults, and burgeoning cultures. One word emerged to describe the second century of our era – *Romanitas*.

Perhaps this sense of belonging both to the Roman world and to one's own small motherland explains the Empire's five centuries of life in the West and its much longer survival in the East. Perhaps the flexibility of its institutions eased the difficulties it encountered during the 3rd century, or perhaps the invention of the tetrarchy helped prolong the Empire's life. For the idea of the Empire survived even the fall of the last emperor of the West in 476 A.D.

Thereafter, the symptoms of decline came thick

left

Bust of an Emperor
This highly restored bust (only the face is ancient) from the Louvre's Campana collection dates from the 4th century B.C., as the severe expression, simplified features, and geometric proportions attest. A ribbon of marble above the bangs suggests that there was once a diadem. He was an emperor, but which one? Some scholars hesitate between Constantine and Valentinian I, but it is likelier that he was Constans I, who ruled the West from 340 to 350.

center left

Transporting Wheat
A regular flow of supplies to a city like Rome (with perhaps one million inhabitants) meant that times were peaceful. To keep supplies coming in, Augustus created an administrative department, toward the end of his reign, responsible for ensuring the wheat supply. This fresco from Ostia, the port that flourished under the emperor Claudius, shows wheat being ferried in small craft up the Tiber to Rome.

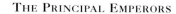

THE PRINCIPAL EMPERORS

Julio-Claudian Dynasty
  Tiberius, 14-37
  Caligula, 37-41
  Claudius, 41-54
  Nero, 54-68
The Flavian Dynasty
  Vespasian, 69-79
  Titus, 79-81
  Domitian, 81-96
The Antonine Dynasty
  Nerva, 96-98

Trajan, 98-117
Hadrian, 117-138
Antoninus Pius, 138-161
Marcus Aurelius, 161-189
Commodus, 180-192

The Severan Dynasty
  Septimus Severus, 193-211
  Caracalla, 211-217
  Elagabalus, 218-222
  Severus Alexander, 222-235

Principal 3rd-Century Emperors
  Decius, 249-251
  Gallienus, 253-268
  Aurelian, 270-275
  Diocletian, 284-305
Principal 4th-Century Emperors
  Constantine the Great, 306-337
  Sons of Constantine, 337-361
  Julian, 361-363
  Valentinian and Valens, 364-378
  Theodosius, 379-395

below, left to right
Caligula, wearing a beard as a sign of mourning for his sister Drusilla. Hadrian, bronze head from a colossal statue raised in the Eastern Empire. Trajan, whose massive head and thick neck hide a subtle intelligence. And the bust of a man, perhaps Maxentius.

GREEK, ETRUSCAN,
AND ROMAN
ANTIQUITIES

and fast. In the spring of 480, Julius Nepos (named emperor in 474 but quickly dethroned) was assassinated. Byzantium began making claims to represent Roman civilization and culture. In the autumn of 593, Pope Gregory the Great wrote that "the Senate has disappeared, the people have perished, and for those few who still live, the pain and the groans increase with each passing day. Empty Rome burns." A series of internal factors, such as civil war, the rise of Christianity, social upheavals, and artistic and intellectual decline, combined with external events like the barbarian invasions, had all helped contribute to the end of the Roman Empire.

right center
Portrait of Constantine
Not so much an emperor as a haloed saint: the emperor Constantine, as depicted in a mosaic from Saint Sophia in Constantinople. Constantine the Great not only legalized Christianity but raised it to the level of a state religion by accepting baptism on his deathbed in 337. The Church of Saint Sophia was built by his son and successor, Constans II.

below right
Interior of St. John of Latran
In 313 A.D. Constantine the Great gave the palace and domain of Latran (from the name of the former owners, the Laterani) to the bishop of Rome. Work on a church began in 326. The church, built on the lines of a basilica, was the seat of the patriarch of the Western Church, who asserted his primacy over other bishops during the 3rd and 4th centuries. It thus became one of the four major basilicas of Rome, with primacy over the others. This fresco depicts the building before Borromini refurbished it in the 17th century.

CHRISTIANITY

Around 30 A.D., an unknown man named Jesus was crucified in Jerusalem. His disciples preached his gospel to Jews and to pagan Gentiles. Having broken from Judaism, Christians were seen as outcasts. Under Trajan, imperial policy toward the Christians hardened: provincial governors could sentence to death anyone denounced as a Christian. There were a few martyrs, but tracking and persecution of the Christians was not systematic. Their numbers rose, their communities became organized, theologians debated doctrine, heresies multiplied, a considerable body of literature was published. Following Diocletian's persecutions in 303 and 304, an edict of tolerance was proclaimed in 311. It was followed in 313 by the Peace of the Church, established by Licinius and Constantine. In the eyes of the law, Christianity had become a religion like any other.

There were dramatic moments, and long periods of remission, but Rome was heading inexorably toward its fall.

In the last half of the 20th century, our historical perspective on the Roman Empire has changed. The label "late antiquity" illustrates the shift in the inquiries of historians. They now approach the Roman era in its entirety and are beginning to realize that behind the devastating events and upheavals (the capture of the emperor in 260, the sack of Rome in 410), a new civilization was coalescing. Christianity had become a religion, with its own art, value system, literature, political bodies, and national territories.

below
Titios Gemellos
This elderly bearded man wears a heavy cloak draped over a tunic. In a cartouche at the bottom of the bust is the following inscription: "Titios Gemellos had this bust of himself cast in his own memory in order to receive burial honors in this place." The bust, found in Gaul, dates from the 3rd century A.D. Originally colored

stones were set into the eye sockets.

The art of Rome has been part of the Louvre since it acquired the Royal Collections. In 1685 Louis XIV purchased the statue called *Germanicus* (in reality it depicted Marcellus). Signed "Cleomenes the Athenian," the statue exemplifies a basic problem: the proper designation of Roman art and its relationship with Greek art. How should replicas and copies of Greek art that were realized during Roman times be classified? Should the Roman artist be taken into consideration? The period? These questions play a key role in determining not only where various works

should be displayed but how their history should be approached.

Fashion and shifting tastes played a role in building the Roman collection. Mosaics were accorded

minor status until France's conquest of Algeria got under way in the 1830s, and the *Triumph of Neptune* was shipped to the Louvre.

The museum's collection of Roman art expanded in the wake of the archaeological expeditions mounted in Eastern Europe and the French colonies during the 19th century, the discovery of Roman artifacts in France itself, and a series of purchases and gifts. Two salient features characterize this collection: the distant origins of the artworks and their immense variety, reflecting the diversity of the Empire; and the quality of the artifacts themselves as seen in the representations in relief of historical scenes on the *Altar Said to Be of Domitius Ahenobarbus*, or in the astounding portraiture, of which the bronze bust of Hadrian, acquired in 1984, is a superb example.

CHRISTIAN ART

From its clandestine beginnings, Christianity gradually became more widespread. Early Christian art of the 3rd century A.D. –that of Dura-Europos, the catacombs and underground burial chambers of Rome –was often influenced by the motifs and forms of pagan art (the Good Shepherd) or by the Old Testament (the story of Jonah). But it imbued these themes with new meaning. As recognition came to the

new religion, its art became more prominent, figuring in liturgical services, pigrimages, and celebrations of Christ's divinity. Its originality found full expression in architecture (for example, the basilica with transept in St. Peter's in Rome, or the martyrium, a crypt where the relics of martyrs were treasured) and, as its iconography grew more elaborate, in painting, mosaics, and sculpture.

Art historians tend to relegate Roman art to a subcategory of its Hellenistic precursor: "There is no such thing as Roman art," André Malraux once decreed, reflecting this tendency. The supremacy accorded Greek art ever since Johann Winckelmann, the idea of a progressive, linear evolution in art, and the enthusiasm with which the Romans themselves received Greek art have all helped persuade scholars of the secondary status of Roman art.

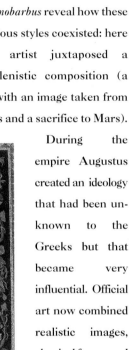

Greek art that were best suited to Roman society, to the glorification of Rome's great families, and to the depiction of scenes from everyday public and private life. Works like the reliefs on the *Altar Said to Be of Domitius Ahenobarbus* reveal how these various styles coexisted: here the artist juxtaposed a Hellenistic composition (a procession of divinities) with an image taken from Roman civic life (a census and a sacrifice to Mars).

Although Roman art was clearly influenced by Greek art, however, it was never merely a selective rehashing of Greek art forms and therefore does exist in own right. It incorporated Etruscan and Italic elements and then selected those elements from

During the empire Augustus created an ideology that had been unknown to the Greeks but that became very influential. Official art now combined realistic images, classical forms, and political messages. At the same time, a more popular art form was gradually taking shape.

THE PORTRAIT

Whether official or privately commissioned, the portrait was an essential feature of Roman art. Its origins date back to the 4th and 3rd centuries B.C., when portraits exalted the power of great families, the "right to images" being reserved for members of the patrician nobility under the republic. In the second half of the first century

B.C., and particularly during the imperial era, the official portrait became more widespread. It reflected ideology and the models who inspired that ideology; and it was influenced by the demands of propaganda. In late antiquity, the portrait became more abstract; function prevailed over the person the portrait was celebrating.

"A storm cloud rose, ash began to fall and parts of Vesuvius glowed, as great flames and large pillars of fire leaped from it, the flashes of light from the flames accentuated by the blackness of the night."

This account was written by an eyewitness of the spectacle, Pliny the Younger, who described the eruption of Vesuvius and told of the death of Pliny the Elder, his uncle, a scholar and admiral of the Mediterranean squadron.

On that day, August 24, 79 A.D., twelve feet of volcanic ash fell on the peaceful city of Pompeii. The light of day did not return to the survivors until the twenty-seventh. When it did, it revealed the full scope of the disaster: three cities had disappeared, Pompeii, Herculaneum, and Stabiae. Pompeii had already been shaken by earth

tremors in 62, and reconstruction work had not yet been completed. This time no reconstruction was possible. An investigating committee came out from Rome, salvaged cultural artifacts, and ordered everything still rising above the debris to be leveled. The city was dead. Even its name quickly fell into oblivion. The site was soon covered by grass, vines, and humus.

In the 16th century, a local nobleman ordered an underground pipe system to be dug in the area. Discovering the inscription *decurio Pompeis*, he conjectured that he had stumbled upon a villa of Pompeii. Not until the 18th century did it become clear that entire cities lay beneath the volcanic ash. Archaeological digs were commissioned. In 1763 the name Pompeii was once again known to the world.

below

Cup from Boscoreale
This silver cup set with gold, part of the Boscoreale treasure, shows the sculpted head of a woman, coiffed

with a flayed elephant head, at its center. The lady personifies either the city of Alexandria or the land of Africa. A diverse mix of religious emblems speaks eloquently of the syncretic tendencies prevalent in ancient Campania.

center

Melpomene
The house of Julia Felix was one of the first sites to be excavated in Pompeii, in 1766. A series of frescoes, representing Apollo surrounded by the muses, were given to Napoleon and entered the Louvre in 1825. Here Melpomene, the muse of tragedy, is depicted with her two emblems, the tragic mask and a sword.

left

Fresco, Pompeii
This fresco from Pompeii remains something of a mystery. Two women are seated, one behind the other, brandishing a branch on which a fawn is nibbling. Between the women and the animal is a basket filled with leaves and fruit. This scene is probably a symbolic glimpse of a mysterious cult rather than a scene from everyday life.

right

Winged Genius, Villa of Faunius Sinistor
This enigmatic winged spirit, with spiked hair and pointed ears, and bearing a tray in his left hand, guarded the entrance to the Aphrodite Room in the dwelling of Faunius Sinistor in Boscoreale. He was intended to drive off evil spirits.

below left, center

Gold Medallion
A coin set in a piece of jewelry was a style of medallion popular during the 3rd century. This gold coin from Constantine's reign, minted in 321, was acquired by the Louvre in 1973. The intricate medallion is less than four inches in diameter.

BOSCOREALE

In 1895 a worker unearthed a *villa rustica* (farm) in Boscoreale near Pompeii and found a wine cistern, jewels, a thousand gold pieces, and a 109-piece silver dish service. This cache is exceptional but far from unique, as another 118-piece service was found in Pompeii. The Louvre possesses the Boscoreale treasure today, essentially as a result of donations by the Rothschild family. The craftsmen respon-

sible for the treasure, skilled at silver repoussé work, were undoubtedly Greek. The service – refined, delicately decorated ladles, paterae, cups, and goblets – was used primarily for pouring libations. Its owner was surely someone of high standing, a prosperous landowner or a gentleman likely to make pronouncements worthy of characters in Petronius' novel *Satiricon,* set in the same period in Campania.

The Department of Near Eastern Antiquities and Islamic Arts

The Department of Near Eastern
Antiquities and Islamic Arts opened
in 1881. It was the third and last of
the Louvre's antiquities sections.
The department grew out of the collection in
the Louvre's former Assyrian Museum:
founded in 1847, the museum had given
awed Frenchmen their first view of the
giant, winged, human-headed bulls brought
back from excavations at Khorsabad by
French consul Paul-Émile Botta. Under
Napoleon III, who became emperor in
1852, and in the decades that followed,
a wave of archaeological discoveries in the
Near and Middle East led to the Assyrian
Museum's expansion and eventually to
the founding of the Louvre's Department
of Near Eastern Antiquities. Since 1993,
the department's collections have been
displayed in the Richelieu Wing, with a
handful on exhibit around the Cour Carrée
and in the Denon Wing. The department
offers visitors a rich collection drawn from
a geographical zone that stretches from
North Africa to the frontiers of India.
It was in the heart of this immense region
that the first literate civilizations
and centralized states were born.

ASSYRIA ON EGYPT'S HEELS: BIRTH OF THE DEPARTMENT

In the early 19th century, knowledge of Mesopotamia and Persia was limited to biblical sources and accounts by Greek and Roman historians. After Napoleon's 1798-1799 expedition to Egypt, French diplomats posted in the Ottoman Empire and Persia started excavating ruins and digging for treasures. The Louvre, closely associated with these scientific and archaeological missions, brought the historic and artistic masterpieces they uncovered into the museum.

Credit for the first discoveries goes to Paul-Émile Botta (1802-1870), French consul in Mosul (present-day Iraq). Botta hoped to find traces of Nineveh, the capital of the Assyrian kings, whose splendor is described in the Old Testament. Instead, he stumbled in 1842 upon the ruins of the palace built by the Assyrian king Sargon II in Khorsabad. His successor as consul in Mosul, Victor Place, continued his work and completed the Khorsabad palace excavations.

From the Middle East, which he visited in 1860, the writer Ernest Renan brought back Phoenician antiquities as well as material for his classic *Life of Jesus*. Then in 1877, Ernest de Sarzec, a French diplomat posted in southeastern Iraq, identified the first traces of the Sumerians, the forgotten people who had invented writing. In 1884, the engineer Marcel Dieulafoy enriched the Louvre's collections with Persian artifacts from Iran. After the First World War, several Middle Eastern countries established active departments of antiquities. The French often assisted them in their archaeological projects, dividing the finds with local researchers and thereby enhancing the Louvre's collections.

previous double page
Sacrificial Procession
Excavated in 1935 from the palace of Zimri-Lim in Mari, this brightly colored fresco depicts the investiture of the king by the goddess Ishtar. In the foreground at left is a bull earmarked for sacrifice.

below
The Khorsabad Courtyard
Gigantic bulls with human heads, lions' chests, and eagle wings

guard the entrance to Sargon II's palace at Khorsabad. Despite its small size, the Louvre's Khorsabad courtyard, which attempts to reconstruct the layout of the reliefs that decorated the palace, gives a clear sense of the greatness of this martial, realistic art.

center left
Map of Principal Archaeological Sites and Modern Cities of the Near East
This watercolor map of shows the principal archaeological sites and modern towns of the Near East. Today the territory of ancient civilizations is encompassed by Syria, Iraq, Iran, Turkey, Lebanon, Israel, and Jordan.

above
Giant with Lion
This immense alabaster relief embellished the gate of the palace of Sargon II. The giant holds a weapon in one hand and with the other restrains a young lion, later to be unleashed to ward off evil spirits.

left
The Assyrian Museum
Gazing in awe at the winged bulls from the palace at Khorsabad, the first visitors pace through the Louvre's Assyrian Museum, inaugurated in 1847 by King Louis Philippe. (Illustration from an 1849 edition of Le Magazine Pittoresque.)

KHORSABAD
EXCAVATED

Appointed French consul in Mosul in 1842, Paul-Émile Botta began digging at the site of Nineveh. He never found the legendary Assyrian capital, but fifteen miles away, in the small obscure village of Khorsabad, he unearthed the palace

Baghdad and then Basra, where they were shipped to Le Havre on a French naval vessel. They reached Paris in February 1847. On May 1 the world's first Assyrian Museum was inaugurated in the Louvre.

previous page
Vigil at Nineveh,
Félix Thomas
*Thomas, an
internationally
recognized artist,
became the valued
collaborator of French
consul Victor Place at
Khorsabad. Besides his
drawings and
architectural plans, he
made several studies of
Arab horsemen.*

above
Portrait of
Victor Place
*Place (1818-1875) is
shown in consular
uniform during his
1848 posting to San
Domingo. In 1870 he
was falsely accused of
embezzlement and was
later convicted.
Although pardoned by
the head of the French
government, he spent
the rest of his life in
self-imposed exile
in Romania.*

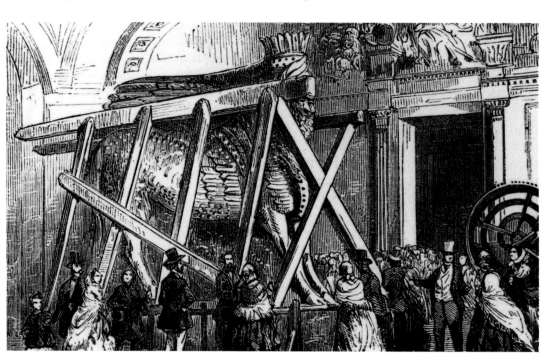

built by King Sargon II at his new capital, Dur-Sharrukin, in the 8th century B.C. During the Byzantine period a new town had arisen on the site of the ruined capital. It was named after the Persian monarch Khorstabad, now shortened to Khorsabad.

Sargon's palace was the first Assyrian monument to be excavated. Six months of digging laid bare a considerable area of the building, the reliefs and inscriptions recorded in precise drawings. The excavated ruins were taken to Paris by a peril-fraught route: transported to the Tigris on carts, they were rafted downriver to

Dispatched to Jerusalem after the French monarchy was swept away by revolution in 1848, Botta had to abandon the Khorsabad site. Pillagers moved in, scattering the Khorsabad antiquities to different parts of the world. French excavation resumed in 1851 under the supervision of Victor Place, the new consul in Mosul. But like Botta, Place was abruptly transferred in 1854. Abandoned yet again, the Khorsabad site became a quarry for local people. It was another seventy years before American researchers resumed exploration of the site.

left
Bull from the Place
Mission
*Place continued the
work started by Botta.
But nearly all the
statues and reliefs he
worked so hard to ship
down the Tigris were
sunk during a Bedouin
attack in 1855. Only
one giant winged bull,
shown here en route to
Paris, survived.*

left center
Paul-Émile Botta,
Charles-Émile
Champmartin
*Son of a historian
from northern Italy,
Paul-Émile Botta
(1802-1870) was
French consul in
Alexandria before his
posting to Mosul. The
findings from his digs
at Khorsabad formed
the core of the Louvre's
original Assyrian
Museum. Given little
credit for his
discoveries, Botta was
posted in 1848 to
Jerusalem, where he
abandoned archaeology
and died a forgotten
man.*

below left
Bulls Traveling
Overland,
Félix Thomas
*The architect and
draftsman Félix
Thomas made a
number of drawings to
illustrate the hardships
of transporting such
monumental works.*

As in Egypt, rediscovering Mesopotamian civilizations meant deciphering their scripts.

In 1802 a young German named Georg Friedrich Grotefend began deciphering Persian script copied from stones and tomb inscriptions. Like Champollion and others who cracked the hieroglyphic code, he took as his point of departure common names known from the works of Greek historians. Having identified a few characters, he went on to pinpoint the remaining forty-two signs in the Old Persian alphabet. He spent the rest of his life pursuing his research alongside other scientists, including the Frenchman Silvestre de Sacy and the Englishman Henry Rawlinson. The latter broke fresh ground with his discovery of new inscriptions, in particular the Bisitun rockface, on which Darius I of Persia gave an account of his victories around 500 B.C.

top right
Georg Friedrich Grotefend
As a young Latin teacher at the University of Göttingen in Germany, Grotefend (1755-1853) succeeded in identifying the names of Persian kings on inscriptions brought to light by excavations. The university failed to recognize the importance of the breakthrough, and this brilliant scholar ended his career as a school principal.

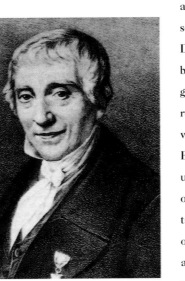

below right
The Bisitun Rock
In 1835 Henry Rawlinson discovered a long inscription carved in rock some 300 feet high on the cliff at Bisitun, about 60 miles from Ecbatana, former capital of the Medes. The inscription, written in three different scripts, commemorates the victory of Darius over rebel kings. Once the first (Old Persian) was deciphered, scholars could understand the second (known as Elamite) and the third (Akkadian).

Once Old Persian was deciphered, scholars turned their attention to the two other scripts found on the tomb of Darius I. One of them did not belong to any known language group. Today this tongue is referred to as Elamite, since it was spoken in the kingdom of Elam in Iran. The other unknown script, which occurred on all Mesopotamian monuments, could only be the script used in ancient Babylon prior to its conquest by Persia. The race to decipher it began. By 1857 scholars had succeeded in mastering this Assyrian tongue, one of two dialects of a Semitic language now referred to as Akkadian.

This took place even before the discovery of new tablets revealing the existence of a still older language, Sumerian. Its decoding in 1905 by François Thureau-Dangin brought back to life one of Mesopotamia's oldest civilizations, which had flourished before the Assyrians, the Babylonians, and the Achaemenid Persians.

center left
Accounts Tablet, Iraq
Discovered at Telloh in present-day Iraq, this accounts tablet bears an inscription in cuneiform script. Such tablets were generally of clay, but if they carried a royal inscription, they could also be of stone or metal.

below
Gudea's Cylinder, Iraq
Also found at Telloh, this imposing barrel-shaped clay cylinder bears one of the longest

Sumerian texts. It tells how Gudea, prince of Lagash, was ordered by the god Ningirsu to build a vast temple in his honor, and it describes the different phases of the temple's construction.

TRACKING DOWN THE SUMERIANS, PERSIANS, AND ASSYRIANS

From the end of the 19th century until the 1930s, archaeologists from all over the world vied for the glory of unearthing the ancient civilizations that flourished between the Tigris and the Euphrates, where the first city-states had flourished.

While living in Mosul (near the French excavations at Khorsabad), the Englishman Austen Henry Layard began exploring the site of Nimrud, where he found a gigantic complex of palaces that had once been Nineveh – the real Nineveh! The ruins and treasures he uncovered there were to enrich the collections of the British Museum.

Meanwhile Ernest de Sarzec, French vice-consul in Basra, uncovered the first traces of the Sumerians, whose earlier civilization had long before fallen into oblivion. His digs, carried out from 1887 to 1904 in Telloh, yielded for the Louvre pieces of priceless value: statues of the Sumerian king Gudea; a silver vase dedicated by Entemena, prince of Lagash; and mace heads dedicated to the gods by Mesilim, king of Kish. Through the study of countless Sumerian tablets, the language and civilization of Sumer were gradually resurrected.

From 1884 to 1886, the French engineer Marcel Dieulafoy carried out digs in Iran, exploring the site of Susa, former center of the Persian Empire. One of his most important discoveries, found in the ruins of the palace, was the Archer Frieze. In 1894 he was succeeded by Jacques de Morgan, an engineer who had begun his archaeological career in Egypt.

These discoveries attracted archaeologists from around the world: Americans came to the site of Nippur, a former religious center, while Germans explored illustrious sites like Babylon, Assur, and Uruk. Between 1899 and 1917 the Germans Edouard Sachau and Robert Koldewey excavated the ruins of the city of Babylon, unearthing some of the more recent

below
Plan of Nineveh,
Paul-Émile Botta
Nineveh, capital of the ancient Assyrian Empire, sits on the left bank of the Tigris. The goddess Ishtar is the presiding deity of this city, which flourished under King Assurbanipal. Here the king established an extraordinary library of 25,000 cuneiform tablets. Botta drew this plan in 1842. He had been seeking Nineveh when he stumbled upon the

ruins of Khorsabad, thus opening the whole field of Mesopotamian studies.

left
Moving a Winged Bull
Under Layard's supervision, dozens of men grapple to tip over a giant winged bull, while an even bigger group struggles to slow its fall. The next stages – transporting the monumental piece by cart, then shipping it by boat – were even more arduous.

below left
Portrait of Adrien Prévost de Longpérier
A numismatist, but also a man with a sound grasp of Oriental languages, Adrien de Longpérier possessed the instincts of a born courtier: he pulled off the feat of opening the original Assyrian Museum in time for a royal birthday.

FIRST CURATOR OF THE ASSYRIAN MUSEUM

In February 1846 Adrien Prévost de Longpérier (1816-1882) was appointed curator of the Louvre's antiquities department, taking over the section on Egyptian and Near Eastern monuments formerly run by the Egyptologist Jean-François Champollion. Longpérier was chosen over the painter Eugène Flandin. A specialist in numismatics (the study of coins and medals), he had also studied the Arabic, Persian, and Hebrew languages. He organized the inauguration of the Assyrian Museum at feverish speed, timing it for May 1, 1847, King Louis Philippe's birthday. In 1856 he supervised the transfer of the Louvre's collections from the east end of the Cour Carrée's north wing to the northern half of the Colonnade, ending his brilliant career in 1870.

above
King Receiving a Dignitary, Khorsabad
Starting with Sargon of Akkad, the rulers of Mesopotamia appointed themselves king. They aspired to rule the earth, an ambition later also held by the Assyrians. On this bas-relief, recorded by Eugène Flandin, two symbols identify the king: the tiara and the staff.

below
The Tower of Babel, Lukas van Valkenborgh
Biblical descriptions of ancient Babylon have fascinated artists down the ages. Here is Lukas van Valkenborgh's version of the construction of the Tower of Babel, painted in 1594 and now in the Louvre.

layers of that fabulous capital, with its double walls, monumental gateways and innumerable towers, temples, and palaces.

Hoping to find an older city, another German, Walter Andrae Jordan, dug between 1903 and 1914 around Assur, the first Assyrian capital. Exhuming the ruins of a number of religious sanctuaries and retrieving several hundred inscribed tablets, he managed to piece together the city's history from the 14th century B.C. to its destruction by the Babylonians and Medes in 612 B.C.

Accompanied by the German archaeologist Koldewey in 1913, and alone in 1928, Jordan carried out digs in Uruk, a Sumerian city located in the desert between Baghdad and Basra. In 1928 the world's oldest written documents came to light there. Dating back to 3200 B.C., they suggested that this

EUGÈNE FLANDIN

The painter Eugène Flandin (1803-1876) had made a name for himself with canvases glorifying the French conquest of Algeria. No sooner had he returned from a mission in Persia than the French government sent him off to help Paul-Émile Botta draw plans of the digs at Khorsabad. The assignment earned him as little fame or fortune as the digs brought Botta, and Flandin's candidacy for the Academy of Fine Arts was rejected in 1858. Although he was primarily a painter in the Orientalist mode, Flandin's drawings of the palace ruins were admirably precise.

region was the cradle of cuneiform writing, with its characteristic wedge-shaped letters. Thirty-five miles to the south, the Englishman Leonard Woolley spent twelve years (from 1922 to 1934) methodically excavating ruins once identified by Rawlinson as belonging to Ur, Abraham's homeland. He made several important finds, particularly the Royal Cemetery, dating back to 2600 B.C.

Like the collections of other European museums, the Louvre's Assyrian section was considerably enriched during the 19th century. By 1856 the two rooms at the east end of the Cour Carrée's north wing no longer sufficed to hold the collections. They were moved to three rooms occupying the northern half of the Colonnade, where they remained until 1992. They were then transferred to the new rooms assigned them as part of the Grand Louvre project.

below
Austen Henry Layard
Shown here in Persian dress, Austen Layard unearthed the ruins of ancient Nineveh in 1849. Initially, he

believed they were located at Nimrud. His finds greatly enhanced the British Museum's collections.

left
Reconstruction of Nimrud's Palace
As a frontispiece to his book The Monuments of Nineveh *(1849), Austen Layard, who discovered the palaces of Calah and Nineveh, chose this romantic reconstruction of the Assyrian king's palace at Nineveh.*

SUMER:
OF WRITING
AND CITIES

In Greek, the word *Mesopotamia* means "the land between two rivers" – the Tigris and Euphrates. Mesopotamia was the setting for a major human revolution: the transition from an agricultural to an urban society, and later to centralized political structure. The first cities in this region rose up around 3500 B.C. and left clear traces of their social and political organization. This civilization is divided into two periods: the Uruk period (3500 to 3100 B.C.), and the Jemdet-Nasr period (3100 to 2900 B.C.).

The Uruk period is named for an ancient city in southern Mesopotamia whose ruins, more or less buried by sand, were methodically excavated by the two German archaeologists Koldowey and Jordan. During this period writing, used to record commercial transactions, made its first appearance. Initially, coins similar in shape to the articles being counted were used, but from around 3100 B.C. they were gradually replaced by coins with phonetic signs. The first statuettes also date from this period, often depicting the "priest-king," a ruler who wielded political authority and interceded with the gods on his people's behalf.

The first dynasties of the Sumerian civilization appeared around 2900 B.C. Their existence was discovered in Telloh (formerly Girsu) in present-day Iraq, by Ernest de Sarzac. He brought back steles, or monumental commemorative tablets, honoring the various members of the Lagash dynasty,

THE SUMERIAN GODS

Each Sumerian city-state had its own god, personified by a human sovereign entrusted with supreme temporal power and with the duty of service to the divinity. These local gods were believed to act as mediators with other divinities who controlled the forces of nature. The belief that a local god ruled both spiritually and through a human surrogate led to a system referred to as "theocratic socialism." The temple assigned work and distributed resources. Writing was developed to maintain a careful check on production. The earliest Sumerian inscriptions dealt not only with religious questions but with administrative and economic ones. Plans of Sumerian cities reflect the temple's predominant role: houses surrounded the sacred precincts, which included the temple, workshops, and scribes' quarters. The temple stood in the center, on an artificial hillock called a ziggurat. These mounds were the abode of the gods, for the Sumerians, who lived on the plains, had no alternative but to create man-made mountains for their divinities.

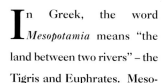

above
Spearhead
This colossal spearhead, carved with a lion and dedicated around 2600 B.C. to Ur-Lugal, king of Kish, was discovered by Ernest de Sarzec.

below right
Leaf-Shaped Necklace
Formed by delicate leaves of hammered gold, this necklace attests to the skills of Sumerian silversmiths and Sumer's taste for luxury articles.

NEAR EASTERN
ANTIQUITIES
AND ISLAMIC ARTS

above
Head of Guardian Lion
The threatening glare of this powerful bronze animal was intended to shield the temple from evil spirits.

left
Head of Prince Gudea
A score of statues representing Gudea, prince of Lagash (2152-2110 B.C.), have survived. The longest Sumerian texts we possess were written during his reign. Most of the statues of Gudea were unearthed at Telloh by Ernest de Sarzec.

below left
"Feathered Figure," bas-relief
Found at Telloh, this limestone bas-relief depicts a Sumerian chief praying before a temple (symbolized by two poles) dedicated to the god Ningirsu.

founded around 2500 B.C. by Urnanshe.

Well before the rise of the Akkadian Empire and the mingling of languages and cultures that ensued with it, Sumerian culture already influenced neighboring civilizations like that of Mari, a Semitic royal city located between present-day Iraq and Syria. A French team led by André Parrot excavated the site in 1933; it unearthed temples and palaces that included the Temple of Ishtar, goddess of love and war, as well as many fragments of furniture. The *Standard of Mari* shows a funeral march following a military victory. Statuettes of worshippers were also found, the most remarkable piece being the statue of the official Ebih-Il.

After Sargon II unified Sumer with Akkadi, there was a blossoming of sculpture glorifying the monarch and celebrating military unification. Since no traces remain of the capital, Agade, vestiges of this period come to us only from Telloh and Susa, where they were taken as booty by Elamite conquerors. One such object is the *Victory Stele of Naram-Sin*, a magnificent relief sculpture of a battle scene. Akkadian now became the official language.

The Sumerian era closed with the second dynasty of Lagash and the third dynasty of Ur. Sumerian again became the official language, but Akkadian remained in common use.

above

Votive Beard

This gold votive beard from the Sumerian period bears an invocation by the queen of the city of Umma for the life of her husband, King Gishakidu.

ASSYRIA FIRES MEN'S MINDS

The Assyrian discoveries worked powerfully on the imagination of painters and artists, from the romantics to the symbolists. Following Eugène Delacroix's renowned *Death of Sardanapalus* (1827), the popularity of Assyrian themes soared with the inauguration of the Louvre's Assyrian section and the first publications by archaeologists. Artists freely mixed styles and periods. In 1865 Gustave Doré depicted Assyrian bulls in his illustrations of the Bible. The influential Symbolist Gustave Moreau inserted references to Assyrian art into several of his paintings, while his friend Edgar Degas did the same with *Semiramis Building Babylon* (1861). Assyria became a favorite theme for Orientalist painters like Georges Rochegrosse (*The Fall of Babylon*, 1892). It also influenced architecture: for the 1889 World's Fair in Paris: Charles Garnier, builder of the opera house on Paris' Place de l'Opéra, designed ten pavilions in the Assyrian style.

bottom left

The Fall of Babylon, Georges Rochegrosse

This painting by Rochegrosse (1859-1938) reflects the impact of Babylonian exoticism on the imagination of artists.

THE KINGDOM OF BABYLON

below

Votive Figure Known as "Scarface"
This statuette, representing a mythological figure with a body covered by snake scales, comes from Bactria, a region with close cultural ties to Iran during the second millennium B.C. The scar disfiguring his face bears witness to a short-lived bout of iconoclasm.

above

Pair of Human-Headed Sphinxes
This small ivory plaque, discovered on the Arslan Tash site in northern Syria, probably decorated a piece of wooden furniture. The theme – paired human-headed sphinxes – is of Egyptian origin.

The beginning of the second millennium B.C. marked a new era in Mesopotamia, witnessing the rise of the kingdom of Babylon under King Hammurabi (1792-1750 B.C.). The sixth monarch of the Amorite (a nomadic people from western Syria) dynasty, Hammurabi destroyed the kingdom of Ur. He succeeded in reestablishing Mesopotamian unity, making Babylon the capital of an empire stretching from Mari and Nineveh to the Persian Gulf. His name is linked to the oldest-known legal code, the Code of Hammurabi, which is now in the Louvre.

In 1595 B.C. the Kassites, a nomadic mountain people, captured Babylon. Assimilating its civilization, they dominated the former kingdom from the 16th to the 12th centuries B.C. They built temples and left behind numerous steles (*kudurrus*) engraved with charters for land grants and royal bequests, along with figures of major divinities believed to be the guarantors of such contracts.

Following the rise and fall of the Mitanni Empire (16th to 14th centuries B.C.), Assyria emerged as an independent power. Taking their name from the Mesopotamian god Assur, the Assyrians soon extended their sway to the shores of the Mediterranean. At its peak, their empire was bordered by the Caspian Sea, the Nile, the Taurus Mountains, and the Persian Gulf. Assyrian art, essentially dedicated to celebrating the feats of kings and their armies, suggests an early attempt at propaganda. These friezes of conquest, slaughter, and the hunt are also the first known narrative art.

left

Birth of Horus
These small sculpted plaques were found in the palace of Arslan Tish, in northern Syria. They depict another theme of Egyptian origin: the birth of the god Horus.

below left

Stele of the Code of Hammurabi
This basalt stele was excavated at Susa by Jacques de Morgan's expedition.

THE LEGAL CODE OF HAMMURABI

The sixth king of the Amorite dynasty, Hammurabi (1792-1750 B.C.), was not only a conqueror but a remarkable administrator and legislator who left an important mark on history. He turned Babylon into the political and religious capital of Mesopotamia. During his reign, a code of law of 282 articles was compiled. A monument of cuneiform literature, these laws resolved both public and private

conflicts. More than a legal code in today's sense, Hammurabi's code consisted of a record of arrests, creating legal precedents. Its professed goal was to uphold justice and ensure that the strong did not oppress the weak. But its real purpose was to protect the interests of lenders against defaulting borrowers. Hammurabi's code had a considerable influence on legislation in the ancient Near East.

right

Salmanassar Gate
The Assyrian king Salmanassar III (858-824 B.C.) commemorated his victories on bronze plaques that embellished the gates of his palace at Balawat. From top to bottom, they depict the army's advance, with the chariot-borne king.

IRAN

Although it was separated from Mesopotamia by high mountain ranges and the valleys of Elam, Iran developed flourishing cultural contacts with the other civilizations of the region, particularly with Susa, the Elamite capital. United in the 4th century B.C. by Cyrus the Great, the Persian Empire expanded under Darius I to fill the entire Near East. Its three capitals were Ecbatana, Persepolis, and Susa. Their colonnaded palaces combined the grandiloquence of Near Eastern architecture with Greek notions of classical proportion.

Artistically, Susa was most renowned for its ceramics, painted with geometric and animal motifs. After becoming a Sumerian city around 2350, it kept alive traditional artistic themes such as the female bird protecting her nest with outstretched wings. The city also continued to specialize in the use of bitumen, a petroleum derivative, for making dishes, jewelry, toys, and sculptures. In the second millennium, funerary heads of unbaked painted clay were placed in Susan tombs, a custom that has yielded for posterity some beautiful portraits.

The divinities from Bactria, unlike those from Mesopotamia, are depicted as primitive mountain dwellers. The Louristan produced a large number of intricately worked bronzes, including luxury dishes, weapons, and saddlery.

The monumental art of Persia produced reliefs like the *Frieze of Archers of the Persian Royal Guard* in polychrome brick; and the capital of a column decorated with cattle heads, from Marcel Dieulafoy's digs in Susa. After Alexander the Great's conquest of the Persian Empire, the Sassanid kings ruled Iran from A.D. 224 to 651, fostering a reaction against Western influences and a return to the sources of Iranian art – a tendency later perpetuated by Islam.

above right
Funerary Portrait of a Bearded King
During the Elamite period (ca. 1500-1000 B.C.) in Iran, it was customary to place funerary heads of unbaked painted clay in certain tombs. This head was probably modeled in the likeness of the deceased monarch..

above
Egyptian-Style Mask
Of terra-cotta, shaped in a mold, this Phoenician mask (1590-1250 B.C.) of Egyptian inspiration once decorated a tomb.

below right
Female Figure
This elegant female statuette is from the workshops of Bactria. It recalls Sumerian art of the Early Dynastic Period.

NEAR EASTERN
ANTIQUITIES
AND ISLAMIC ARTS

below
Frieze of Archers of the Persian Royal Guard
The invincible Persian army was the dominant theme at the palace of Darius (522-486 B.C.) in Susa. These archers in polychrome glazed brick wear uniforms derived by Persian artists from a Greek model.

right
Detail of Vase
Detail of polychrome design from a painted Iranian terra-cotta vase: it depicts an eagle with outspread wings, a two-faced sun, and a human head.

above:
The Mistress
of Beasts
*This sculpted ivory lid
once covered a round
box carved from an
elephant tusk – a
specialty of the city of
Ugarit, on the
Phoenician coast. It
shows a fertility
goddess seated on an
altar and offering
wheat stalks to a pair
of ibexes, shown
face to face.*

center
Seated Syrian God
*Seated on a throne, a
Syrian god wears an
oval tiara and
ceremonial dress. A
narrow, bulky sash is
draped around him.
His attitude and
gesture of benediction
suggest that this is a
divinity offering
protection.*

THE LEVANT: CROSSROADS OF HISTORY

A region inhabited since prehistoric times, the Levant now encompasses Cyprus, Lebanon, Syria, and Israel. Agriculture here can be traced back to the 7th millennium B.C., and its first cities were founded in the third millennium. The Levant was a vital passageway and trading center whose prosperity attracted repeated invasions by Egyptians, Mesopotamians, and Anatolians. During the second millennium, the Levant was still nominally a dependency of Egypt, but Tyre, Ugarit, Byblos, and Sidon all fought for supremacy in the region. By the beginning of the first millennium, the Phoenicians dominated the Mediterranean.

The Levant then fell under Babylonian domination, which involved the deportation of whole populations. The arrival of the Persian kings brought a period (593-330 B.C.) of prosperity and peace, opening the cultures of the region to Hellenic influences. Striking examples of this cultural hybridization are anthropoid sarcophagi, mummy-shaped tombs of Egyptian inspiration, cut from Cycladean marble by Greek-trained artists for Phoenician clients.

The Louvre's collections reflect these multiple influences. Among them are works from Cyprus, including a remarkable boat with early second millennium figures and several

top left
Head of Syrian God
*This head was found
at Jabboul, near
Aleppo in Syria, and
dates from 1500 or
1400 B.C. The oval
tiara, decorated with
rows of cattle horns, is
a mark of rank.*

lower left
Gods and Goddesses
of Ugarit
*The first two figures
are representations of
the storm god Baal.
In the first, a bronze
statuette from the site
of Ras Shamra
(formerly Ugarit), he
wears a horned tiara.
His upraised arm
brandishes a spear or
thunderbolt long since
lost. The second, a
bronze figure with a
gold head, shows Baal
in a loincloth and
cone-shaped helmet.
This figure has also
lost its symbolic
attributes, a mace and
a spear. The final two
figures, in ceremonial
costume, are spirits of
peace.*

PHOENICIANS, CONQUERORS OF THE SEA

This Semitic people from the Gulf of Oman settled on the eastern Mediterranean coast at the beginning of the second millennium B.C. Skilled navigators and clever traders, the Phoenicians founded a succession of ports – Tyre, Sidon, Byblos, Arad, and Ugarit – that soon prospered. The needs of their trading vocation impelled them to invent a new phonetic alphabet. After the invasion of the Sea People, Tyre replaced Byblos as the power center of the region, forging an alliance with the Hebrews of Palestine. The Phoenicians then expanded westward, founding mercantile outposts from the Gulf of Libya to the Moroccan coast and from Sicily to the Balearic Islands. The arrival of the Assyrians in the 8th century B.C., followed by the Neo-Babylonians and later still by the Persians, brought the supremacy of the Phoenician cities to a close.

Divinity in Tiara
(Three Views)
*The Phoenician
pantheon included
junior and senior
divinities. This well-
endowed Phoenician
goddess is one of the
younger divinities.*

goddesses. From Byblos, a city long courted by Egypt in its quest for control over Lebanon's fabled cedar trade, come many pieces of jewelry and Egyptian-made plates, as well as a "golden calf," the animal divinity condemned by Old Testament prophets. Ernest Renan located the site of Byblos in 1860 and 1861; it was excavated by the Egyptologist Pierre Monet in 1919, then by Maurice Dunand in the 1920s and 1960s.

objects, as well as vases and other objects made of paste coated with colored glaze.

While the heartland of Syria was marked more by Mesopotamian, Hittite, Hurrian, or Sumerian influences, Palestine was stamped with Egyptian power and culture: it developed an urban and palatial civilization that produced furniture and luxury objects similar to those of the rest of the Levant.

The Louvre's collections have been

right center
Stele of the
Storm God
*In this stele the storm
god Baal brandishes a
mace; foliage springs
from his spear,
symbolizing the
beneficial effects of the
rain he releases. Such
steles are found in
shrines to Baal
throughout the Levant
region.*

left, mid-page
Pectoral from Byblos
*Executed for a
Phoenician sovereign
from Byblos, vassal of
an Egyptian pharaoh,
this hammered-gold
pectoral is decorated
with a falcon with
outspread wings.
Although inspired by
an Egyptian model, the
local craftsman has
created an original
work of art of great
beauty.*

The influence of Egyptian art is also evident in Phoenicia, as in the statue of the Pharaoh Osorkon I and various divinities portrayed in metalwork. At Ugarit, a site excavated by the Frenchman Claude Schaeffer between 1929 and 1971, beautiful representations of the storm god Baal emerged, as well as luxury articles from throughout the Levant. Ugaritic craftsmen specialized in carved ivory

enriched by numerous digs carried out by the French in this region, from François Thureau-Dangin and Maurice Dunand at Tell Ahmar (1929-1931); Robert du Mesnil du Buisson in the Orontes valley; Jean Margueron in Meskene (1972-1976); and Maurice Pézard and Edmond Pottier (1929-1930) in Kadesh, site of the great battle between Ramses II and the Hittites.

left
Funerary Mask
*This wide-eyed terra-
cotta mask probably
served a protective
function.*

HISTORY OF THE ISLAMIC DEPARTMENT

The Department of Islamic Arts grew up independently of the Louvre's Mesopotamian and Egyptian sections and is not associated with any large archaeological expeditions. Islamic art is of more recent origin than Near Eastern antiquities, and while Islamic civilization has known many periods of change, its original inspiration has never entirely disappeared.

In 1890 the Islamic section at the Louvre was created on the initiative of two curators from the Objets d'Art department, Émile Molinier and Gaston Migeon. Since the transfer in 1945 of Far Eastern works to the Musée Guimet, the section has been attached to the Department of Near Eastern Antiquities.

Private donations account for the bulk of the collections. Among the most important donors: Baroness Alphonse Delort de Gléon in 1912; Raymond Koechlin in 1932; the renowned Egyptologist Gaston Maspero; David David-Weill, financier; and his son Jean David-Weill, curator until 1969 of the Islamic section.

By allotting the section a new suite of thirteen rooms, the Grand Louvre project has accorded unprecedented importance to the presentation of these collections. They are among the most important in the Western world and include ceramics, metal and woodwork, glass and ivory objects, carpets, miniatures, drawings, and papyrus and illuminated manuscripts. The Louvre's collections include objects drawn from all periods and regions; presented chronologically, they group the objects by their geographical origin.

below

Ewer with Ducklings, Egypt or Syria, 1309
Decorated with the twelve signs of the zodiac, this ewer is signed and dated at the base by al-Hadj Muhammad Ibn al-Hajadj.

below left

Dish with Peacock, Turkey
The style, theme, and colors of this ceramic dish characterize late-16th-century Iznik ware.

below center

Plate with Fish Roundel
This Iranian ceramic plate with an opaque green glaze is decorated with a roundel of small fish and a solar motif.

NEAR EASTERN ANTIQUITIES AND ISLAMIC ARTS

top left

Basin Known as the "Baptismal Font of Saint Louis"
This masterpiece of Mamluk art comes from a royal collection and is thought to have been used for the baptism of Louis XIII. The beaten brass basin is decorated with a frieze of animals and mythical beasts framing official figures and horsemen.

center

Carpet with Elephant
Draftsmen, weavers, and dyers collaborated to transform this carpet, decorated with floral, vegetable, and animal motifs (here, an elephant and a deer) on a red background, into a work of art.

left, below

Plate with Young Man, Northwestern Iran, 17th century
Executed in a gentle range of colors, a reproduction of a miniature from the same period, it is typical of work from the city of Kubaitcha in Dagestan. An ivory glaze covers the red clay.

THE ISLAMIC RELIGION

Youngest of the monotheistic faiths, Islam (or "submission to God's will") originated in Arabia, where it supplanted polytheistic paganism, in the 7th century. Its founder, Muhammad, was born around 570 in Mecca. When Muhammad was forty, the Archangel Gabriel appeared to him, urging him to become God's messenger. It was only after a second visitation that he accepted Allah's mission. Muhammad never perceived himself as the founder of a religion, but as a religious reformer and heir to the patriarchs and prophets from Adam to Jesus.

But the Prophet could not have won victory for his teachings without also being a man of action – a military leader, a diplomat, and a statesman. Treated with hostility by the inhabitants of Mecca, he fled to Yathrib (soon renamed Medina, "town of the Prophet") on July 16, 622, marking the beginning of the Muslim era. From Medina, Muhammad launched a holy war (*jihad*) against Mecca, which he finally subdued in 630. The Ka'aba became the shrine it remains to this day. By the Prophet's death in 632, nearly all of Arabia had been won over to Islam.

In the 8th century, its influence spread throughout Arabia, Asia Minor, Mesopotamia, Persia, North Africa, Spain, and parts of India. The simplicity of Allah's message, the humanity of his values, his fusion of the spiritual and temporal planes, and the energy with which his teachings were spread all account for this rapid expansion.

THE POWER OF ISLAM

* 632: Muhammad dies in Mecca, but Islam is on the brink of dazzling military expansion.
* 711: As the empire's geographic center shifts westward, Damascus, in Syria, becomes capital of the Umayyad dynasty.
* 750: With the Abbasids, the center shifts again, this time to Baghdad, in Mesopotamia.
* 9th century: Rival caliphates arise in Spain and Egypt.
* 1096-1291: The Crusades challenge Islamic supremacy.

* 1258: The Mongols take Baghdad.
* 14th to 15th centuries: The Ottoman Empire expands. Islam is divided into three rival empires: the Ottomans; the Persian Safavids (1501-1732) in Iran; and the Great Moguls (1526-1858) in India.
* 1492: Completion of the Spanish *reconquista* signals the end of the Arab presence in Spain.
* 1571: The naval defeat at Lepanto puts an end to Ottoman military supremacy. Slow decline of the Ottoman Empire leads to its disintegration in 1922.

top left

Bookbinding Plates
The rich colors and fine drawing of these Iranian bookbinding plates recall miniature painting. They depict princely leisure activities, both athletic and cultural, against a stylized natural background.

ISLAMIC ART

Despite the diversity of the countries conquered by Islam, an authentic Islamic art exists, an art that obeys rules accepted throughout the Islamic world. After the Umayyad rulers made Damascus their capital in the 7th century, a shared artistic vision developed and spread throughout all Islam, strongly influenced by the Great Mosque in Damascus. With the transfer of the capital to Baghdad in the 8th century, Asian elements began to influence Islamic art. Although the relative fragmentation of the Islamic world in the 12th century allowed each culture to maintain a certain autonomy and uphold some of its own traditions, individual Islamic cultures continued to share common artistic traits. These included the predominance of color and decoration; a taste for ornamentation, geometry, and arabesques; a preference for stylized representation over realism; the use of calligraphy; and a relative scarcity of human representations, which appeared only in the treatment of courtly themes such as hunting and war.

The mosque is the best reflection of this common heritage. Architechtally, the "Arab plan" is characterized by a vast inner courtyard (square or rectangular), closed off in the direction of Mecca by a prayer room. Mecca's orientation is indicated by a plaque on one of the mosque walls. Another type of mosque is shaped like a cross, formed by a room with an open facade and covered by a vault. Originally from Persia, this ground plan spread to Syria, Iraq, Anatolia, and Egypt.

Since Islamic tradition largely prohibits the representation of living beings, it gives an important place to the complex floral and geometric designs known as arabesques, and to calligraphy, executed with extreme care, in accordance with Muhammad's words: "God is beautiful and loves beauty." A rich tradition of miniatures also prevails, especially in Persia, where despite Islamic conquest traditional figurative art survived: human representations are found on tapestries, pottery, and engravings.

center

Apothecary's Jar
This large apothecary's jar, of Egyptian or Syrian origin, dates from the 14th century. Executed in a composite style blending Syrio-Egyptian, Iranian, and Mamluk influences, it bears an inscription on its belly indicating that it was meant to contain musk – and referring to the magical uses of this substance.

right

Red Carpet, India
The colors of the floral motif of this Indian carpet have kept all their freshness. Made during the late 17th or early 18th century, this type of carpet was designed for use on a terrace or as a wall hanging. Its design was in vogue under the Mogul emperors.

below

Fabric with Palmettes, Egypt, 8th century
Egypt's Arab conquerors employed Coptic craftsmen from the workshops of Dar el-Tiraz to produce local fabrics. The word tiraz *designated the inscribed bands that adorned ceremonial robes awarded by rulers to their subjects.*

below right

Prayerbook Binding, Iran, 16th century
A fine example of the bookbinder's art in the first half of the 16th century.

NEAR EASTERN ANTIQUITIES AND ISLAMIC ARTS

In the absence of representational painting, Islamic artists put particular emphasis on the beauty of objects – furniture, carpets, and manuscripts. This ornamental art is heavily impregnated with religion, even when it decorates art objects and nonreligious architecture. Regional differences arose and, as they traveled from one Islamic country to the next, were enriched with local touches. Fourteenth-century Chinese decorative motifs, for example, were adopted throughout the Islamic world.

This diversity is reflected in the Louvre's collections, from a 7th- or 8th-century Iranian bowl in the Sassanian tradition, decorated with a young partridge, to the *Portrait of Shah Abbas I with One of His Pages*, done in 17th-century Iran at a time when Western influences fused with Asian stylization. Muslim art from Spain also provides many examples of this crossover process. Mamluk art, which developed in Egypt from the 13th to the 16th centuries, borrowed

Far Eastern motifs like the lotus flower and the phoenix from the Mongols. The latter conquered Iran in the 13th century and embraced Islam a century later. An extremely refined art developed under their domination, like a wall panel from the mausoleum at Khurasan, whose animal, vegetable, and figurative motifs are interwoven with great delicacy.

The Louvre's collections recall the high scientific achievements of medieval Muslim civilizations, for example in 12th-century celestial spheres and a wide range of measuring instruments. They also reflect the sophistication of Islam's funerary art (in principle forbidden by the Koran, which says that the dead must be buried in a simple grave without any monument to distinguish them from other mortals). The collections also evoke the martial fire of Islamic civilization, with finely worked and decorated weapons and armor, as well as the art of carpet making, perhaps the most characteristic feature of Muslim art.

below and right
Lion and Peacock
Both of these bronze animals are from 12th-century Muslim Spain. The lion has an articulated tail – probably the spout of a fountain. The peacock appears to be screeching as it is bitten by another animal. Latin and Arabic inscriptions adorn the peacock, undoubtedly commissioned from a Muslim artist by a Christian king.

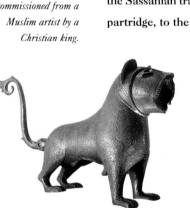

below right
Page from the Book of Wonders
This illuminated page is from the Book of Wonders, *a work on cosmography by the 15th-century Arab geographer al-Qaswini. Beginning with the Middle Ages, Arab scholars acquired a more sophisticated knowledge of the world than their Western counterparts, whose Christian vision was obsessed with superstition and faith in the miraculous.*

right
Man Giving a Fish to a Woman
Christian themes were not unknown to the Muslim world: this illuminated page by the painter Husayn presents an extremely loose interpretation of a subject borrowed from Christian iconography.

Arabesques
Arabesques, as the name suggests, are a dominant feature of Islamic art. Very early on, these intricate traceries of boughs, leaves, blossoms, and animal heads became a key to the identification of Muslim ornamental art – even though Christian art also used flower garlands and vines to adorn church capitals. Arabesques unfold in infinite geometric variations that evoke the mathematical and speculative spirit of Muslim civilization.

BOOKS AND CALLIGRAPHY

Early on, the book achieved central status in Islamic culture. Very elaborate surviving copies of the Koran, reflecting the sacred nature of Arabic script, attest to that status. Despite precise rules governing the size of Arabic letters and their spacing, the writing varies in style according to medium, period, and region.

The Arabian school is characterized by symbolic representations of nature coupled with realistic and often humorous depictions of animal life. Artists

presented their scenes against a neutral background with no horizon line and ignored the rules of symmetry. By contrast, calligraphers of the Iranian school preferred a poetic atmosphere to realism and anecdote. Nature held a more important place in their work. In the 14th century, the Iranian school evolved toward greater realism, aiming for perspective in its depiction of scenes from everyday life. Individualized portraits appeared soon after.

GREEK ART

ROMAN ART

ROMANESQUE ART

Western art's primary wellspring, the art of Greece has remained our point of reference. No civilization better illustrated the canons of classicism. Yet the material vestiges of Greek art are fragmentary: architectural ruins, defaced sculptures whose originals we know only from Roman copies, paintings whose beauty we can glean only from mosaics or pottery. Nevertheless, we deduce universal values from this art that developed through the first millennium B.C. and endured until the Roman era. Historians have traditionally broken Greek art down into a series of periods: the Geometric (from around 1100-725 B.C.); a period of Near Eastern influences (around 725-610 B.C.); the Archaic period (around 610-480 B.C.); and the Hellenistic period (around 480-31 B.C.). "Man as the measure of all things" was the determinant concept in Greek art. It was an art based on reason, on the urge to achieve objective awareness of the world in order to master that world. Equilibrium, harmony, order, clarity, proportion, and moderation were the universal values invented by Greek classicism and transmitted as an ideal to posterity.

Essentially urban, Roman civilization borrowed heavily from Greece. But it also developed an art that belongs to it alone, one turned more toward the pleasures of the living than to celebration of the gods. Architecture was perhaps the greatest Roman art form. Temples – hitherto extremely simple in form – evolved during the Empire in the direction of excessive ornamentation. Meanwhile, by the 2nd century B.C., purely civil monuments had multiplied, and soon constituted the distinguishing characteristic of the urban landscape. In the last years of the Republic, a crucial innovation revolutionized architectural techniques: rubble wall construction. Walls were no longer made entirely of solid blocks of stone, but of a central core composed of a mixture of sand, lime, and stone fragments, coated by a decorative outer covering. This swift and economic technique made the boldest of constructions – such as vaults – possible. In other artistic forms – sculpture, relief, painting – Rome's dependence on the Greek model remained marked, although Roman art was never solely one of imitation.

The term "Romanesque" was coined in 1818 by a French archaeologist, Charles de Gerville, to designate artistic forms developed in the Christian West between the early 11th and early 13th centuries. The historical context from which Romanesque art arose was marked by demographic and urban growth and economic expansion. It was also the era that saw the development of feudalism and the first "national" states, the Crusades and reform of the Church, and the rise (with the abbeys of Cluny and then Cîteaux) of monasticism. All these factors contributed to the birth of Romanesque art, which soon filled monasteries, seigneurial dwellings, and rich bourgeois homes. But it was above all religious architecture, and its painted or sculpted ornamentation, that gave Romanesque art its distinctive features. Its great innovation was its systematic recourse to the vault, freeing buildings to assume entirely new proportions. Romanesque art had many faces, as the domed churches of the Angoulême, the Périgord, and the Quercy attest.

GOTHIC ART

The word "Gothic" was first uttered by Raphael in the Renaissance and then popularized by the art historian Giorgio Vasari. It was used, with slightly pejorative intent, to designate art forms that succeeded the Romanesque style. Rehabilitated during the Romantic era by the archaeologist Arcisse de Caumont, the term was taken up by the first historians of medieval art in preference to the expression "ogival art." The new style's major innovation was the use of the ogive or of the ribbed vault, making vaulting much lighter and ensuring a better distribution of weight upon supporting walls, which could now be pierced by large bays. This redefinition of architecture would be duplicated in all the other arts, from sculpture to precious metalwork. As with Romanesque art, it was from religious architecture that Gothic drew its defining characteristics. Gothic art gradually distanced itself from its Romanesque predecessor, reaching its apogee in the 13th century and utterly dominating the 14th and 15th centuries. After 1500, Gothic art fell into disuse, although isolated aspects survived until the 17th century and were reborn in the next century when the Romantic movement adopted the Gothic manner.

THE ART OF THE RENAISSANCE

The Renaissance was a vast cultural movement born in Italy in the 1300s (the Trecento), evolving through the 1400s (the Quattrocento) to reach its height during the 16th century (the Cinquecento). It was originally a scholarly and literary movement (triggered by the rediscovery of the great works of Antiquity), but it rapidly developed into a scientific and philosophic revolution that challenged traditional views of the world. The medieval age of faith gave place to the age of reason and doubt. In medieval art, the often anonymous artist effaced himself before his creation, intended to celebrate God's work. Renaissance art celebrated individualism above all else. It was also a profane art, bent on extolling life and earthly happiness. Reflecting the new humanist ideal born in Italy, artists strove to infuse everyday life with beauty. Man became the measure of all things; painters no longer hesitated to celebrate the beauty of the female body. In place of Christian virtues, this resurgent art harked back to "antique virtues," in other words to courage and energy, values whose models were to be found in the heroes of ancient history and mythology.

MANNERISM

This term, which appeared at the beginning of the 18th century, designated a trend that emerged in painting in the twilight of the Renaissance. It was a trend that stressed the artist's "manner," in other words his virtuosity, as an end in itself, rather than fidelity to nature. The artists who embodied this anti-naturalist trend included Rosso Fiorentino, Parmigianino, Daniele da Volterra, Bronzino, and Giovanni da Giambologna. Starting in Italy, the style spread all over Europe, particularly in France, with Primaticcio, Niccolo dell'Abate, and the School of Fontainebleau. Essentially a court art, Mannerism was marked by the cult of formal elegance, virtuosity of execution, and aspiration to the creation of artificial beauty, which flattered the tastes of an aristocratic and refined public. Until the 20th century, Mannerism was synonymous with what was seen as the decadence of the Renaissance, a decadence that was finally stemmed by the classicism of the Carracci brothers. Reassessed during the 1920s, Mannerism is no longer considered by art historians as a corruption but as an original development of the art of the Renaissance.

CLASSICAL ART

The notion of classicism took root in France in the 17th century in opposition to late-Renaissance Mannerism and to the naturalism of Caravaggio and his school. The term designated artistic forms deemed worthy of consideration as classical in any given period, in other words forms whose perfection attained exemplary levels. "Classical" art thus encompassed the Greek art of 6th- and 5th-century Athens, Roman art from the periods of Augustus and Hadrian, the Carolingian Renaissance, Florentine art in the reign of Lorenzo the Magnificent, and French art of the Sun King's century. For the theoreticians of classicism, its main characteristics include: concern for order and symmetry, respect for reason, and nobility of theme. Classicism, committed to the Greek ideal of beauty and goodness, thus linked esthetic to moral values. These constants remain operative today. The primacy of reason is perhaps the most characteristic mark of classicism, an art aimed above all at an intellectual and cultural elite.

BAROQUE ART

Of Iberian origin, the term "Baroque" was synonymous in the 17th century with "irregular," in other words unregulated, stripped of rules. It remained a pejorative term until the end of the 19th century, when it was reassessed by the Swiss historian Jakob Burckhardt, then by his pupil, the art historian Heinrich Wolfflin, who defined its characteristics in opposition to the values of Renaissance and so-called classical art. After Wolfflin, the Spaniard Eugenio d'Ors and other critics proposed Baroque as a vision of the world that was opposed to the classical ideal, a vision present in all forms of civilization and to be found in every period of history. However, the historic field of Baroque can probably be confined to the 16th and 17th centuries, and its origins in Counter-Reformation Rome, whence it spread to the rest of Italy, to Europe, and as far as Latin America. While the Renaissance and classicism advocated the imitation of reality through a system of harmonious relationships, Baroque sought, by means of spectacular visual effects, to establish a relationship with the spectator based not on reason but on emotion.

ROCOCO ART

Known in France as "Rocaille," Rococo, which spread to most major countries in Europe, was essentially a decorative art. It reached its peak in France during the Régence and the early years of Louis XV's reign, with the work of the goldsmith Juste-Aurèle Meissonnier and the cabinetmaker Gilles-Marie Oppenord. Meissonnier, the official Cabinet decorator, was charged with creating the decor for court ceremonies. Oppenord, who had discovered Baroque art in Rome, became the Regent's favorite decorator and was assigned the refurbishing of the Palais-Royal. His drawings were influential in spreading the Rococo style to other countries. But it was above all in the ornamental arts (goldsmithing, furniture, woodwork) that Rococo, with its joyful predilection for curves and whorls, found its most exuberant expression. In painting, François Boucher, with his voluptuous nudes, was the major representative of the Rocaille style, with its Rococo counterparts in Central Europe and Italy.

Neo-Classical Art

This movement was born around the middle of the 18th century in reaction to the excesses of Baroque and Rococo, and endured until the beginning of the 19th century. A complex phenomenon, neoclassicism sought to restore the ideals of rigor and harmony typical of the art of Antiquity. It operated not only in the figurative arts but across the whole cultural spectrum. Its birth was stimulated by the excavations carried out at Herculaneum and Pompeii in 1738 and 1748, and by the rediscovery of the Doric order, which was illustrated by the temples at Paestum, near Naples.

The major theoretician of neoclassicism was the German archaeologist Johann Jakob Winckelmann, while the Italian painter Giambattista Piranesi celebrated the austerity and sternness of Roman monuments. Sculpture, marked by the rediscovery of the marbles of the Parthenon and Phidias' statuary, was chiefly represented by the Italian Antonio Canova and the Dane Bertel Thorvaldsen, while the Frenchman Jean-Louis David was the leading exponent of neoclassical painting. He presided over a galaxy of pupils who furthered the spread of neoclassicism until the movement vanished before the shock of Romanticism.

Romantic Art

The Romantic movement left its powerful mark on the European art of the first half of the 19th century. By the last years of the 18th century a distinctly romantic sensibility was making itself felt in European literature. This sensibility was distinguished by the primacy it accorded to the emotional and the irrational, by the rejection of esthetic or moral rules, and by the importance given to the individual and to contemporary events. Artists abandoned classical Antiquity and the rule of reason in favor of Shakespeare, of Germanic and Nordic myth, the mysterious powers of the imagined, of the fantastic, the erotic, even of the insane. The pioneers of Romanticism were the English painters Blake and Fuseli and the Germans Runge and Friedrich, as well as the visionary French architects Boullée, Ledoux, and Lequeu. The second generation was led by Delacroix and Géricault in France and by Turner in England. Powerful craftsmanship, the exaltation of color, and harsh contrasts of light and shade characterized the Romantic style in painting, overthrowing the traditional hierarchy of genres inherited from academia.

Realism

Reevaluation of contemporary themes drawn from the everyday world in order to make them accessible to all; affirmation of total fidelity to nature; depiction of reality without the pathos or the heroism dear to Romanticism – such were the goals of the Realist movement, which began around 1830 and endured until the end of the 19th century. The principles of the movement were expressed in 1857 by the critic Jules Husson Champfleury in his essay entitled *Realism*. The heritage that Realist painters claimed was that of Caravaggio and his school, the Le Nain brothers, Chardin, and – more recently – Daumier. Among the leading Realist painters were Jean-François Millet, Gustave Courbet, Jean-Baptiste Corot, and the painters of the Barbizon School, who painted their subjects in situ.

PHOTO CREDITS

PHOTOGRAPHS: Nicholas d'Archimbaud.

A.K.G. : 268b ; 290b. Archives Photos : 29d. Archivio Scala : 242-243 ; 280m ; 294. Artothek : 292. Biblioteca Apostolica Vaticana : 293h. Bibliothèque Nationale : 15 ; 54b ; 56hg ; 57 ; 235g,m et b ; 237h et m ; 238g ; 244b ; 265 ; 266 ; 267d ; 280b ; 283b ; 290g ; 291 ; 306b ; 308h ; 311b ; 313b. British Museum : 240 ; 263m ; 311d. Bulloz : 311h. Christian Larrieu : 308g et b ; 310 h et g. Christophe L. : 28m. Dagli Orti : 21mb ; 22m ; 24g ; 27m ; 263h. D.R. : 16h et b ; 19d ; 23d ; 24m ; 26h ; 27d ; 29h et 29b ; 54m ; 75d ; 190b ; 241 ; 244 ; 263d ; 267g ; 268g et m ; 280g ; 285b ; 290h ; 294m ; 306h ;307 ; 309h et b. Edimédia : 54d ; 238m ; 241m ; 244m ; 263g. ENSBA : 291h. Gallimard : 244d. Giraudon : 14h ; 21b, 26m ; 241d. Jean-Loup Charmet : 22g ; 24hd et b ; 27b ; 237d ; 268d. Keystone-L'Illustration : 26b ; 81h, 293d. Lotos Film : 295b. Luciano Pedicini : 293m. Metropolitan Museum of Art : 321d. Monumenti e Gallerie Pontificie : 280h. Musée cantonal des Beaux-Arts de Lausanne : 14b. Musée de Fontainebleau : 16m. RMN : 12-13 ; 14g et d ; 18m et b ; 19m ; 20h et b ; 21h, d et mh ; 22h et b ; 23 ; 24hg ; 25 ; 26g ; 27h ; 28b ; 36b ; 41m et b ; 56m ; 61b ; 65b ; 66b ; 70 ; 71 ; 72h ; 78b ; de 96 à 159 ; 191 ; 193g ; 194g ; 206m ; 217h ; de 218 à 229 ; 232b ; 234 ; 236 ; 238h ; 241b ; 246g et m ; 247 ; 248 ; 249h ; 264h ; 270 ; 271h ; 273h et b ; 294g ; 300h ; 301 ;302g,m et b ; 308m ; 310b ; 311g ; 316d. RMN/Chuzeville : 319h. Photothèque de la ville de Paris : 17 ; 18h ; 19b et h ; 20m ;162met b ; 163. Roger-Viollet : 28h ; 235h ; 245 ; 282. Royal Institute of British Architects : 263b. Tallandier : 16g ; 24hm. Thames and Hudson : 268h. Tyne and Wear Museum : 293b. Victoria and Albert Museum : 239.

Acknowledgments

I wish to thank all the people

who have assisted me with patience and enthusiasm in the preparation of this book,

in particular the whole editorial staff of Editions Laffont:

Anne-Isabelle for her presence and her efficient work;

Anne-Rita and Céline;

Anne de Margerie and Catherine Bellanger;

and Daniel Czap.

Contributing Authors

Bruno de Cessole: Introduction of the Departments; History; Department of Paintings; Department of
Sculpture; Department of Decorative Arts (major texts); Graphic Arts
Department; Department of Near Eastern Antiquities and Islamic Arts.

Annie Forgeau: Egyptian Antiquities.

Frédéric Valloire: Greek, Etruscan, and Roman Antiquities.

Yves Saint-Hilaire: captions, boxes, Sculpture, Decorative Arts

Anne Chêne: Architecture section.

Artistic Direction: Nicholas d'Archimbaud and Who's Partner

This work was printed on Euroart 170 grams matte SCA Fine Paper;

typeset by SCCM in Paris, France;

engraved by MP Productions in Montrouge, France;

printed by Clerc in Saint-Amand-Montrond, France;

bound by Brun in Malesherbes, France.